Methods for the Study of Religious Change

Methods for the Study of Religious Change

From Religious Studies to Worldview Studies

Edited by
André Droogers and Anton van Harskamp

SHEFFIELD UK   BRISTOL CT

Published by Equinox Publishing Ltd.

UK: Office 415, The Workstation, 15 Paternoster Row, Sheffield, South Yorkshire
S1 2BX

USA: ISD, 70 Enterprise Drive, Bristol, CT 06010

www.equinoxpub.com

British Library Cataloguing-in-Publication Data
A catalogue record for this book is available from the British Library.

ISBN-13 978 1 78179 042 7 (hardback)
978 1 78179 043 4 (paperback)

Library of Congress Cataloging-in-Publication Data
Methods for the study of religious change: from religious studies to
worldview studies / edited by Andri Droogers and Anton van Harskamp.
pages cm
Includes bibliographical references and index.
ISBN 978-1-78179-042-7 (hb) -- ISBN 978-1-78179-043-4 (pb)
1. Change--Religious aspects. 2. Methodology. 3. Religion--Philosophy.
I. Droogers, A. F., editor of compilation.
BL65.C53M48 2013
201'.7--dc23
                        2013013232

Typeset by CA Typesetting Ltd, www.publisherservices.co.uk
Printed and bound in Great Britain by Lightning Source UK Ltd., Milton Keynes
and Lightning Source Inc., La Vergne, TN

Contents

Chapter 1
Introduction

ANDRÉ DROOGERS* AND ANTON VAN HARSKAMP**

GETTING STARTED

Faster than ever before, religions and religiosity are changing. Modernization, by which we mean the application of the results of science and technology in society, is an important driving force. Various modernizing processes are at work simultaneously, generating complex and diffuse worldviews. The trend towards individualization presents many people with the freedom and the impetus to devise their own authentic worldviews, including secular views. Not only new forms of individualism, but also new social forms are emerging. In this new constellation, the concept of spirituality has gained popularity, sometimes replacing "religion" as a label for the personal worldview.

Much is going on at a global level, including the so-called end of ideologies, the expansion of fundamentalisms, the appearance of syncretistic religions, the spectacular growth of Pentecostalism, or the rise of New Age and other new religious movements. Religions continue playing multiple roles in society, including global society, as both a cause of and a solution to problems. Global migration has taken believers beyond their familiar environments, making for transnational religious connections and new influences in the host society. The picture of a world neatly divided geographically between the five world religions has become outdated. Migrants need to build an identity in their new environment, and religion often provides the building blocks for this to happen.

* André Droogers is Emeritus Professor of Cultural Anthropology, especially the Anthropology of Religion and Symbolic Anthropology, at VU University, Amsterdam. He is co-editor of *"Studying Global Pentecostalism: Theories and Methods"* (University of California Press, 2010). A selection from the articles that he has written over the last 30 years was reprinted, together with an autobiographical Introduction, in *"Play and Power in Religion: Collected Essays"* (De Gruyter, 2012).

** Anton van Harskamp is a philosopher of religion, and Emeritus Professor of "Religion, Identity and Civil Society" at VU University, Amsterdam. He is co-editor of *"Playful Religion: Challenges for the Study of Religion"* (Oberon, 2006) and author of books on new religions and civil society. He is the co-editor of volumes on conflicts in social science, on individualism and on moral philosophy. His main research interest is the social theory of the impact of new religions on civil society.

The public context has changed as well. The mass media provide information and opinions that are seen by many people to be more important than those from traditional religious institutions. Non-institutionalized phenomena now represent an important component of the religious field. Thus in the public sphere mass rituals have emerged that lack an institutional background. At the same time, the views of atheists have obtained an accepted place in public debates, and a few atheist spokespersons have penned bestsellers that eloquently argue for the non-existence of God. Secularization and "sacralization," the process by which the sacred is adopted or embraced anew as a major frame of reference, seem to occur simultaneously.

In looking at this dynamic situation and considering the methodological consequences, we have set a new course for our discipline, re-negotiating several of the established approaches. An effective methodology connects the philosophy of science with theoretical approaches, thematic choices and fruitful methods. We have made a number of choices, with consequences for future research. We take religion to be a sub-category of the term worldview, by which we mean that religion needs to be viewed as part of a larger field in which people struggle for and with meaning. We also intend to pay close attention to similarities between religious and secular views, instead of remaining prisoners of the perceived binary opposition between them. One of the unfortunate results of modernization is that differences have been emphasized, setting religion apart from secular worldviews, partly because scholars of religion identify themselves as scientists of religion. A move in the other direction is needed, just as in art history both religious and secular art are studied in one discipline, even though there are specialists on religious art. Focusing on meaning-making seems the best way to make room for the study of secular worldviews based on scientific knowledge. Moreover, we propose to view scholars as meaning-makers, not dissimilar from the people they study. We suggest that a constructivist view of the mission of science corresponds with the demand for an effective study of current worldviews. This leads us to argue for the rehabilitation of qualitative methods. A playful way of dealing with duality will be outlined in detail. In addition, we make a demand for the applied study of religion and for scholarly engagement.

In order to study the concrete dynamics of the late modern worldview, the researcher needs an updated methodology. For this to happen, a profile of current worldviews must be sketched. The consequences of these can then be appraised. A perspective on the mission of science must be chosen along with a complementary family of methods.

So far in the study of religion, methodological concerns have not received much attention, although there have been several initiatives over the last decade (e.g. Davie 2007: 111–132, Hjelm and Zuckerman 2012, Kurth and Lehmann 2011, Olson 2003, Spickard et al. 2002, Stausberg and Engler 2011, Woodhead 2012; see also the journals *Annual Review of the Sociology of Religion*, *Fieldwork in Religion* and *Method and Theory in the Study of Religion* and the Kent University website http://www.kent.ac.uk/religionmethods/). Commonly however, social science methods and techniques, both quantitative and qualitative, were applied in the study of religion without much reworking. Or sometimes the methodology was inspired by theological, historical and literary methodologies, extended to the study of the world religions, in which sacred texts featured as the main object of investigation, and rituals were given less attention. Disciplinary borders have been established. The field is divided, the choice between quantitative and qualitative methods serving as another watershed. Although occasional strife occurs, the usual business is one of live and let live. Limited resources are distributed accordingly. However, the present situation asks for a different approach. The authors of this book seek to fill the gaps. Part I of this book presents a general perspective, whereas Part II offers a number of thematic case studies. Part III looks to the future, exploring the prospects for the renewed study of worldviews.

BETWEEN SECULARIZATION AND SACRALIZATION

Our joint experience and expertise as authors of this volume stem from a research programme called "Between Secularization and Sacralization" (BSS), focused on Dutch society (see Droogers 2007). The Netherlands is an interesting laboratory for religious and worldview research. In some ways it is unique in its idiosyncrasies, such as the "pillar" system, including the secular worldviews of the socialist and liberal kind, entrenched in the Netherlands for almost a century. The Dutch are an interesting tribe indeed in religious and other respects. At the same time however, Dutch society is subjected to supranational processes such as secularization, migration and globalization. The country today is an interesting experiment in multiculturalism, since it has so many co-inhabitants who come from a variety of continents, cultures and religions. The typically Dutch "pillar" system, as the living-apart-together of sub-societies with religious and ideological identities, was a way of practising tolerance. Nowadays tolerance is no longer a matter of course. Recently the country is known for the religiously motivated assassination of columnist and film director Theo van Gogh. An anti-Islam climate has been nourished through public statements by Pim Fortuyn (also assassinated), Ayaan Hirsi Ali (now in the USA), and MP Geert Wilders.

Every decade since the 1960s, surveys called "God in the Netherlands" have been conducted. They show that Dutch society is now, in terms of de-churching, the most secular society in the world (Becker and Vink 1994, Becker et al. 1997, Dekker et al. 1997). Had the German Democratic Republic continued to exist, then the Netherlands would take second place, but thanks to the demise of the wall, the Netherlands assumes first place.

Yet in recent years there are also signs of what has come to be called de-secularization in Dutch society (e.g. Berger 2002), a return to religion, usually lacking any clear institutionalized expression, and manifesting itself increasingly in the new phenomenon of "free-floating believers" (De Hart 2011, van

Harskamp 2000). Moreover, the faithful, who in those decades of secularization remained connected with their churches, are no longer a homogeneous
category, if they ever were one. They now hold a very mixed bag of views,
sometimes contained within the same person. As a consequence, the current
situation is confused and confusing. Philosophers, theologians and sociologists speculate on the question of where religion is heading in Dutch society.
This makes Dutch society interesting to foreign scholars as well.

The BSS programme was organized around five themes: ritual, experience, language, morals and identity. Each theme was thought to offer an entry
point into the field of changing worldviews in the Netherlands. Together
these themes cover most of the issues raised when changing worldviews
are being examined. Each theme was approached by means of a qualitative
monographic case study. In selecting a concrete context for our research, we
sought out rich or "thick" ethnography, nourishing and nourished by theoretical and methodological debates. In qualitative work, the researcher is supposed to influence the way the case study is to be put into practice, because
the researcher's personality is thought to be his or her most significant tool.
The so-called subjective aspect of this type of research was opened up to close
scrutiny, the researchers becoming self-conscious of their own role in fieldwork encounters. The study of religion has always to come to terms with the
ongoing tension between religion and science, the latter often used as the
measuring stick for the relevance of the former. Moreover, qualitative methods also pretend to be scientific. Thus the question of just how objective or
subjective a researcher should be in order to gain access to believers' views,
experiences and practices, remains a constant area of debate. The methodology of participant observation in particular raises the problem of how the
researcher can be both an outsider and an insider at once.

QUANTITATIVE AND QUALITATIVE METHODS

Although the authors choose to explore the possibilities that qualitative
methods represent in the new situation, they do not mean to deny that the
quantitative approach was helpful in verifying trends statistically. The Dutch
sociologists of religion, the "bookkeepers" of secularization, as one author
(Post 1998: 47) called them, did a good job. But as Dutch sociologist of religion
Gérard van Tillo once observed (quoted in Wijsen 2002: 15), we know now how
religious the Dutch population is, and yet we hardly know in what senses the
people are religious, or irreligious for that matter. The results are available,
calculated to two decimal places, but the processes that led to the formulation
of these results are virtually unknown. What cannot be read, categorized and
determined from the tables, diagrams and graphs are people's personal stories and the idiosyncratic uniqueness of individual meaning-making, or the
fulsomeness of religious life. The "mystery" of religion, "the-rest-of-what-is"
in religion, cannot even begin to be considered in quantitative forms of social

observation (Van de Port 2011). Particularly in the context of the current confused situation, exploratory qualitative studies are badly needed.

Quantitative work still predominates in the sociology and psychology of religion, despite a recent revival of qualitative approaches. The usefulness of qualitative methods is not immediately obvious, and this in itself is in need of explanation. There is a certain respectability, a reputation that surrounds quantitative work that implies that it is objective, especially when it is presented in statistical form. "Research has shown" usually means that statistics have been produced that suggest some inescapable conclusion about a correlation or causal relation. Policymakers are used to working with statistics. They routinely employ research results derived in this way, and they even frequently pay for them to be produced.

Qualitative research, in contrast, appears to produce much "softer" results, to take much more time and to provide a much less objective result. Policymakers have less experience working with sometimes very nuanced research results expressed in narrative form. The qualitative researcher is the Calimero of social science research, the ugly duckling. His or her work seems to be concerned with the leftovers, after the quantitative researchers have been publicly applauded for doing their job. Whereas qualitative research is often defined by its lack of concern with quantitative methods, one almost never comes across the inverse statement.

And yet, as will become clear throughout the course of this book, a renewal of interest in qualitative research is taking place. Several authors have claimed a place for qualitative research under their social science sun. Sometimes they defend splendid isolation (e.g. Smith 1993), sometimes they emphasize the complementary nature of the two methods (cf. Denzin and Lincoln 1998b: 8–11, Tashakkori and Teddlie 1998). The qualitative tool kit has been debated and expanded and the range of possible applications extended. It seems therefore worthwhile to take stock of the current favourable prospects for qualitative research, specifically in such fields as worldview studies. In fact, the present situation calls for explorative qualitative research, and not only in the secularized and multifarious Netherlands.

Thus in Chapter 3, we try to kill two birds with one stone. On the one hand, the general rehabilitation of qualitative approaches is argued for. On the other hand, a qualitative methodology for current worldview research is proposed, as an illustration of the usefulness of that approach. This double focus has the advantage of providing a practical and concrete illustration of a more theoretical and abstract discourse, just as the theoretical and abstract considerations can be shown to clarify a complex and sometimes chaotic worldview.

In doing this, we will simultaneously and perhaps paradoxically defend both the uniqueness of the qualitative approach, and its complementarity with quantitative approaches. Since the debate around the use of either quantitative or qualitative methods is loaded with dichotomies, special attention is given to the question of how to avoid binary choices. André Droogers has coined the term "methodological ludism" as a way out of seemingly impossible dilemmas

(Droogers 1996, 1999, 2012). He makes a demand for a playful way of dealing with exclusive options. This position is described in more detail in Chapter 4.

The dichotomous opposition between qualitative and quantitative methods may serve as the basic dilemma of a wider debate, since the options are linked to other sets of alternatives. As we will see, much depends on the view one holds of science's mission in society, and more particularly of the humanities and the social sciences. This view is influenced in turn by the theoretical perspectives used to analyse society. The different perspectives show traces of old philosophical oppositions, such as that between mind and matter. To these methodological, theoretical and philosophical puzzles, the thematic dimension must be added, because what one takes to be the object of research makes a difference, as does the question of what one wants to know about the object of research.

This combination of methodological, theoretical, philosophical and thematic elements opens fascinating perspectives. In the case of worldview research, it is obvious that researchers give meaning to the people who give meaning to life and death. Scholars develop ways of knowing about ways of knowing. This double hermeneutic, as Anthony Giddens (1984: xxxv, 284) has called it, also means that this theme, and therefore this book, offers a fruitful means by which to explore validity problems, thereby illustrating the dichotomies and opportunities that the debate around qualitative research presents. Current worldview research is definitely subjective and therefore offers a test case *par excellence* for some of the methodological problems of validity that characterize the qualitative approach.

STRUCTURE OF THIS VOLUME

The structure of the book follows the pattern described so far. In Part I, André Droogers looks at methods for the study of the changing contemporary religious and worldview situation. In Chapter 2, the term worldview will be defined in relation to the meaning of two similar concepts, religion and ideology. In this chapter the current global situation is summarized with regard to worldviews, showing how useful qualitative methods can be in the study of new phenomena. Chapter 3 is dedicated to a comparison of the quantitative and qualitative approaches. Their complementary relationship will be discussed, as well as their singular nature. Chapter 4 contains a presentation of the concept of methodological ludism as a way of combining seemingly contrasting approaches, perspectives and methods.

The second part of the book consists of five illustrative chapters of monographs in which aspects of qualitative methods are discussed.[1] In every chapter, transitions in worldviews are presupposed. The cases described in the successive chapters refer to the key themes of the research programme

---

1   These chapters have appeared in 2011 in a special issue of *Fieldwork in Religion* 6 (2).

"Between Secularization and Sacralization" (BSS): ritual, experience, language, morals and identity. The authors explore the connections between their theme, their theoretical approach, the processes at work in the transformation of the situation they study and the idiosyncrasies of their fieldwork experience. All of these aspects together have consequences for the methodological approach taken. Though each chapter takes a different theme as a starting point, the authors have in common their commitment to the praxis of current worldview research. The authors show how they dealt with dichotomies. The double perspective that honours both poles and the whole spectrum is sought. The pitfalls of unilateral choices are shown.

Chapter 5, on ritual, by Kim Knibbe, Marten van der Meulen and Peter Versteeg, focuses on the question of what participation in ritual praxis "delivers" in religious research. The authors demonstrate that being a participant in rites may enhance the understanding of social processes among the group of believers who are regularly involved in ritual. Experiencing the emotional and physical sensations that often accompany ritual can give the researcher some clues into what other participants experience. The authors discuss the tendency in ritual studies to objectify ritual phenomena as parts of a symbolic network, thereby overlooking the experiential meaning of ritual. The authors envisage a methodology for the study of religious ritual that consists of making the transition from insider to outsider and then to insider again.

Chapter 6, on experience, by Peter Versteeg and Johan Roeland, addresses the processes of deinstitutionalization and individualization, since these increase the scope for the experiential dimension of religion. The authors avoid the pitfall of limiting the study of experience to the individual level. In their view, the social and political dimensions need to be included, despite individualizing tendencies. Religious experience, even authentic experience, is socially constructed. Focusing on subjectivization, they also apply this insight to the debate around the concept of spirituality. This has consequences for the methodological choices made. In a case study about a meditation course, the authors show how the dual social and individual construction of experience can be uncovered in fieldwork.

The contribution on language, by Rhea Hummel, is the most interdisciplinary of the five chapters in Part II, as it is written from the double disciplinary perspective of literary studies and the anthropology of religion. In her analysis of worldview language, as used by artists and writers, Hummel seeks to enrich anthropological qualitative analysis of life histories by showing how language students study and interpret narrative discourse. Individualization, fragmentation and secularization are the modernization processes that stand out in her approach. Artists and writers pose as authentic individual meaning-makers *par excellence*, exploring the frontiers of signification. Interestingly the majority of respondents use their discourse to emphasize the inchoate nature of life, rather than presupposing coherence and consistency. Despite the strong individualism of the artists and writers, Hummel distinguishes four types of worldview language, thus showing that her respondents convey supra-individual tendencies, despite the confessed uniqueness of the life stories and worldviews presented. Here again the individualizing tendency is shown to have social and cultural dimensions. This is also visible in the role model that artists and writers present to others in a de-churched society. She also pays attention to the ways in which the researcher establishes rapport with this type of respondent.

Morals are discussed in Chapter 8 of this volume from the perspective of Kim Knibbe's fieldwork in the south of the Netherlands in a predominantly Catholic environment. Knibbe draws attention to three aspects of her research that were crucial to understanding how moral orientations changed and to gaining insight into the role of religion in these changes. She looks at the role of gossip and secrets, stories about fallible priests, and the ways in which the image of the "Other" is constructed in liberal Catholicism. At first sight, it seems counter-intuitive to take gossip seriously, or to include secrets in a general analysis. However, from Knibbe's research it became clear that any kind of analysis of the role of religion in moral orientation would not be complete without taking into consideration these suppressed genres of speech. Her approach goes beyond an individualizing methodology, calling attention to the social roots of individually experienced phenomena, especially the clergy's former moral dominance. In describing her methodology, she shows how a researcher becomes complicit in social processes involving secrets and gossip, and subsequently how writing about this can come to feel like a long series of small betrayals. This leads Knibbe to a discussion about some ethical considerations.

The last chapter in Part II, written by Edien Bartels, Daniëlle Koning and Martijn de Koning, focuses on the identity of young Muslims living in the Netherlands. In fact, identity has become part of the vocabulary of the faithful, in this case Muslim identity. Identity in this chapter is seen from the perspective of the researched, but also from that of the researcher. The authors suggest that focusing on the interaction between the researcher and the people that he or she studies is instrumental in constructing a sense of the complex identities of fieldworkers and the people they study. They also show that in the wider context of Dutch multicultural society and the dramatic events taking place within it, such as the assassination of Theo van Gogh, this interaction weighs heavily on the process of identity formation. The influence of migration and globalization is taken into account, especially the politicization of Islam. The dynamics of these processes are made visible in the examples the authors describe and in their identity formation as researchers. The fine line between the role of insider and outsider and between participation and observation, is illustrated by focusing respectively on the roles of consulting partner, believer and youth worker.

Part III, "Moving parameters," contains two chapters that remind us where we started and that look forward to the overall method in the study of religion and to the mission of the discipline. It is here that the contours of the new study of worldviews are drawn. In Chapter 10, André Droogers summarizes his views on applied and engaged worldview research. He points to the new themes that are on our agenda. They demand a new mission statement for our discipline, a corresponding theoretical and conceptual framework, as well as a new methodology. In Chapter 11, the Epilogue of this volume, Anton van Harskamp comes back to the central idea in the new methodology of the study of religion: doing qualitative religion research is not only a detached study of worldviews of others but also the meeting, that is playful interfering, of the very own social-scientific worldview with religious worldviews. He suggests that in the meeting of worldviews, the symbolic order of both worldviews, the religious and the social-scientific one, can be surpassed, making religion for the researcher a simultaneously intimate and strange phenomenon.

Together these chapters make a significant contribution to answering the central question posed throughout this collection: what is the most useful methodology for the study of worldviews in our era? We, the editors, believe that in answering this question, we are opening a crucial and urgent conversation about the importance of better worldview research for our times.

Part I

Methods for the Study of Contemporary Worldviews

Introduction to Part I

ANDRÉ DROOGERS*

Methodology tells scholars how to proceed. When it is our intention to study religion and religions, we must be aware of the concepts we use, such as "religion," since they define the limits of our field. They also fill our toolbox. If we wish to extend our field, as is proposed here, to include worldviews, whether religious or secular, the same condition prevails. We may have to change the contents of our toolbox.

At the same time, in defining our concepts we must be aware of the characteristics of the phenomena we wish to study. We may use abstract and general notions, such as "fundamentalism" or "ritual," but at the same time we deal with concrete examples of the categories of "fundamentalism" and "ritual." So we must move back and forth between the abstract generalizations and the concrete cases. Otherwise we cannot be sure that our conclusions correspond in some way with the reality we do research on.

We usually think, as a working hypothesis, that we may presuppose consensus between scholars on terms and what they stand for. Just as dictionaries reflect such agreement on our language, textbooks are thought to offer the correct vocabulary, applicable in our work. That is how students are trained and what books like this one are supposed to offer.

Yet there are at least two reasons why this straightforward format must be corrected. One is that scholars are meaning-makers, like the people they study, and may differ in the way they make sense of their study field. The differences stem from choices that have to be made, such as the decision on what the mission of science is and what type of knowledge is demanded in a particular case. The answer is not really a matter of course. This condition introduces arbitrariness into the picture.

The other reason is that the field is rapidly changing and that today's phenomena are not necessarily the same tomorrow. This is in fact our daily bread in studying religion. Some of these changes are rather drastic, as can be seen in one's own context from a comparison of the changes in the religious behaviour of three successive generations, say over the last century.

* André Droogers is Emeritus Professor of Cultural Anthropology, especially the Anthropology of Religion and Symbolic Anthropology, at VU University, Amsterdam. He is co-editor of *"Studying Global Pentecostalism: Theories and Methods"* (University of California Press, 2010). A selection from the articles that he has written over the last 30 years was reprinted, together with an autobiographical Introduction, in *"Play and Power in Religion: Collected Essays"* (De Gruyter, 2012).

So we take as our point of departure that not all scholars agree on the nature of the profession, or on the tasks ahead, or on the tools to use, and to top it all the field is changing as well. Therefore it is useful, as we will do in this part of the book, to take stock of concepts, of views on the mission of our trade or on the type of knowledge we wish to gather, and of the changes that are occurring in our field.

Not that this will result in an easy recipe of how to proceed scholarly under the circumstances. One superficial look in the monographs and articles that are being published makes us aware of the different approaches available. Though the next three chapters present a particular view, the main purpose is to map the landscape, so that the reader may obtain sufficient resources to plan his or her journey through this study field. In other words: each scholar – newcomer or established – should be aware of the options made and the degree of arbitrariness involved. Like the people we study come to have their worldview identity, we will have to construe our academic identity, in a continuing dialogue with our world and our colleagues. As scholars we can together make our profession prosper and progress, using our differences in our debates as our academic working capital. Accordingly newcomers are primarily introduced to the trade's differences, and much less to its consensus.

Thus we must first of all list our options in defining our concepts. What can be called a worldview, a religion, an ideology? We will explore the wider conceptual framework of these terms, including notions such as culture, secularization, globalization, identity and power. Inevitably this inventory reflects a particular approach, but it also presents the options that we face. Usually proposals that are made in such debates are the result of a specific way of handling these options. Though this is only rarely successful, the intention is to challenge other scholars to agree and reach consensus. Yet more often the debate continues.

Thus this part of the book contains the proposal to substitute "religion" as our main topic with "worldview" and rename the Study of Religion (or Religious Studies) as Worldview Studies. One reason to do so is the current variety in worldviews, ending the monopoly that religions had in that area. Of course we should continue studying religion and religions, but under the current circumstances the inclusion of secular worldviews is an appropriate update. Besides, after working for decades with the contrast between religion and science, neglecting the common characteristics between religious and secular worldviews, the worldview banner opens a new perspective. Finally, in defining worldview, it will be suggested that doing academic work also presupposes a worldview. Accordingly, when looking for commonness between science and religion, the comparison between scholars in the study of worldviews and the people they study, whether religious or secular, can be included.

Thinking of methods in the current study of religion, two families of methods and techniques dominate the field, either working in a quantitative way, or taking a qualitative approach. The difference is common in the social sciences. In Chapter 3 the alternatives are compared, making the options explicit. The choice for a particular view on the mission of science, either neo-positivist or more constructivist, will be shown to be central to the comparison. Another option regards the combination of the two or, in contrast, their exclusive use. In any case, the current worldview situation appears to demand a more ample use of qualitative methods.

Chapter 4 discusses an underlying problem in these discussions, which is that very often the options regard two contrasting and exclusive positions. Thus the opposition is presupposed between science and religion, quantitative and qualitative approaches, neo-positivist and constructivist views of science, and many other sets of alternatives. Though the contrast is fuel for the debate engine, the arbitrariness of many standpoints must be acknowledged as well. As a way to deal with this aspect of the academic worldview, play is proposed as a way of dealing simultaneously with alternatives. This is not a plea for eclecticism, though it may result in such a position. However, the playful approach opens the possibility to better appreciate the other point of view. For example, in studying religion from a secular scientific perspective, the playful way of looking at phenomena can be fruitful. Using this "methodological ludism," even a secular scholar may gain a more ample insight into what motivates a religious participant.

Chapter 2
The World of Worldviews

ANDRÉ DROOGERS*

FIRST THINGS FIRST

Definition precedes method. Before I can discuss the methodological implications of the study of contemporary worldviews, the field itself needs to be defined and mapped. It does not make sense to start filling our toolbox before we know precisely what our task is. Moreover, we must have a developed sense of the changes that have taken place in the recent past. So first I will explore the meanings of the concept of worldview, including the terms that can be considered sub-categories of that general category; religion, ideology and spirituality. In addition, I discuss other characteristics of the field, especially in relation to recent developments.

I do not intend to reinvent the concept of "worldview." The knowledge I need to map the field has in large part been set out in previous research. Any science is cumulative and in this field there is an impressive body of general methodological literature. As a scholar I stand on the shoulders of my predecessors, even during the moments that I think of their contribution as being outmoded. As we mentioned in Chapter 1, in the study of religion method has recently received greater attention. I am trained to move between case studies and generalizations, from intuition to plausible conclusions, from general models to particular instances, and back again, hopefully in an upwards spiral of understanding. In this chapter however, for didactic purposes, I begin with theory and concepts, fully aware that they are the result of previous movements in the empirical cycle. Regardless, it is my personal perspective on the state of the art, along with some of my own reflections. Defining phenomena is in large part an arbitrary business, posing choices that others might make differently. In producing knowledge, we are in some ways all conditioned by our biographies (see Droogers 2012: 1–32 for mine). Disciplinary frameworks

* André Droogers is Emeritus Professor of Cultural Anthropology, especially the Anthropology of Religion and Symbolic Anthropology, at VU University, Amsterdam. He is co-editor of *"Studying Global Pentecostalism: Theories and Methods"* (University of California Press, 2010). A selection from the articles that he has written over the last 30 years was reprinted, together with an autobiographical Introduction, in *"Play and Power in Religion: Collected Essays"* (De Gruyter, 2012).

often prompt unilateral decisions. Accordingly, each scholar will blaze his or her own path through the terminological jungle. Thus it becomes clear that my disciplinary frame of reference is the cultural anthropology of religion.

Though it may seem that this chapter is primarily about concepts and definitions, the focus is in fact on methodology, in the general sense of the term. It is about the scholarly effort towards observation and meaning-making. Scope and perspective provide greater direction than the vocabulary that results from them. It is important to know the toolkit, but also to see that it is derived from the reflections of generations of scholars.

This is why I begin from a broad perspective, via which I describe worldview as a category that is derived from an even wider concept: culture. The attention given to culture has been dubbed the "cultural turn" (Davie 2007: 249–253, see also the special issue of the journal *Sociology of Religion* 65 [4] 2004). Culture is therefore the first concept I discuss. Beginning here allows me to look at worldview and its dynamics. I continue working my way through the sub-categories that belong to the category called worldview: religion and its corresponding secular worldview, but I also consider ideology and spirituality. When discussing religious and non-religious worldviews, secularization must be granted attention. In addition, ritual becomes an issue, in view of the debate surrounding its definition. Is ritual religious or does secular ritual exist? In considering these matters, recent processes of globalization must be taken into account. The rest of the chapter is dedicated to considerations that the student of worldviews should be aware of when seeking out an appropriate research strategy. For this reason, processes of identity formation, meaning-making practices and power processes will also be discussed.

CULTURE

My starting point is very general and universal. Humans possess culture and cultures. They are able to develop and assimilate knowledge and thereby attribute meaning to their natural and social worlds. Each human group does this in its own way. People display this cultural capacity not only as individuals, but also as members of the group they are born into, or become part of. Humans are cultural beings in all of the contexts to which they belong, both in the course of a day, and throughout their lives. Anything can be subjected to this act of attributing meaning, and the interpretations that result may differ widely, between societies and also between individuals. People and peoples are accorded status. Subjects and objects are named. Events become routine. Chaos becomes order. We seek and find our way around, conferring and recognizing labels. Through this act of meaning-making, the puzzling aspects of existence are made familiar and reality becomes accessible. Reality also comes into being and takes form through people's meaning-making. Worldview is the workshop in which humans labour over their image of reality

Culture distinguishes human beings from other animals. Some authors would omit the word "other" from the previous sentence. Their choice to do so is in itself the result of meaning-making. A certain amount of arbitrariness can therefore be detected in any position taken. When comparing animals and humans, the emphasis may either be put on the common elements, as primatologists and physical anthropologists tend to do, or on the differences, as most cultural and social anthropologists would suggest. As a consequence, the concept of culture has been used in relation to animal behaviour as well, in the sense of considering a particular way of life of a species. On the other hand, the fact that the human species knows literally thousands of cultures can be emphasized as a point of difference, and provides an indication of what the exceptional human capacity for culture has brought about. No other animal shows this immense and constantly transforming diversity.

Although animals also understand meanings and may learn new ones, as any dog owner knows, the capacity of animals to produce new meanings on their own, beyond their genetic and instinctive conditioning, is much weaker in most cases than the capacity of humans. Humans, as animals of one particular genus, are conditioned as well, and therefore undeniably share fundamental characteristics with animals. Yet, by a fluke of the evolutionary process they are equipped with a meaning-making capacity that is exceptional among animals. To survive in their habitat, the members of all other animal species depend very much on their command and understanding of available meanings. This basic set of repertoires remains more or less the same from generation to generation. Unless challenged by a changing environment or new events, they will not of their own initiative produce alternative systems of meanings. Humans, in contrast, have developed a huge variety of meaning systems and are able to modify them, not only from one generation to another, but also in an individual's lifetime. In human cultures, even the naturally conditioned sets of meanings, for example, those regarding food and reproduction, come under scrutiny. Animals do not consciously or explicitly fast or take vows of celibacy, because of cultural or religious custom. In this sense, other animals do not possess culture, let alone religion.

So far I have used the world culture in the singular, to refer to a general and exclusively human characteristic. But I have also used the plural. Whereas any animal species has only one way of living, the human animal chooses from among diverse ways of living. In each of these concrete cultures a different set of shared meanings is developed and adapted. What makes the scope for variation even greater is that people have their own idiosyncratic preferences. Moreover, a culture's and a person's repertoires commonly contain contradictory meanings. It might therefore be said that the human animal distinguishes itself by having both culture in the singular, and in the plural, while other animals only exhibit cultures, as distinguishing ways of life, in the plural.

Ignited by modernization, contemporary society sees a massive amount of meaning-making, stimulated globally and transmitted through various means of communication. This is happening today on an unprecedented scale. The

search for cultural and personal meaning has been intensified. Modernization conferred numerous components of cultural repertoires to the dustbin.
Cross-cultural interactions have proliferated, appealing to a universal human
cultural capacity that extends beyond cultural boundaries and becomes applicable in any new situation. The universal schemas of airport terminals are
an example, as are the traffic rules on the World Wide Web. More and more
people use two or more cultural and religious repertoires to negotiate their
path through the global world. The contemporary dynamics are so compelling that they demand a reconsideration of research methods in the area of
religion and religions. In fact, the social sciences were stimulated immensely
by modern dynamics, and the founding fathers became puzzled by what they
saw being changed. Society and culture became increasingly puzzling.

In short, the universal human capacity to link persons, social relations,
objects, events, time, space and any other perceived phenomena, with meanings and words, could be called culture in the singular, implying an exclusive
and uniquely human potential to establish a relationship with reality. Such a
definition must be added to the typical approach to culture, in which the concept is primarily understood to refer to everything that results from the application of the afore-mentioned capacity for meaning-making, in terms of ideas,
beliefs, artefacts, customs, actions, social patterns, and so on, thereby taking
culture as a plural category, more or less synonymous with way of life. The
plural meaning of culture was coined in a period when the boundaries were not
as perforated as they are today. The singular version has more recent origins.

In my use of the term, the singular and plural versions should be kept
together, since both the human capacity and the results of that gift are important ingredients in what makes human beings human. In this way the universal and particular can be combined. Such an approach will prove to be useful
when discussing the dynamics of worldview and worldviews as well, especially now that meaning-making and communication have reached unprecedented levels on a global scale.

Interestingly science has a particular way of being culturally active. Like
religion (bien étonnées de se trouver ensemble), it is not satisfied with the
image of the world as it appears in daily life (Bellah 2011: 4, 9). Scholars seek to
give meaning in a systematic methodological manner, obeying the rules of logic
and method that have come to characterize academic culture. In the case that
human beings are being studied for their social and cultural makeup, scholars
act as human meaning-makers, studying their fellow human meaning-makers.
In Chapter 5 the authors discuss how fieldworkers, in studying ritual through
participant observation, act as meaning-makers in their own way. This double
layer of meanings has to be taken into account when discussing worldviews and
the methods of studying them. As scholars, we have to decide on the numerous
meanings we attribute to the field of meanings that we seek to understand. We
are of the same nature and kind as those we seek to study: meaning-makers.
Academic culture, with its paradigm shifts, ongoing debates and gamut of concepts and definitions, characterizes the trade of the scholarly tribe.

A REINVIGORATED CONCEPT

Culture as a concept is not without problems, however. Although cultural anthropology derives its name from the notion of culture, several anthropologists have criticized the concept (for an overview see Brightman 1995, Eriksen 2004: 26–31). Anthropologists reject the essentialist approach in particular, because it presents culture as a determinant of human behaviour. For example, the Bongo-Bongo, seen as a quintessential supra-individual localized culture, is treated as a reified abstraction, with a supposed autonomy and cohesion, and with closed boundaries. "Culture" in this sense is seen to act as if it were a subject, imposing itself upon all the Bongo-Bongo, who behave like its objects.

Yet, the current context of interaction between cultures (in the plural sense of the term) and of migration streams across the world, has opened our eyes to the perforation of cultural boundaries and to the active way in which individuals use their cultural capacity and accompanying fluid repertoires as a sextant in their voyage through life. As a consequence, power mechanisms have also received more attention than before, since these determine the margins within which individuals are both treated as objects and allowed to actively deviate from the course of their society. Accordingly, culture, seen as a capacity more than as a constellation of customs that is typical of a society, has gained attention. In fact, even obligation or imitation can be understood as acts. In retrospect, perforation and repertoires were probably already occurring when anthropologists saw the model of culture as a closed and supra-individual unity. Bound by the disciplinary methodology of their time, they were not yet able to see all that was happening in relation to meaning-making. Each generation of scholars has its own type of blinkers.

In my view, an emphasis on the meaning-making capacity and process, including the power dimension, reinvigorates the term culture for continued use, free of the defects that first led anthropologists to criticize the concept. It has the advantage of pointing to the process through which people produce, use and reproduce repertoires of meaning, according to circumstance, within or outside the boundaries of "cultures" (in the plural sense), and using their own strategies in dealing with the powers that be. No reification occurs, and the tension between the person's double roles, as subject and object, can be appraised. Culture then becomes the human capacity for meaning-making, and all that results from it.

WORLDVIEWS

Worldviews, whether religious or secular, emerge as an important part of cultural repertoires. Analogous to culture, worldview can be understood as both a human capacity and the result of exercising that competence. Admittedly this is an arbitrary construct, but as in the case of culture, it offers a helpful way to pay attention to both the process and the result, to change as well as continuity, to the actual meaning-making and to the concrete output.

Some provisos must be made. This focus on meaning-making may sound as if a worldview is both a rational and perceived system. Yet experience, behaviour and emotion nourish the form it takes as well. Of course there is always a class of specialists whose rather cerebral work reflects on the idea system and the rituals, but they are a minority, albeit a powerful one.

Besides, though I stress the importance of meaning-making, the major component of the practice of worldviews is routine work. The worldview wheel is not re-invented every time people raise existential questions. Answers are available. That is also the reason to keep an eye on both competence and outcome.

One last caveat that must be mentioned relates to the fact that basic questions are often not answered, either because they are too difficult to answer, or because the perspective experienced cannot be put into the right words or into adequate symbols. The worldview experience can bring both orientation and despair, bliss and misery, consolation and disquiet, as well as sense and its lack. Though moral questions are part of the worldview domain, worldviews are not by definition morally good – except perhaps by their own definition. In the course of history several worldviews, religious as well as secular, have felt legitimated to wreak havoc in human lives, laying entire countries, cultures and societies to waste. Worldviews can present themselves as final and exclusive. Yet, meaning-making can also be meaning-seeking. One might say that any worldview that claims to have all the answers should be mistrusted. Most probably the system appears so convincing because it is accompanied by effective power mechanisms that discipline followers and discourage debate on presuppositions. Worldviews have open ends, simply because the human capacity for meaning-making is limitless. It may seem paradoxical when we observe what is presented as true and certain, but meaning-making is in fact oversized, offering much more than is functionally necessary, as evidenced by the enormous variety in worldviews. The wealth of meanings comes with the difficulty of choosing between options, as the meaning-maker always searches for better alternatives, none of which are fully adequate. All said and done, the mystery is inexpressible. Fullness is transcendence's prerogative (Taylor 2007: 5–12).

Having presented these conditions, we will now look at worldviews, starting with the existential questions that constitute their raw material. Ellen Hijmans and Adri Smaling (1997: 17) suggest that there are five basic and ultimate questions that humans universally ask about themselves and their world:

What is considered beautiful (aesthetics)?
What is morally good behaviour (ethics)?
Why do humans live and die (ontology)?
What can be trusted as true (epistemology)?
And, in summary: How can groups and individuals, in answering these questions, distinguish themselves from others as authentic human beings (identity strategies)?

In raising and answering these five ultimate questions, about what is beautiful, good, significant, true and authentic respectively, people act as cultural, that is, meaning-making beings. The human animal is able to raise and answer these ultimate questions because of its exceptional position as a meaning-maker. In part the questions belong to a self-reflection on that surprising aspect of the human condition. We might well ask, "For heaven's sake, what are we?" or: "Who the hell are we?" Heaven and hell may play a role in the answers that are given, including their explicit denial.

As already suggested, like culture, worldview can be understood in the singular form, as a human capacity to raise and answer life's ultimate questions. Understood in the plural, it points to the variety of answers given, in religions, secular worldviews, ideologies and spiritualities. Again the universal and the particular, the process and the outcome can thus be combined. In appreciating the differences, the common background can become part of the comparison as well. One way of summarizing what is common, despite the many differences, is the classical phenomenological approach, coined in the comparative study of religions and labelling common phenomena. Ninian Smart's distinction of seven dimensions is a well-known example of naming aspects that occur in any worldview, including secular ones, such as nationalism or Marxism (Smart 1992: 12–25). Smart lists the following dimensions:

The practical and ritual dimension
The experiential and emotional dimension
The narrative or mythic dimension
The doctrinal and philosophical dimension
The ethical and legal dimension
The social and institutional dimension
The material dimension.

Together these seven dimensions help to map the world of concrete worldviews, opening them up to comparison. These dimensions also serve to house the answers to the five basic questions mentioned above. Although there is not a clear one-to-one relationship, connections between questions and dimensions can be traced. A clear case is that of the moral question, directly linked to the ethical and legal dimension. Although many answers to the basic questions appear primarily in their cognitive form, as part of the doctrinal and philosophical dimension, they are also expressed within the other dimensions, most clearly in the experiential and emotional dimensions. Meaning may take the form of abstract affirmations, but can also be expressed in very concrete behaviour (the ritual dimension), or in stories (myths, legends, fables), and taken up in narrative or mythic dimensions. Art objects and temples are part of the material dimension. To preserve any theological or philosophical stance, an institutional framework is necessary.

These seven dimensions are distinguishable from each other, but they are also interconnected. Thus a strong institution will build impressive temples, filled with art objects, where extensive rituals take place, generating strong emotions among followers. A moral and doctrinal system will legitimize the institution and its leadership, perhaps also justifying them with an authoritative myth of origin.

The advantage of the five questions formulated by Hijmans and Smaling (1997) is that the focus on meaning-making is acknowledged. Similarly, the value of Smart's typology of dimensions (Smart 1992) is that the ritual, experiential, mythical, philosophical, moral, social, and material characteristics of worldviews receive due attention, as answers to basic questions. The five basic questions and the seven dimensions are therefore complementary with each other, combining inquiry with the potential for solution.

In the present situation, especially in Western Europe, secular minorities have consciously adopted worldviews, such as atheism, Marxism or humanism, that are critical of religion and religions, yet at the same time provide answers to the ultimate basic questions and develop their own seven dimensions. The concept of worldview makes it possible to combine non-religious solutions to the ultimate questions and the seven dimensions together with religious views, into one category. They can be compared, not only for their differences, but also for what they have in common. Together they are an important factor in the way human society, nationally as well as globally, is given form.

Worldviews can be said to derive from the human capacity to seek answers to basic aesthetic, ethical, ontological, epistemological and identity questions. Worldviews are also the set of ritual, experiential, mythic, doctrinal, ethical, institutional and material dimensions that together provide answers to the questions that human beings raise. This definition of the concept does not include any reference to the sacred or the divine. Thus the common characteristics of religious and non-religious worldviews can be emphasized. This however does not prevent us from looking for differences when we wish to distinguish between these types of worldviews, and we turn to this next.

WORLDVIEW DYNAMICS

At first sight, worldviews guarantee some continuity in the practices of groups, societies and individuals. Any worldview offers a more or less systematic and normative perspective on the meaning of a group's world and life, defining the group's role in it. The result can, for example, be read in textbooks on world religions.

Through socialization, children learn the answers to questions that previous generations have provided and begin to find their own way through the maze of life. The worldview may be part of an oral tradition, transmitted from generation to generation, but in literate groups it can also take the form of written texts that codify answers to the five basic questions in a fixed literate form and legitimate a concrete form of the seven dimensions.

At the same time, in daily practice, worldviews have their own dynamics, and are influenced by societal change and changing personal circumstances. At this point, routine can be no longer enough and these life events and changes need to be interpreted. In one of the five categories, a new and crucial question is raised, either by the individual or the group. This can happen in the wake of being lucky or experiencing happiness (How have I become so prosperous?). Satisfaction and fulfilment flows through the life of a person or community. But similarly, the experience of affliction and crisis, minor or major, creates a sense of deprivation and loss (Why was I, of all people, the victim of that calamity?). When a shift in worldview is caused by unexpected negative events, such as calamity or catastrophe, personal reflection on bliss and blessing does not always happen as systematically as may be suggested within philosophical or theological literature. Meaning seems to come to light in an ad hoc manner, in the course of living the experience. It may even remain implicit, without being directly verbalized, as an intuitive model or script that is readily available for future use. It may be filed away to be retrieved again one day, usually in fragments, when it is needed.

The human capacity to raise basic questions is an ever present competence, just as the cumulative work of preceding generations is always contained in the individual, transmitted via socialization. This duality is typical of culture and cultures, and it is also present in worldview and worldviews, combining human capacity with all that results from it, in a constant tension between continuity and change. Followers play the twin roles of being both active subject and passive object. They are both subject and subjugated, depending on the power context in which they live and on the ways they deal with its demands.

This duality was articulately expressed by Peter Berger and Thomas Luckmann (1972: 79) when they wrote, "Society is a human product. Society is an objective reality. Man is a social product" (italics in the original). They distinguish between three stages within an ongoing cycle (Berger and Luckmann 1972: 78):

1. First of all there is the act of externalization. In expressing themselves, human beings produce their society and culture. This is the meaning-making stage. In the case of a worldview, answers are sought to Hijmans' and Smaling's five basic questions.
2. The result, however, given form in Smart's seven dimensions, tends to lead a life of its own, as if it exists independently of its creators. Berger and Luckmann call this stage the objectivation of society and culture. The seven dimensions represent this objectified result.
3. Subsequently, through socialization, people learn how to behave in a particular society and culture. This phase in the cycle is called internalization. Worldviews have their own forms of socialization. This third stage is not a dead end, and may lead on to other innovative efforts to change society and culture, or a worldview, for that matter. Then the cycle makes a fresh start, and externalization starts all over again. In modern times, this cycle has accelerated.

Worldviews obey the threefold cycle. New religious or ideological movements may serve as examples. Innovative meaning-makers come up with a new solution to the ultimate human problems, externalizing a new point of view or a new practice, thereby proposing a change in one or more of the seven dimensions. If there is a plethora of potential meanings and people sense that full and final insight is never reached, initiatives that re-open the cycle will always be welcomed. Yet success is not automatic. There are always failed prophets. This can take tragic forms, like an endlessly repeated rehearsal, without there ever being an opening night. However, when innovative meaning-makers prove to be successful *externalizers* and a substantial number of people adopt their views and practices, the worldview moves on to the following stage, of *objectivation*, as a system itself. In the third stage, new followers are socialized by this approach to understanding life, *internalizing* questions and dimensions. But after some time, a decade or a generation later, new meaning-makers will come up with proposals to change the system, especially when new circumstances demand new answers to old questions (as happens constantly in our era), or when power structures become too demanding and incite resistance. Of course change may also happen simply because people love the fun of reinventing meaning-making anew, for its own sake.

Even if there is very little visible change, people actively consider their worldview. Those choices that appear to be about mere replication and imitation, as for example happens between generations in traditional or orthodox groups, may in fact involve change, perhaps on a minor scale. This is change nevertheless. Even when internalizing worldview, the human meaning-maker is active.

RELIGION AND IDEOLOGY

If worldview is a subcategory of culture (by which I mean the human competence for meaning-making), the concept also contains other terms as sub-subcategories. The best known are religion and ideology. The definition of both terms has led to much debate and resulted in a variety of approaches (Asad 1993, 2003, Bocock and Thompson 1985, Clarke and Byrne 1993, Droogers 2009, Platvoet and Molendijk 1999, Saler 1993). The variety is such that to some authors, any religion is a form of ideology, whereas to others, ideology is a form of religion. Other people again understand religion and ideology as totally distinct from each other. Asad (2003) presents the religious and the secular – *mutatis mutandis* including ideology – as constructs that now prevail but earlier on did not serve as public categories.

Instead of hastily accepting any one approach, it is better first to draw the map of the options that present themselves. The advantage of such an approach is that the reader may follow his or her preferences. Besides, by describing the alternatives, the field is depicted in the process. Since methodology requires taking a perspective on the limits of the field of study, this debate over definition has direct relevance. Moreover, even the boundaries one may wish to draw can eventually prove to be rather nebulous. On either side of the supposed boundary, there may be a coalescence of ideas or practices, such as occurs between religious and secular worldviews when united in a category called worldview.

One important option in defining religion is the question of whether it should be defined substantively, that is, as a worldview based on a relationship with supernatural entities (e.g. God, gods, spirits, saints etc.) that are held dear by believers, or functionally, as a worldview that serves certain needs (e.g. raises the ultimate questions of life, guarantees social or mental stability, reduces anxiety, acts as the opium of the masses, etc.) (Berger 1967: 175–77). An early example of a substantive definition of religion was provided by E.B. Tylor in 1871, when he spoke of religion as "the belief in spiritual beings" (quoted in Van Baal 1971: 35). An example of a functional definition was provided by Erich Fromm in 1950, when he spoke about "any system of thought and action shared by a group which gives the individual a frame of orientation and an object of devotion" (quoted in Clarke and Byrne 1993: 7). The substantive approach is closer to the believers' and thereby the ethnographers' point of view, because it describes the human beings' relationship with the supernatural. The functional view is closer to the interests of the sociologist beholder, who looks to religion for explanations of occurrence and persistence.

Since in a functional definition there is not necessarily any reference to supernatural entities, the substantive definition, with its reference to the divine or the sacred, may be absent in specific secular cases that fit perfectly within a functional definition, simply because they fulfil the same functions. A functional definition of religion is therefore close to the definition of worldview given above, including secular views. Thus humanism rejects the religious point of view, and yet comes with answers to basic human questions. The advantage of a functional definition is that worldviews that are excluded from the substantive definition (because they lack any reference to sacred entities of the type mentioned above), would fit within it very well. Thus the similarities between the functions of religious and secular worldviews are emphasized, in spite of substantive differences. In recognizing this, the value of the umbrella concept of worldview is highlighted. However, one problem remains. Representatives of secular worldviews do not like to be called religious, because they usually take the term religion in the substantive sense and this is precisely what they oppose. The denial of the existence of the substantive supernatural is usually central to their position. So in defining religion, much depends on the focus chosen.

Similarly, in the case of ideology, different approaches may prevail. If ideology is given the broad meaning of being a set of ideas and practices that help people orient themselves in life, in ways that are in fact more or less identical to the definition of worldview I gave above, then religion becomes a sub-category of ideology. Even if ideology is defined more specifically, as

I would suggest it should be, and understood functionally as a particular form of worldview, namely one that serves to justify a particular form of society, existing or utopian, it is still difficult to distinguish it from religion, since religions may also contain blueprints for society. Accordingly, ideology understood in this narrower sense may have religious characteristics, in the substantial, but also in the functional senses mentioned above.

Still there may be a difference between this approach and commonsense language. Marxism is commonly viewed as the prime example of an ideology. Frequently it is seen as a powerful example of a secular and even anti-religious ideology. To many people the term ideology carries the connotation of being secular, despite the fact that it would fit perfectly within a functional definition of religion. Marxism itself polices its own terminology as far as ideology is concerned, viewing any usage of the term outside of Marxist contexts, including religious contexts, as false consciousness.

Therefore much depends on definitions of ideology and religion. A religion that obeys the substantial definition may very well, in the terms just expressed, legitimate a particular form of society, admittedly with an appeal to sacred entities, but nevertheless ideological in function. Fundamentalists, regardless of whether they are Hindu, Jewish, Christian or Islamic, are notoriously adept at toying with religious ideology. Precisely because they have ideological commitments, their religious groupings are considered to be political. Religion, in the substantive sense, thus serves in the wider context of a society as an ideology. In case a substantive reference is lacking, ideology, in the sense of a set of ideas used to justify a particular form of society, may still overlap with a functional definition of religion, depending on what function is emphasized. For example, as Fromm would have it, as soon as people live and die for an ideology, such as happened with Marxism or with national-socialism, devotion, in Fromm's terms, is implicit.

So there is a subtle interplay between terms and cases, definitions and examples, idiosyncrasies and generalizations. We may think that in the process of defining a concept, we do little more than describe, in a standard manner, what has been known for some time already, albeit as commonsense knowledge. Yet, our definitions, especially if they are adopted and reiterated by colleagues, may indeed call a phenomenon into being. Thus Michael Jackson (1998: 6) argues:

> what we commonly call "subjectivity" or "selfhood" are simply arrested moments artificially isolated from the flux of "interindividual" life...the subject-object partition is an artifact of our interventional acts of *measuring* reality; in fact, selves are no more single existences than are atoms and molecules. (italics in original)

New views and cases may highlight the arbitrariness of established terminology. Thus Dany-Robert Dufour (2007) defends the thesis that, thanks to theologian-economist Adam Smith, the Christian God was substituted by the market of liberal ideology as a new God, with surprisingly similar characteristics. A God that was central to a religion in the substantive sense was succeeded by a God that had similar functions, who thus would fit the functional type of definition. And here's the rub. Ironically, liberalism as a profane ideology defends a principle that can be said to contain divine characteristics. So much for defining religion and ideology!

A DEFINITE MESS

It is clear that the concepts of religion and ideology have been given varied and even antithetical meanings. One way out of this definitional mess might be to accept the relative and arbitrary character of definitions and to remain conscious of the various alternatives, opting for working definitions that are able to give a logical and, where possible, a mutually exclusive place to the terms worldview, religion and ideology. The intention is not to become the prisoner of definitions but instead to view definitions as rather arbitrary tools, as servants, not masters. In order to clarify the meaning of concepts, it is necessary to know the discourse that sustains them.

In choosing to take this path forward, religion and ideology can be viewed as subcategories of worldview. Religion should then be understood primarily in the substantive sense, as a relationship with sacred entities, nevertheless recognizing that it may make some use of functional definitions of religion, even though it is not defined by these. Within this approach the substantive side predominates, the concept of ideology can be taken primarily in the functional sense, and serves as a blueprint of and for society. Within this approach, religion and ideology may overlap and reinforce each other. They are not mutually exclusive to each other, as religious and secular views are, but clearly focus on different criteria: the relationship with the supernatural, or the blueprint of and for society, respectively.

This view of working definitions suggests that substantial and functional approaches to religion and ideology are taken to be complementary, and are not necessarily mutually exclusive, as if all non-religious worldviews were to be called ideologies, for example. Just as a functional focus on religion is possible, emphasizing what it does, such as solving ultimate problems, ideology can be looked at in a substantive way, by thinking through what its basic ideas include, such as references to class struggle or entrepreneurial liberty. As we saw, all examples of the substantial definition serve functions, though perhaps not in all cases providing the blueprint of society that ideology, as defined above, requires. Similarly, not all examples that obey the definition of ideology include a substantive reference to the supernatural, yet come with a substantive content.

All of this obliges us therefore to reserve a space for non-religious worldviews. The difficulty is that we do not have a term that clearly fits this type of worldview. The adjective "non-religious" takes religion as its reference point. In part this corresponds to the anti-religious position that this type of worldview often adopts, yet it can be felt as a sign of religious dominance that even religion's opponents are adorned with a label that takes religion as its reference point. Secular worldview, as it is employed above, is then the least subjective term perhaps.

SPIRITUALITY

When addressing the terms used in discussing the worldview spectrum, "spirituality" is a term that needs to be considered as well. Spirituality has a long history, especially in the Christian tradition, referring specifically to the experiential side of monastic and mystical life. Recently it has gained new meanings, connected with the modern non-institutionalized religious experience. Secularization, understood as de-churching, has opened the possibility of religious activity outside of the control of the institution and its clergy. The aspects of worldview that facilitate the exercise of choice have become more important (Taylor 2007: 3). As a consequence there has been a peculiar change in the connotations surrounding the terms "religion" and "spirituality." In non-academic but politically correct speech, "religion" is now sometimes understood as the institutionalized form, whereas "spirituality" represents the non-institutionalized, and yet religious in the older sense, worldview.

There is some continuity with the older meaning of spirituality, since the new de-institutionalized forms depend to a large extent on the believer's personal experience, as was previously the case with monastics and mystics. Unlike the monastic type of spirituality and closer to the experience of independent mystics sometimes viewed by the institution as heretics, the new spirituality celebrates the believer's liberation from the institution. Without the control and discipline imposed by an institution, people roam freely through the realm of religious feeling. Yet, as shown in Chapter 6, even individualized experience has a social dimension. In Chapter 7 it is shown that even such highly individualized meaning-makers as artists and writers can be shown to belong to one of a mere five types.

Since experience is the focus of spirituality, the body is its main vehicle. This has led to a rediscovery of the role of the body (Csordas 1999, McGuire 1990, Meyer 2008, Simpson 1993). In a broader sense, the material dimension of religion has become a topic of interest. This approach complements the cerebral, rational aspect of worldviews. As a concept "worldview" has not only a visual/sensory connotation, as in a view or observation, but also a cerebral, cognitive bias, with an emphasis on ideas, beliefs and reflection (another visual term). World religions are commonly identified first by their doctrines and only secondarily by their rituals. The term "spirituality" points to the experiential and corporeal, downplaying or even ignoring the doctrinal, rational connotation of worldview.

SECULARIZATION

The terms outlined here can be put to the test when the process of secularization is given a place in the discourses described so far. This is not an easy task, because here too definitional confusion reigns. Secularization can be given a variety of meanings. As we will see, the weight given to the contrast between religious and secular worldviews shifts accordingly. In reflecting on the methodology for the study of secularization, some clarification of the concept and its definitions is needed (Bruce 2002, Casanova 1994: 12–17, Davie 2007: 46–66, Dobbelaere 2009, Taylor 2007: 1–4, 423–535).

The most radical approach would use the term secularization to indicate the end of religion, as an expected consequence of modernization, understood here as the application of the results of science and technology in society. Science is thought to prevail over its opposite, religion. This is a direct reference to the substantive aspect of religion, since it is the existence of the supernatural that is drawn into question. However, predictions about the demise of religion formulated in the 1960s have now been proven to have been inaccurate. The other meanings given to the term, as set out below, have nevertheless retained their currency.

Secularization has also been understood as referring to the loss of influence in society that religion has suffered. In other words, religion has lost much of its ideological function, no longer providing the blueprint for the organization of society. This is also the perspective chosen when secularization is defined as the relegation of religion to a separate sector of society, or more precisely, to the private and individual sphere. This may take a functional form when religion functions in the service of the individual believers by, for example, enabling them to cope with life's vicissitudes.

Secularization can also be viewed as de-churching, or put more generally (in order to avoid Christian bias), de-institutionalization. Individualization has affected the power of institutions in society in general, not only in religious affairs but also in politics and labour organizations (Davie 2007: 92). As far as religion is concerned, many people in Western Europe no longer go to the temple, synagogue, church or mosque, even when they still consider themselves to be religious. They no longer let the institution or its clergy influence their decisions about how to organize their life. The increased freedom in worldview matters has made people aware that they have an option: "faith, even for the staunchest believer, is one human possibility among others" (Taylor 2007: 3). However, those who leave their church do not necessarily take leave of religion. Even in countries like the Netherlands, with its reputation for secularization, massive de-churching has not significantly augmented the number of atheists. Over the decades, the percentage of non-believers has been a constant 10 to 15 per cent. Currently about two-thirds of the Dutch population can be said to see themselves as (regularly or irregularly) following religious ideas and practices, although they do not participate in organized religious institutions. In other words, the substantive side does not disappear when people leave the institution, although some erosion and erasure may take place in relation to followers' opinions and practices.

The way the term "secularization" is understood varies with the definition of religion that is used. Suppose we were to employ a functional definition, extending the substantive category of religion to include secular worldviews that serve functions similar to those of religion (in the substantive sense). The consequence would be that secularization can no longer be defined as the loss of religious influence in society, since religion would then possess a much wider functional meaning. Functional religion could be said to survive, albeit in secular forms, for example, as we saw in Dufour's (hypo) thesis regarding the market as the new God. Again the terminological confusion would increase, making room for the paradox of a secular religion. The advantage would be that a certain similarity and continuity in viewing the world is given emphasis, despite the secular worldview's rupture with the sacred dimension. It depends on the focus of the comparison: on the differences or on the similarities.

In contrast, a substantive approach to religion fits much better with the concept of secularization, especially if it is implied that the belief in supernatural entities (God, gods, spirits etc.) is rejected by secularized persons. However, if we were to define secularization as de-institutionalization, the rejection of the existence of the sacred need not necessarily be a defining characteristic of secularization, since once outside the institution, people maintain beliefs. "Believing without belonging" has become common (Davie 1994).

The answer to the questions of what has actually happened within a particular society and which definition of secularization would apply best, differs according to context. The inhabitants of the most modernized society on earth, the United States, are in the majority religious, some fundamentalist. This example contradicts the notion that modernization puts an end to religion. Yet some of the above-mentioned secularization processes occur in the United States as well. Western Europe, once seen as the epicenter of processes of secularization resulting in the disappearance of religion, is now recognized to be the exception and not the rule (Davie 2002).

Where secularization seems to have weakened institutionalized church religions, in Western European countries for example, many people look for religion outside the churches. New Age religions represent a strongly individualized alternative, just as there are people who accept a self-styled version of Hindu or Buddhist views. Pentecostalism and Evangelicalism are examples of rapidly expanding forms of personalized Protestantism. They place an emphasis on individualized experience, and yet often develop strong vertical institutions. These forms of Protestantism mark their presence in Latin American as well as African countries, in South Korea and in the Philippines.

When studying secularization and seeking out appropriate methods, it is important to first determine which type or definition of secularization corresponds most closely with the situation to be studied. Although it can be difficult to determine this in advance of undertaking the research itself, an awareness of the traps and pitfalls that abound in the field of secularization studies is indispensable.

RITUAL: RELIGIOUS OR SECULAR?

The term "ritual" is surrounded by the same conceptual confusion as religious and secular worldviews. It is for this reason that I discuss the term here. Ritual usually refers to religious rather than to secular worldviews, indicating forms of standardized, formal, repeated, symbolic behaviour in communication with supernatural entities. Some scholars look at ritual in order to understand the origin of religious feeling (e.g. Rappaport 1999).

The history of the definition of the term "ritual" (Asad 1993, Bell 1992, Boudewijnse 1995) includes at least three approaches. The first approach defines ritual exclusively as religious, the second as inclusive, combining religious and secular ceremonial behaviour, whereas a third approach would abandon the term altogether. In the latter case, it is suggested that the concept distorts the reality to which it is applied, because it is primarily a scholarly nineteenth-century construct, revealing a Western Christian, anti-magical, rational bias, and is therefore of no use outside the Christian context.

Of the two approaches that choose to retain ritual as a concept, the question remains as to whether the religious aspect is essential to all ritual, or whether as was the case with worldview, both religious and secular forms can be said to exist. As I observed earlier, a focus on differences need not make one blind to similarities. For this reason, it is good to keep an eye on the wider context of a phenomenon. Keeping this in mind, ritual, whether referring to a sacred reality or not, is primarily a form of repeated formal symbolic behaviour. It may occur within the context of a religion, but can, at least within this wider definition, also form part of a secular worldview or an ideology.

Interestingly, the exclusively religious connotation surrounding "ritual" as a concept, seems to have played a role in the supposed absence of ritual in the context of secular worldviews, especially those that take an anti-religious position. Sometimes "ceremony" is used as a substitute. Nevertheless, similarities can be observed between religious rituals and so-called ceremonies, and this justifies the use of the term ritual in the wider sense, including secular ritual.

GLOBAL TRENDS

In discussing worldview as an umbrella concept, the emphasis is placed on what is shared among otherwise discrepant views. For this reason, I have approached worldview as a specific form of the universal human cultural ability to signify and create meaning. Though there is an enormous variety of concrete worldviews, the same human capacity can be shown to be active everywhere. This capacity is universal, but expresses itself in always different forms. Each worldview can therefore be placed within a wider context, understood not only or primarily for its idiosyncratic exclusivity, or within its own social or geographic boundaries. Each worldview can be considered as belonging to the domain where a particular category of human competence is at work. This process is facilitated by the fact that in almost every human context the five basic questions are raised. Similarly, the seven dimensions highlight points of convergence that can be observed, despite the many differences.

The meaning-making subject is the central actor, who either voluntarily accepts a worldview (internalization), or resists it and acts autonomously (externalization). This presupposes different power constellations, making room for individual initiatives or, on the contrary, limiting them. Yet, this emphasis on individual agency tells only half of the story. At the macro-level of a worldview, supra-individual trends may occur that appear as unintended consequences, sometimes causing changes in the structures themselves. Even the leaders can become objects of these structural trends, despite their power to steer the behaviour of followers.

Nowadays, the emphasis on universal commonality is gaining relevance. Because of globalization, people adopt a universal perspective. Globalization can be defined as the process by which the world is experienced as one place. This perspective was influential in previous eras as well, when the oikumene, the inhabited known world, was much smaller. Yet, in constructing and adapting their current worldview, world citizens are now challenged and inspired by the wider global context and all that is available in the global worldview market. The neat separation of world religions, for example, that is typical of textbook content, is no longer reflected in followers' understanding. More and more people freely combine those aspects that they find attractive and useful.

But there is a flip side to this coin. Reactions to globalization that reinforce the exclusive and the local are just as likely as reactions that focus on the freedom to explore self-styled meaning-making. If worldview boundaries are perforated, leaders and followers may close borders and guard them more closely than ever before. Fundamentalism has been stimulated by both modernization and globalization. It has been nourished by feelings of uncertainty that have arisen in response to the globalized spread of liberty. If familiar views are eroded, one reaction may be to take leave of those views. Another reaction might be to cling to them more tightly than ever. These choices involve constructing and maintaining one's own identity.

WORLDVIEWS – THE CURRENT SITUATION

Globalization (as the experience of the world as one place) has meant that world religions are now part of repertoires adopted by many people around the world. Whereas Hinduism and Buddhism were once primarily Asian religions, forced or voluntary migration has helped to encourage their global spread. Westerners have brought both religions to the West. Judaism, Christianity and Islam, having spread and expanded over the course of many centuries, are found far beyond the regions in which they originated. Modernization did not only bring about processes of secularization, but especially in colonial contexts also furthered the expansion of these religions. In the case of Africa, slavery took African tribal religions to the New World, where they were combined with Christian and American Indian elements. This resulted in the rise of Afro-American religions such as Haitian Voodoo and Brazilian Candomblé. Those Africans who were not carried to the Americas by the slave-traders and who stayed in their towns and villages were also confronted with the expansion of Christianity, just as Islam made its way through the continent.

For a long time worldviews around the world were religions, whether they belonged to the so-called world religions or to the many religions that characterized the world's tribal societies. Although philosophy began its course in the sixth century bce, for a long time it had a religious dimension as well. In the nineteenth and twentieth centuries, in the wake of modernization, secularization, in several of the senses mentioned above, put an end to the monopoly of religions in the field of worldviews. Secular views started to play a significant role, as a consequence of the Enlightenment idea that virtually anything, including society, can be developed by human efforts. European societies in particular were approaching their world as an entity that could be developed and cultivated. This stimulated the development of science, including the social sciences. Although religion was recognized to play a role, as suggested by the Weberian thesis on the contribution that Calvinism made to the rise of capitalism, the loss of influence of religion in society created the conditions under which secular worldviews could become popular. Secular ideologies, and most notably liberalism and socialism, presented a challenge to religious views on the way society should be organized.

The worldview situation has become even more complex since Industrialization, when human connections were strengthened by travel and improved communications. The simultaneous presence of different religions in one area stimulated interaction and exchange, but also strife, isolation and withdrawal. Depending on context and the historical moment, new religious movements evolved, especially in Africa and Oceania.

In the twentieth century, the redeployment of the ideologies of the long nineteenth century marked their presence and influenced the political and economic organization of world society, leading to the formation of a capitalist and a communist bloc. Fundamentalisms, especially Christian, Islamic and Hindu varieties, are political powers to be reckoned with. Although seemingly traditional and conservative, current fundamentalisms nevertheless can be seen as products of modernization as well, representing a reaction against what modernization had brought in terms of moral and secularizing transformations.

IDENTITY

In raising and answering the five basic questions, and giving form and content to the seven worldview dimensions, people position themselves and determine their identity. Simultaneously however, people with particular worldviews are also perceived by others, and this partially also constitutes their identity. The process of positioning therefore is social in a double sense. First of all, any person either identifies with others or distinguishes him or herself from them. And secondly, people are the objects of the attribution of a particular worldview identity by others. In both cases, real, ideal and stereotypical versions of worldview identity are conflated. In their effort to manage this repertoire of different identities, people act and react. The result need not be consistent, but may change by the hour, depending on context. There are many strategies involved in the formation of identity. People use all, or many of these when negotiating their way through the social labyrinth.

This process is as old as humanity itself, but in our times there appears to be a greater variation in the degree to which the social framework makes itself felt. Many people in the world today no longer experience a limited set of social interactions with more or less the same people, as they once did, for example in traditional villages. The human objects of the imposition of social structures act more and more as subjects, construing their own environments. In modern society, the individual has gained greater freedom in fulfilling an expanded range of social roles. There are more options and alternatives. Nowadays people play an increasing number of roles and in the course of the day they come into contact with different groups of people, in a variety of contexts: at home, at work, as consumers, or as people with leisure time. These contexts may be perceived as being global, building identities that transcend traditional boundaries. Alternatively, these contexts can be seen as being strictly local, as people exist in just one place at a time. Even the global is primarily manifest at the local level.

Identity as a concept reflects the dynamism in the human capacity for culture (Hall 1996). As with culture, for a long time an essentialist view of identity predominated. Identity was seen as a constant and stable core essence, the person as unchanging as their "identity" card image. One was supposed to be oneself, one self always and anywhere. This was even maintained in the criteria for mental health. The notion of a constant identity corresponded to the above-mentioned, now widely critiqued, understanding of culture, which presupposed that people living within the same social setting were expected to show similar forms of socialization and behaviour, and to share the meanings given to their reality. They would adapt by sharing with others a constant identity across all sectors of their life, for example, with regard to race, religion, gender, class, profession etc. This shared identity sustained the social order and was protected by it. Its consistency can be traced in quantitative research and expressed in statistics.

But this view too was soon drawn into question. The growing awareness of the active role played by individuals led to an emphasis on the more complex dynamics of identity formation. Instead of being one self, a person is now understood to wield a number of selves, choosing from among a stock of behavioural repertoires with which she or he has been socialized, or that are commercially available, according to the changing context. The one single identity as a criterion for mental health was substituted with the understanding that people behave differently in changing contexts with a different process of identity formation at work each time. It is not society as a whole that demands the making of just one consistent self, but a society divided into multiple contexts that demands the making of many and even opposing selves.

This interpretation of identity is better able to explain the modern, or even postmodern complexities of context-dependent identity formation. Instead of collective identities, the various individualized and contextualized identities serve to distinguish a person from other individuals, with their own idiosyncratic multiplicity of selves. In many contexts, it is not conformity but differentiation that matters and is considered functional. Different contexts allow for a certain degree of contradiction and inconsistency, without the social order being eroded. The consistent meaning-maker would not survive, or might soon be regarded the neighbourhood idiot. Rather, the strategic signifier positions her or himself according to her or his interests as a stakeholder in a situation. This has consequences for social science research, and also for worldview research, since complex, fragmented and changing identities are much more difficult to study than a collective simple identity.

ROUTINE AND REFLECTION

Meaning-making as a term implies constant activity. However, cultural behaviour may take place in a routine and implicit manner, as in the daily process of dealing with persons, objects and events. People behave, without explicit reflection, in the ways they have been socialized to behave. Culture need not be reinvented each time it is redeployed. Many activities, such as driving through traffic, do not even allow time for reflection and depend on conditioned responses. In daily life, even some existential questions can be dealt with without a second thought, on autopilot almost.

However, whenever routine actions fail to solve a problem, reflection is demanded. In worldviews, a revival reintroduces old meanings within a new context, usually adding new meanings as well. Any reformation or schism results from new meaning-making. Moving to a new and unfamiliar context also demands conscious adaptation. New meanings must be discovered or given, or at least old meanings must be applied to new situations, demanding some adaptation of the old and familiar. Conversely, reflection may in turn feed routine, once a new solution comes to be regarded as having wider application. Especially in times of personal or social change and conflict, the exchange between reflection and routine becomes more obvious. There may be special occasions, provided within the context of many religions, for explicit reflection, such as retreats. This explicit act of reflection may become institutionalized in a division of labour, in which some persons are liberated to spend time on reflection, or on counselling clients or followers. In modern societies, tutored meaning-making, called psychotherapy or psychoanalysis, has become an established professional domain.

It is possible that a crisis might have such devastating consequences that reflection is simply not possible. Then the context becomes completely different. Whatever kinds of meaning-making remain possible stem directly from deep-lived experience and are not recognizable as answers to the questions that emerge from the crisis situation. Body and soul coincide. Cognition becomes embodied experience.

Quite a different way of dealing with routine and reflection can be observed in meditation techniques that are meant to stop routine reflection. These techniques dwell on the paradox that meaning only comes into being when everything has become meaning-less, and emptied of sense. This may invoke the experience of crisis as well, as expressed in Zen metaphors such as "knocking where there is no gate." This approach to reflection may also be understood as a reaction to the extraordinary, almost unmanageable human capacity for meaning-making.

Usually believers will speak more readily of meaning-finding than of meaning-making. It is part of the religious experience that much of the meaning that people perceive to exist in their lives is experienced as coming from the outside or, more specifically, from above. The active making of meaning is viewed more as a passive act of receiving revelation from the divine or the sacred, or whatever name is given to this transcendental experience. This raises the methodologically significant question of where religion finds its origin: in the transcendental or in the human? I will return to this question in Chapter 4.

VARIATION

By reflecting on the world they live in, people in principle have the opportunity to choose from a huge repertoire of meanings. The existence of a large variety of worldviews offers proof of this. Though people are commonly socialized within one particular worldview, they may alter aspects of their worldview, or switch to another worldview. Even by conservatively imitating the preceding generation, people may bring about change, since perfect replication is not possible. Reproduction is very often re-production. The worldview is produced anew, adapted to an individual situation and personal demands. Understood in this way, structures do not represent the static and orderly side of life, but can be said to have their own dynamics, simply because they need to be reproduced (Moore 1975). Choice may therefore be part of reproduction.

Yet, in comparison to reproduction, there are more radical deviations from the heritage of the past. These may of course only concern a person's life. But there may also be dramatic consequences that affect society as a whole. Thus the personal desire to reform a worldview may lead to the creation of a new one. In that originally strictly personal way, Buddha became the founder of Buddhism, Moses of Judaism, Jesus of Christianity, and Mohammed of Islam. None of them started from scratch, all were socialized into and marked by an existing religious framework. Similarly, variations and modalities within the so-called world religions have come about. But even ideologies such as Marxism originated from a radical personal change in views. Ordinary everyday people may be inspired by the cumulative presence of different repertoires for meaning-making and thus come to accept new perspectives, comparing and contrasting all available views. When people become acquainted with other worldviews, they may switch allegiances or make their own selection from among the views they have become familiar with.

There are other reasons that can be used to explain the variation in the practice of worldviews, whether religious or secular. These arise from the strategies that followers adopt when wheeling and dealing in worldview. What people say, may differ from what they really think. When asked a question by an interviewer, respondents may appear to cherish a certain opinion, while at the back of their mind an antithetical view is more strongly held. They may say yes and mean no, express agreement and yet regret or even contradict their response. They are able to make calculated or so-called "correct" use of available meanings and of questions and answers, depending on the context they find themselves in. Virtually all followers deviate from their chosen path at times.

POWER

Particularly in individualized modern society, worldview carries the connotation of occurring primarily at the level of idiosyncratic personal meaning-making. People, however, are not ever fully free to choose. Externalization, as defined above, does not occur in isolation The objectified worldview is located within a power context. Though usually implicit in worldview vocabularies, power obviously steers believers in a certain direction. I use Max Weber's widely accepted definition of power, as the human capacity to influence other people's behaviour, even against their will. The exercise of power can be sustained by exclusive access to resources such as weapons, money or knowledge. These become effective tools for those in power.

Both religious and secular worldviews contain mechanisms and constellations of power. By influencing other people's behaviour, even against their will, worldviews, both religious and secular, are drawn into question. An elite will control the reflection and practices that constitute a particular worldview. Power may, for example, be based on exclusive access to essential knowledge, core views and ritual practices, or economic, or legal control. Power and meaning-making may be more closely related than the adherents of such a worldview may realize. Yet, despite the mechanisms of power and the small margin for freedom, people always find ways to play with the variety of meanings and do so according to their own interests, or even for altruistic reasons. They do this in spite of power. On the other hand, people may find little room for play and then will suffer dearly from imposed worldviews that act "against their will."

Individuals share views with each other and seek affirmation through agreement with others. Though individuals may feel free to express themselves, they will also reckon with mechanisms of social control. A leadership may, for example, exercise censorship, either rewarding or disciplining followers' views and practices. Wherever the act of meaning-making is the prerogative of the leadership, a specialized category of leaders will emerge who dedicate themselves completely to reflective activity. The worldview is then institutionalized. The social order that rules society may result from this top-down production of meaning, the worldview containing a blueprint for what it considers the ideal society. Some visionary or wise person then develops a systematic worldview that is satisfactory to both the individual and the group, or even to society as a whole. Disciplinary strategies, based on coercion and control, may be used by those in power to impose their view.

The process of meaning-making occurs between the poles of individual agency and the structured social order. People in the act of meaning-making are always both active and passive, subject and object, and this determines the degree of variation between them. People may take initiatives that lead to changes in structures, just as they may be fully socialized, subjected to the social structures imposed through education and sanctioned by authorities. Followers are both externalizing and internalizing. They may be restricted from doing what they would do of their own volition, but there are always margins, narrow or wide, for deviant or innovative behaviour. Social mechanisms of exclusion and inclusion influence views on what is true and what is false.

A visionary may defy established structures and be rejected by the social order, as happened to Moses in Egypt, to Jesus when he was put on trial and executed, or to Mohammed when he discovered that he had to flee Mecca for Medina. Karl Marx, for all his life, was a displaced person. Innovative meaning-makers may also be architects of a new social order. Moses, Jesus and Marx did not live to see the societies they envisaged, but Mohammed lived at the centre of his new order in his final years. That which was considered by many to be heresy became truth, at least in the eyes of a significant number of the population.

In sum, worldviews, as the result of reflection on human life, have not only an individual, but also a social aspect, as they are shared and entrenched within a given society. Power is therefore an important issue. Worldview research should include this dimension.

In the case of a religious worldview, the power dimension is even more significant. Whereas a secular worldview limits its frame of reference to the observable human world, religion as a worldview refers not only to the human world, but also to the existence of a non-human, supernatural world. Sometimes the human and sacred worlds are not even distinguishable as different "worlds," but are experienced as one reality. This supernatural level has consequences for the practice of meaning-making, and thereby for the methods we use to study it. Believers may understand meaning as having been granted or revealed by the divine power, for example through visions and dreams. In this context, people do not so much understand themselves as meaning-makers, but more as meaning-receivers. Deeper meaning is experienced as insight that has been given, received or granted. How is it then possible to do justice to this, understanding methodologically? It is difficult to undertake scientific research on a source that science tells does not exist. How, for example, do we take informants seriously, including their convictions about supernatural reality? As one of my students once said, "It is a pity we cannot interview God in our fieldwork." I return to this in Chapter 4.

Not all believers need to experience divine inspiration for themselves. They may view it as the privilege of the members of a religious elite. The active meaning-making role presumed to be typical of human beings is transformed into a passive role for most believers. Where this is the case a worldview is thought to have been revealed, and not constructed, through the intermediary of divinely elected believers. It may even be that only a select few have access to this source of revelation, of deep sacred knowledge. This elite is thought to "walk with the gods." Even more exalted still is the position of persons understood to be the incarnation of a god or God. Some founders of religions have occupied this special position, Jesus being the best-known example.

Power and meaning-making are connected in another way. Power can be detected in the symbols that are used to express supernatural or divine power. When believers feel overwhelmed, they inevitably express this in metaphors that they find in the religion's power arrangements, or in profane power contexts. Thus terms like "father," "lord," "master," "king" are evoked to imply a perceived connection with God or an ancestor spirit. Many of the meanings given to these metaphors in daily life will apply to the supernatural entity as well, influencing the image people invent of that being. This may result in a distortion of the experience being interpreted. For example, "a father" may be depicted as a caring person, but can also be a castigating relative. The net effect will be that the legitimization of the power structure is reinforced.

CONCLUSIONS

When thinking about choosing methods for the study of contemporary worldviews, an awareness of the field and its rapid transformation is needed.

The changing modern world has stimulated people's capacity and desire for meaning-making in general, and especially for worldviews in particular, adding new religious and secular views to their repertoires. In addition, it is necessary to be aware of the concepts that we employ in studying new circumstances since they direct our attention, revealing and also concealing important things. The public awareness of secular worldviews justifies the use of the term "worldview" as a general category in which the secular and the religious are brought together. Whereas the traditional perspective focused exclusively on religion, a wider view is now needed, in view of the rapid changes generated by modernization, individualization, de-institutionalization, migration, globalization and secularization. As we will see in Chapter 4, this involves ethical issues, also for the researcher, especially when worldviews take anti-human positions, sacrificing life and prohibiting free meaning-making.

Identity formation is the arena in which meaning-making can be observed. The dialectics of humans as subjects and objects must be kept in mind, including constellations of power. Ideology can be viewed as part of the field of worldviews. Taking culture as our starting point, by which I mean the human capacity to give meaning to reality, the different forms of worldview can be accommodated. Even the study of worldviews can be understood as a form of meaning-making. In our search for appropriate and effective methods, this approach, beginning with culture, is helpful.

Chapter 3

Quantitative and Qualitative Approaches Compared

ANDRÉ DROOGERS*

MAKING A START

What roles do quantitative and qualitative methods play in the study of the contemporary worldview situation? This question suggests the need for a general appraisal of quantitative and qualitative methods. Although I intend to launch my demand for the rehabilitation of qualitative methods, emphasizing their usefulness in their own right and in the present context particularly, I do not argue for the exclusive use of this approach. As I will show, both qualitative and quantitative methods are useful. Together they reflect the dichotomy between individual and social aspects of meaning-making processes.

The strength of the qualitative approach is that it enables us to uncover insights that cannot be proven with numbers and yet remain crucial to our understanding. This suffices as a justification for the stand alone use of this approach. In comparison, the advantage of the quantitative approach is that its results can be generalized, revealing structural and causal consistency. This approach can also be employed in a self-contained and exclusive manner.

Yet, the two families of methods can also be used in ways that complement each other. For example, an emphasis on a substantive definition of religion, which focuses on the believer's relation to the sacred, invites qualitative, narrative work on individual believer's idiosyncratic experiences. A functional definition by contrast, which seeks to understand what religion does, would search for structural consistencies in the behaviour of a group of believers and in the process of developing and inscribing worldviews.

* André Droogers is Emeritus Professor of Cultural Anthropology, especially the Anthropology of Religion and Symbolic Anthropology, at VU University, Amsterdam. He is co-editor of *"Studying Global Pentecostalism: Theories and Methods"* (University of California Press, 2010). A selection from the articles that he has written over the last 30 years was reprinted, together with an autobiographical Introduction, in *"Play and Power in Religion: Collected Essays"* (De Gruyter, 2012).

The positivist model of the so-called empirical cycle, moving constantly from hypothesis to data testing, to conclusions, to theory and returning to a newly formulated hypothesis, combines both approaches. The newness of the global worldview situation, as described in Chapter 2, including its confused, individualized nature, appears to call for much exploratory research, commonly prompting the start of a new cycle. For this purpose qualitative methods present themselves as being particularly effective, especially because individual difference is such a striking characteristic of the new situation. Qualitative studies may produce hypotheses about regular structural characteristics of processes of signification that can be tested by quantitative means. Each approach can be useful under certain circumstances.

In this chapter, first I will make some general preliminary observations regarding the mutually exclusive views that exist on the role and mission of science. I do so because these competing views often form the starting point for making a choice in favour of either qualitative or quantitative methods. In fact they represent two radically different academic worldviews, with their own practical, experiential, mythical, philosophical, ethical, institutional and material dimensions. In their meaning-making on aesthetic, moral, ontological, epistemological and identity questions, scholars are as human as anyone. They form special tribes, each with its own culture and worldview. They believe in what they do. My next step will be to actually compare quantitative and qualitative methods. I will review the consequences of the comparison for the study of worldviews and suggest two complementary ways of making good use of the two approaches, one within, the other outside the empirical research cycle.

STATEMENTS

Abbas Tashakkori and Charles Teddlie (1998: 3) label the various positions regarding the potential and mission of science as "worldviews," thereby confirming that scholars are meaning-makers as well. In drawing comparisons between qualitative and quantitative approaches, the risk of exaggeration exists. Some of the related debates, such as those concerning postmodernism, are fierce and have led to much polarization. A few elements keep recurring and have proven to be resilient, surfacing regularly. They still appear to form part of the scholarly habitus on both sides.

A simple way of measuring the degree to which polarization still exists would be to present two lists of statements and ask the reader to count the number of times that he or she agrees. Below are the two lists. Each contains 13 items. The lists reflect the inventories that are made in the vast literature on the two approaches (e.g. Bernard 1998, Brink 1995, Denzin and Lincoln 1998a, 1998b, 2005, Flick 2009, Huberman and Miles 2002, Maxwell 1996, Murchison 2010, Newman and Benz 1998, O'Reilly 2005, Silverman 1999, Tashakkori and Teddlie 1998).

LIST I

Scientific knowledge is verifiable knowledge.

Verification is reached through experience, i.e., observation through the controlled use of the senses.

Verification produces hard empirical facts.

Science formulates laws and rules, and therefore is able to predict in a deductive manner.

To measure is to know. To know is to measure.

People's behaviour is regular because humans are rational beings.

People's behaviour is regular because they act goal-oriented, strategically, and in their own interest.

People's behaviour is regular because they are social beings, integrated into a social order.

Just like persons, groups develop behaviours. Individuals submit themselves to these processes.

To explain is to uncover causal relationships.

Science is the most trustworthy form of knowledge.

A statement is true if it is confirmed by the facts.

A statement is true if it can be integrated into the set of already accepted statements.

And here is List II:

A statement is true if it can be confirmed by concrete behaviour.

A statement is true as long as people accept its validity.

Verification of theories is not important. Falsification of theories is much more important.

Science is one of the human modes of knowing.

Rational and strategic behaviour can have unintended and unforeseen consequences.

Clarification of concepts (i.e. the effort to establish relations between meanings) precedes establishing relations (correlation, causal relation) between facts.

In the social sciences, what matters is understanding the meaning people give to their behaviour.

Knowledge is conditioned by context and theory, and therefore cannot be objective.

Variables have been made by us: "We defined them into being" (Deutscher, quoted in Patton 1987: 18).

Since respondents are able to react and to interpret, to study them demands a different type of science model than that provided by the natural sciences.

Social scientists are humans and therefore are signifiers, meaning-makers.

Much causality occurs in the black box between input and output, and can therefore not be studied.

What really matters is Verstehen: putting yourself in the position of the persons you study.

NEO-POSITIVISM AND CONSTRUCTIVISM

A high score on List I locates you on the neo- or post-positivist side of the spectrum (Guba 1990). This point of view has also been labelled systematic (Johnson 1998: 138, 139), modernist or foundationalist (Seale 1999: 9). Neo-positivists are realists in that they maintain that reality exists out there. This reality can be studied and generalizations, about the social functions of world-views, for example, can be formulated because that reality is rule-oriented and even laws can be discovered. To reach maximal objective understanding, scholars should maintain a distance from what they study and interaction should be avoided. This applies to natural science laboratory situations, but should also be the rule when people study people, as in the social sciences. In such a way it is believed that the interviewer's values will, for example, not influence survey results. The empirical cycle is the model copied from natural science. It demands that hypotheses about regularities be formulated and fal-sified via empirical testing and that conditions and variables are to be strictly controlled. Only then will it become clear what causes or influences what.

In less orthodox versions of this position it is acknowledged that com-plete understanding is not possible. The need for a variety of data sources is emphasized, more attention is given to the role of contextual conditions that cannot be fully controlled, there is an explicit awareness of the delicate rela-tionship between theory and empirical data, and sometimes the use of quali-tative methods is advocated. The need for verification as the sciences' "hard" goal is viewed as less absolute and attempts at meaning-making are placed in the "soft" company of intuition and discovery.

Those readers who had a high score on List II seem to be more sympa-thetic to the viewpoints of the so-called constructivists, and if the score is really high, they are comfortable among the postmoderns (Guba 1990). Their approach has also been called interpretive, phenomenological, hermeneuti-cal, and even deconstructionist (constructivism that is led to its paradoxical end!) (Johnson 1998: 139, 140). This view of reality is influenced by idealism in the sense that emphasis is placed on the cognitive constructions that people develop in their efforts to understand what reality is about. Instead of the focus on reality "out there," typical of the neo-positivist position, reality in this case is located "in here." The meaning-maker is given the central role. One would almost say that scientific views are as constructed as religious views were said to be according to their secularizing positivist critics. As a consequence, there is not just one picture of reality, but there are many images, contained potentially even within one person. Since there is a ten-dency to identify the picture with reality itself, it can be said that there exist many realities. Our understanding is limited and dependent on context. Knowledge formation is conditioned. It therefore leads to diverse results. But beware, this does not necessarily result in the denial of the existence of a reality out there, though it may. At the very least, one consequence is the creation of uncertainty about the current images of reality and its existence, even when we are not talking about a sacred or supernatural reality. In this sense, all humans are believers.

Be this as it may, a person's cognitive processes are not developed in isolation. Communication works as a sieve, since people generally prefer to be understood. Knowledge is produced in a social environment and is constantly tested to guarantee its "truth." Here, the word truth is placed between inverted commas because it is a relative concept. Therefore concepts are important but also insufficient tools. This is a consequence of the presuppositions of the constructivist view.

According to this view, the researcher whose task it is to discover "truth" must be aware of the role of his or her own cognitive parameters. As a consequence, research in the humanities is not only *about* thought processes, but *itself* becomes a cognitive process in which researcher and researched are engaged. Their interaction is vital, and the data are not tapped from the informant as a vessel of information, but emerge in the course of the research as the result of contact between researcher and researched. Rather than distance and objectivity, closeness and rapport are understood to generate successful research. Of course individual views must be compared with those of others so that a certain degree of provisional consensus can be reached, though usually more constructs and corresponding realities will crop out.

A characteristic of this approach, which highlights the relativity of views, leads the snake to bite its own tail. This constructivist approach provides not more and not less than a cognitive construct that does not possess eternal value and that may be replaced in the future by better paradigms. But as long as it continues to work and produce results, it is a practical solution to a number of problems posed by the neo-positivist views. A consequence of such a relativist position is also that the neo-positivist approach is not condemned outright. As a construct it has its own relevance (Guba 1990: 27).

FUNDAMENTAL QUESTIONS

The two lists and the task of comparing them raise many questions. Is there a way out of this dilemma? Which view is right? What is the wisest approach to take in this situation? Do both approaches refer to the same reality? Do they represent different language fields, different citation communities (groups of scholars who tend to cite each other), and opposing academic subcultures with different concepts and varying versions of reality, the proponents of which often reify their interpretations and promote them to the status of reality? Or is it a matter of personal preference? What weight should the exalted natural sciences model carry in the practice of humanities research? Is human behaviour sufficiently consistent to warrant the adoption of such a model? Is it possible to copy the laboratory model, controlling for certain causal factors and at the same time excluding the possible influence of other variables? Can the laboratory situation be imitated in real social life? If the natural science model must be followed, how natural and therefore universal are human beings? What does culture do to specimens of the genus *homo sapiens*? What does cultural variation mean in comparison with the common cerebral, meaning-making outfit? How do the physical apparatus and the cultural capacity relate to each other? Since this book is about methodology, the following questions must also be asked: should data always take the form of numbers and statistics? Must one measure in order to know? Or can researchers tell stories and talk about particular instances of how people construct their worlds?

This dilemma has ancient roots. T.L. Brink (1995: 462), basing his argument on J.E. McKeon's, tells us that the neo-positivists are in the immortal company of Aristotle, Aquinas and Comte, whereas the constructivists can call in as witnesses great names like Plato, Augustine and Dilthey. The last name suggests that the choice between neo-positivism and constructivism is similar to that between the nomothetic law seeking and the idiographic descriptive alternatives (Brink 1995: 462). Realism and idealism have been mentioned in passing already, and it is evident that the corresponding distinction between mind and matter belongs among the options outlined above. Mind, or spirit, is utterly uncontainable, whereas matter is measurable in time and space. Mind and spirit are subjectively understood categories, whereas in relation to matter, a certain degree of objectivity is more easily sought.

If mind and matter form such a fundamental schema for our thinking, it might be observed in an ironic sense, that any person in Western culture, scholar or not, perceives many cognitive constructs in relation to mind and matter – and thereby to objectivity and subjectivity – as natural rather than as cultural. Again we perceive the scholar as a culturally biased meaning-maker. That which in fact is culturally determined and open to alternatives, is taken to be universally valid. Though we are condemned to thinking in contrasts, we tend to reify one pole and invest in it the status of exclusive reality. Our toolkit certainly facilitates our work, but it also represents our cultural limitations. The mutual exclusiveness of the two approaches seems to be part of this cultural heritage. The question is whether this is inevitable, or whether some form of inclusiveness and complementarity can be uncovered. Is there a methodology that would enable us to go beyond dualist binary thinking? Is there an approach that is dialectical?

THREE SOLUTIONS

There are three solutions to the problem presented here. The first solution accepts the distinction between the two approaches as inevitable, and considers each approach as a ship that passes the other in the night. Each approach may be valid in its own right, but to retain their validity they should not be combined. The presuppositions of each approach exclude the alternative. The gulf between the two is viewed as being too wide to bridge.

The remaining two solutions seek out some form of coexistence and mutual compatibility. The first of these maintains the model of the empirical cycle, but assigns different roles to the two approaches (e.g. Newman and Benz 1998, Tashakkori and Teddlie 1998). The neo-positivist mode sustains the cycle itself to test hypotheses, especially in relation to causality: if this, then that. This approach also helps to establish theories. It is basically deductive in that it looks at reality from a pre-established idea that can either be confirmed or falsified.

Still part of this second solution, the constructivist approach is much more inductive, because it takes the subsidiary role of developing hypotheses and theoretical insights that can be put to the test through investigations of the neo-positivist type. If the latter type of research draws attention to new topics of research, as is intended within the cyclical nature of the model, then constructivist methods can help to prepare for the next course of the cycle, developing hypotheses for the new round, especially if old theories fail the test.

Thus the objectivity of the neo-positivists, though never perfect, and the subjectivity of the constructivists, though never fully controllable, can complement each other. They serve each other. This solution to the problem further explores the above-mentioned neo-positivist tendency to use qualitative methods as a way to compensate for the negative characteristics of positivism.

The third solution, also based on complementarity, identifies neo-positivist work as precise and constructivist work as rich (e.g. Brink 1995). Each type of approach has its value and none can claim primacy. This view entertains constructivist doubts about some of the exclusive claims held by defendants of the empirical cycle in relation to verification, validity, generalization and reliability. Such claims can only be made with regard to data that can be expressed in numbers, not to all data, or to all research in general. A constructivist method can, for example, serve to show the "uniqueness of individual subjects and instances" that statistics fail to capture (Brink 1995: 464). What is measurable is not necessarily what is most relevant (Brink 1995: 468). Objectivity is not guaranteed by counting, since "[n]umbers do not protect against bias... All statistical data are based on someone's definition of what to measure and how to measure it" (Scriven in Patton 1987: 166). The neo-positivist approach is useful in studying quantifiable data, but its proponents should accept that their research strategy does not cover all social or cultural reality. In giving up on such a pretense, validity claims should be adapted accordingly. Constructivist research is valid in its own right and can therefore be more than a catalyst of hypotheses. Its main contribution is to explore the richness of the data. To use Brink's words (1995: 464, 467), the neo-positivist approach can be characterized as "necessary but limited," whereas the constructivist alternative can be said to be "essential but inadequate."

QUANTITATIVE AND/OR QUALITATIVE METHODS?

The description of the neo-positivist and constructivist approaches has already hinted at and thus prepared the way for a comparison of the quantitative and qualitative methods. The contrast should not be over emphasized. Many researchers who work with quantitative methods are as critical of positivism as constructivists, and are not seeking to discover laws, but only want to "produce a set of cumulative generalizations based on the critical sifting of data" (Silverman 2000: 5). Besides, there are qualitatively sensitive neo-positivists, as in so-called grounded theory, just as constructivists may apply quantitative methods. Yet, to a large extent quantitative work finds its roots in positivist traditions, whereas qualitative work, though not a consequence of constructivist efforts, reflects several of its presuppositions. The presupposition of consistency in human behaviour invites the use of methods in which numbers and counting play a central role. Unpredictable and idiosyncratic human meaning-making can only be grasped through narrative methods and case studies. But at this more concrete level of actual research, a few other components can be added to the comparison.

Precision and richness have already been mentioned as keywords in relation to the two approaches. To these, the terms generalization and plausibility can be added. In offering general statements based on statistical verification via surveys, a neo-positivist quantitative approach fails to recognize the differences between people. In providing identical answers, people may statistically belong to the same category, and yet they are not the same. When observing these people in their context and asking them to tell their stories, it is possible to give them flesh and blood. The plausibility of the image given of these people is reinforced. As has often been said, in quantitative surveys a limited number of questions based on a few variables are put to many people, in qualitative interviews many questions are put to a small number of persons regarding a large number of variables. Quantitative research produces quantifiable answers that can be compared, whereas qualitative fieldwork results in answers that are not able to be put into numbers and which are therefore not comparable. Qualitative research results in stories and cases. In quantitative research, people tell the researcher how they behave. In qualitative research, the researcher observes and checks whether oral statements and real behaviour correspond.

Another distinction is that the quantitative researcher, in going through the empirical cycle, works towards a result, an end product. Qualitative approaches lack this cyclical framework and move as it were from one section of the jigsaw puzzle to the next, constantly adapting the methods used. The qualitative researcher will usually continue until informants fail to tell new stories. This may take a long time, and not just because the respondents are communicative. The quantitative researcher considers his or her work to be finished within in a limited and usually short period of time, when a sufficient number of responses guarantee the representativeness and validity of the data. During the survey, the methods and research design remain unchanged. In Bruno Latour's terms (1987), although quantitative research results are often presented as final and ready-made, they too are manifestations of "science in action."

As I already noted in the preceding section, the quantitative researcher seeks to maintain distance from his informants. In fact it should not make a difference to the results whether scholar A, or scholar B conducted the survey interviews. The researcher is by definition anonymous. In qualitative research in contrast, the scholar's personality is to a great extent his or her tool. His or her personality influences the success or failure of the fieldwork. As shown in Chapter 9, this may involve the researcher's identity, also as viewed by the persons under research, taking politicized forms. He or she seeks rapport and participation. Thus friendships often develop, enabling access to additional information that would otherwise remain hidden. In the same situation, quantitative scholars would avoid friendship in order to remove the potential for bias.

There is one more difference that must be mentioned. Because quantitative research can be undertaken within a short time span, and moreover because the results of this kind of research can be expressed in generalizations, policymakers frequently make use of this type of research. Qualitative researchers take more time, experience greater difficulty generalizing from their data, and are seen to have produced research that is subjective. It takes greater explanatory effort to prove the usefulness of data that are not representative, but that uncover deeper layers of social and cultural behaviour in plausible ways.

Quantitative research is more easily accepted and may sometimes carry such prestige that, as is often the case in the pre-election polls used in the world of politics, indicative results may become self-fulfilling. For this very reason, in some countries polls cannot be conducted directly before the elections. If people are sensitive to trends and readily accept what is presented as "accurate" and "scientifically verified," quantitative prophets may seem always to be right. Thus, if sociologists of religion suggest that the trend towards secularization is irreversible and that a majority of people in a society has no religious affiliation, this may make it easier for ambivalent or uncommitted members of a particular church to take a final step and sever their membership. On the other hand, continuing members of a church, on hearing about secularizing processes or influences, may step up their efforts to support their church.

METHOD AS A CULTURAL PHENOMENON

Science as a cultural phenomenon arose within the context of a particular era and type of society, and has developed its own social mechanisms. Just as anthropologists may study a tribe of hunters and gatherers, a street corner gang, or a migrant church, thus the anthropological perspective may also be applied to communities of scientists who work with different methodologies. The advantage of such an approach is that seemingly absolute claims can be located within the cultural context in which they were produced, where they come to be seen as more relative. In the preceding section, because of the way I chose to write about them, approaches and methodologies were enlivened in order to imply they were able to reflect and produce effects. But once the cultural perspective is invoked, then the people belonging to a specific culture really come into focus and their centrality can be emphasized.

The two communities, with their different methodologies, are in a way like social science tribes. They have forebears in common, but as happens between siblings, they may go their separate ways. Each has been subjected to diverse influences and made selections from what was available on the cultural market. Neo-positivists with a preference for quantitative work show a warm appreciation for the natural science model, an ancestor with a well-earned reputation for reliable long-term duty and service. Constructivists working with qualitative methods seem to have been impressed by the individualism that for all sorts of reasons developed in Western societies as part of the process of modernization.

The application of its scientific work influences an academic tribe's customs. Qualitative methods, for example, via anthropology, were advanced by changes during the colonial period. The growing awareness of cultural differences and the administrators' need for advice in colonial political matters, stimulated participant observation as a method of fieldwork. Similarly, in Western societies, sociology came to provide an advisory function for government policymaking. Sociology in turn, was transformed within this context, stimulating – and stimulated by – the development of quantitative methods.

Parallel disciplinary boundaries developed within the social sciences. Sociology, through its founding fathers, focusing on Western society, developed a preference for quantification and for the social structural framework, whereas anthropology, for a long time limiting itself to non-Western societies, took culture, as a holistic concept with different aspects, as its central concept and adopted the method of participant observation as its trademark. Within the sociological discipline, sub-disciplines emerged, focusing on an aspect of social life. Thus sociologies of the family, labour and religion developed into autonomous branches, each with its own methodological preferences and specialties, though often emphasizing a penchant for quantification by means of surveys. Anthropology, given its holistic approach, and through its sub-disciplines, in its way did for non-Western societies what several other disciplines did in Western society. Thus social anthropology corresponds with sociology (especially British anthropology), whereas economic anthropology, more recently posing as a branch of development studies, is the non-Western equivalent of economics. Political anthropology corresponds with political science, and the anthropology of religion is akin to the study of religion and the sociology of religion.

The development of disciplines and sub-disciplines has contributed to the rise of various "tribal" cultures within the social sciences. An anthropology of these tribes would show that within each social science tribe there are theoretical clans, each with its own ancestor and founding myth. These myths, as paradigm charters, colour the way the world is looked at.

It thus may be that a rather mechanistic view of society is adopted, according to which people are thought to exhibit certain forms of behaviour under the influence of social structures. People are socially controlled and therefore show a high degree of conformity and similarity. They respond to stimulus in predictable ways, especially when negative or positive sanctions are imposed by those who maintain social control. Continuity is important in this rather neo-positivist view of the world.

However, the clan of social scientists may also adopt a more subjective view of the world, closer to a constructivist position. Then the subject, as a thinking actor, receives heightened attention. An emphasis on reflection will increase awareness of the individual actor's way of attributing meaning to social structures. Forms of deviation and resistance against authority will become visible. The order in society and culture is seen to be based not so much on an external social structure, as on an internal cognitive order, internalized by participant actors. Their perceptions and intentions are given much more attention than social control and sanctions.

FASHIONS

It is obvious, as I argued in previous sections, that these clans do not develop their ideas in isolation, but are influenced by other clans and tribes, for example, by philosophers, some long dead, but still of fundamental significance for the way people think, others alive and kicking, *en vogue*, and continuously quoted in the present. Thus some Anglo-Saxon clans of social scientists admire the work undertaken by clans of French philosophers. Every time a new version of reality is presented and becomes popular, the question remains as to whether reality has the characteristics that are being emphasized because they were always present, or whether they are a product of the current era. Perhaps they are even the invention of philosophers who, usually without recourse to empirical verification, tell us what the world is like. In the latter case, the same self-fulfilling mechanism previously mentioned makes itself felt, especially when scholarly publications become bestsellers and their authors celebrities.

An interesting example stems from how postmodernism has wrought havoc in some sectors of the humanities and has led to discord and conflict within academic departments. The characteristics that postmodernists point to in their analysis of contemporary Western society, such as fragmentation, unpredictability, contradiction, play, and so on, may always have been present but have escaped attention because the focus was always on order and continuity. If this is true, it is not the postmodern human that is new, only his/her discovery, just as America was there before Columbus. An observation that is coloured either by the presuppositions of List I or List II above, may influence what one sees. It may also be that postmodern sensibilities are the by-product of contemporary society, and it is possible that they have been stimulated, if not created, by the immense popularity of postmodern ideas. I suspect that here, as in other debates, there are at least some mutually reinforcing exchanges taking place between the set of ideas on the one hand, and the identity of the persons who position themselves as either modern or postmodern on the other. It may be hypothesized that personal preferences correspond with the insights that the theoretical models under debate confer. The reader might put this hypothesis to the test by showing a preference for either List I or List II above, based on strictly personal reasons, involving autobiographical elements.

Trends in the field may be mirrored in academia. I am reminded of a study by Peter Fry and Gary Howe (1975) who developed a hypothesis to find out which of the migrants to Brazilian urban centres were predisposed to becoming converts to Pentecostal churches and which would find their way to the terreiros of Afro-Brazilian Umbanda. The authors predicted that the first group would be looking for continuity and order in their lives, which would be provided by the compelling demands placed on the Pentecostal faithful. The second group was expected to improvise much more and to use the Umbanda sessions only when they felt the need, otherwise living their lives as they wished, and attending other religious groups if they wished to do so. No Umbanda leader would think of rebuking random attendees. Scholars may not differ much from these two categories of Brazilian urban dwellers in their appreciation of some theoretical or methodological viewpoint, who are either selective and mono-paradigmatic or more eclectic and poly-paradigmatic. In Isiah Berlin's terms (Berlin 1953), there are always sedentary hedgehogs and roaming foxes.

A few decades ago Thomas Kuhn (1962) drew attention to the inner mechanisms that influence academia as a sub-society. Though he was reluctant to apply the concept of paradigm to the humanities or the social sciences, the phenomenon he described can be seen at work there as well. Networks of authors, reviewers, departments, conference organizers, sponsors and editors, with their own codes and tacit knowledge, play a role in sustaining a particular approach. Citation communities exist and often correspond to the hedgehogs and foxes I described. They usually ignore each other, thus avoiding debate on the basis of arguments, especially if funding can be guaranteed without the polemics.

Funding decisions can be made in isolation from the in-depth exchange of academic arguments. For practical reasons, sponsors may restrict the range of options on which scholars have to develop a stance. As was suggested above, policymakers usually have a strong preference for quantitative research, and this may mean that this sector of academia is indirectly stimulated, even financially, at the expense of disciplines and faculties that produce qualitative research. In the Netherlands, for as long as sociologists of religion continued to predict the end of religion, it was difficult to obtain funding for qualitative projects on religious topics. Secular members of funding committees were especially unlikely to deem research on religion to be worthy of funding. This was particularly true when the research in need of funding happened to be qualitative.

ASYMMETRY

The Kuhnian framework is cultural relativist in the best sense of the anthropological tradition. Each paradigm forms an autonomous universe of its own, and like some of the great civilizations, it may rise to great heights of power and glory and then subsequently fall into oblivion. Time takes its toll and thus academic life goes on. But in anthropology, cultural relativism has never barred the quest for a supra-cultural form of communication and level of reference. Especially in this time of globalization, some forms of intertribal contact within academia become viable, and so begins a multicultural academic society. Anthropologists have studied multicultural societies and might apply the lessons they have learned to their own communities. In terms of the phenomena under discussion here, more academic and methodological syncretism and less academic fundamentalism is needed in order to develop an improved methodology to study the present religious situation in the world. The boomerang thought lost amid the study of culture and religion, a study focused around the process of meaning-making, will return to the scholars once they admit that they are not fundamentally different from the people they study.

What would a syncretistic, complementary approach look like? How could it do justice to the identity of each approach and yet combine them into a workable formulation? As suggested above, leaving aside the ships-that-pass-in-the-night model, two modes remain for combining the different perspectives. Either each has its proper place in the empirical cycle, qualitative research serving quantitative work, or, if the constructivist critique of that cycle is too devastating, the two ways of knowing may derive their justification from the differences in the questions and data they represent. The first, an asymmetrical case is discussed in this section, and the second, a more balanced case, in the next.

The first way of combining them is unequal, with the quantitative approach taking the lead in the empirical cycle. Its neo-positivist background prepares it for this role. Verification of a thesis or hypothesis, with a generalizable statement as its goal, demands an approach that quantitative work is able to provide. The validity of an idea, verbalized in the hypothesis and derived via qualitative methods, must be tested. Such a hypothesis usually suggests a correlation or a causal relation between two variables.

Let us consider, for example, the hypothesis that the better-educated are also the more secularized. Education, as part of modernization, is suggested as a cause of secularization. Measurable criteria must be established, for example, for the level of education attained (diplomas, degrees, years spent in tertiary study) and of secularization (church membership, church attendance, compulsion to appeal to religious ideas or rituals in situations of crisis). A representative sample of people must be chosen, composed of a group of well-educated people (group A), and a control group of less-educated people (group B), otherwise the influence of education, or lack of education, cannot be established. The design of the survey demands that variables other than education do not intervene, and therefore the two groups may only differ with regard to education and must otherwise be similarly composed, corresponding to the composition of the general population. As happens in the laboratory, variables are controlled as much as is possible. Once the survey has been administered, the results can be summarized and elaborated statistically. A conclusion can be drawn with regard to the significance of education as a factor in the secularization process.

In the empirical cycle, neo-positivists may decide to use the qualitative approach as supplementary and subservient to quantitative work. They may do this before any research starts and after it finishes. In the example described above, the idea that education may be a significant factor in secularization processes may arise from preparatory qualitative inductive work. From the study of a limited number of situations, a pattern may surface that points in that direction. People may respond in open interviews by saying that once they went to college or university, they were faced with questions they hadn't previously considered. It is possible that there are differences among students in terms of the extent to which their chosen discipline of study raised existential questions. For example, biologists will probably have directly considered the question of whether evolutionary theory and a creationist approach are mutually exclusive, whereas social scientists may not have been confronted with this question directly. What is suggested on the basis of a relatively small number of open interviews with a small number of informants, or through any other qualitative method, such as case studies, life histories and so on, will lead inductively to hypotheses that can be verified in quantitative research.

It is clear that the preparatory role of qualitative research is repeated following the completion of the quantitative study that it helped prepare, once it becomes obvious that further research is needed. It may be that the hypothesis could not be proven, or that unforeseen correlations were established. In this case qualitative research forms the link between two empirical cycles, because it helps to prepare for a new round of research. The role attributed to qualitative research, as a continuation of quantitative work, is essentially identical to the preparatory work described above.

Qualitative research demands open-mindedness and a lot of intuition. It is the work of an explorer in *terra incognita*. This means that the methodology cannot be too strict. It must leave room for the unexpected, the unthinkable. Whereas quantitative work can only begin from an already formulated hypothesis, explorative qualitative work would be frustrated by pre-conceived ideas. The qualitative researcher is constantly taking stock of what seems probable, trying to find out more, so as to know for sure that he or she is on the right track, getting to know each square inch of the landscape. Every cautious inference must be checked in another way and through another source, because it might be that what seems to be the rule is actually only the exception. Though generally inductive, there is thus a series of movements from induction to deduction and back again, thereby creating the pre-conditions for successful quantitative verification of the hypotheses initially formulated through this preparatory, heuristic qualitative research. In this way quantitative research depends upon qualitative research to begin with. Accordingly, it can be said that in this way neo-positivists and constructivists need each other, perhaps more than they are ready to admit following the decades of trench warfare that has been waged between them. The promising insights constructivists develop will only gain value and become plausible when tested with quantitative methods among a larger group of respondents. Neo-positivists will only be able to know what they are looking for if more or less probable hypotheses have been formulated on the basis of earlier qualitative work. In view of the fierce philosophical divide between the two schools, it may come as a surprise that in a very practical manner, the two might be mutually inclusive instead of mutually exclusive. Each approach is right in a sense, precisely because each is referring to a different phase of the research process.

BALANCE

The picture so far might suggest that qualitative methods are subservient to "real" quantitative work. This need not be the case. From my research experience, I know that the situation can be otherwise and that it may even be that the inverse is true, especially in terms of the function that quantitative techniques serve. In 1976–1977, I undertook a year of fieldwork among the Wagenia fishermen tribe of Kisangani (Congo), in the same context where from 1968 to 1971 I had undertaken research for my PhD on Wagenia boys' initiation (Droogers 1980). In 1976–1977, the focus was on religious change among the Wagenia, brought about since the end of the nineteenth century by the Protestant and Roman Catholic missions. I spent nine months interviewing a dozen people and I spoke with some of them more than 20 times. At the same time, I did participant observation, living the village life as much as possible. I spent a good deal of time in the Sunday church services of the four denominations that existed in this particular setting, including Roman Catholics, Baptists and Salvation Army, as well as the local community of an independent national Congolese church, the Kimbanguist church, named after its founder Simon Kimbangu (1887–1951). At the end of these nine months I devised a list of statements on the basis of the open interviews and the participant observation. During my last three months in the field, my list of statements was presented to 250 people, 50 from each of the four churches and 50 who did not belong to any of the four churches. Though real representation was difficult to obtain with such numbers, I took care to include a more or less representative sample of people in each of the five groups. The results (Droogers 1981) showed that Wagenia selected any Christian denomination according to how well it accommodated traditional beliefs, and not the other way around. Western influence was shown to be a stimulus to religious activity. Modernization therefore did not lead to secularization, as the sociologists of secularization had suggested, but to "religionization" (by which I mean increasing acceptance of religion or the sacred into everyday life) instead. Moreover, the members of the Kimbanguist church, the most African church of the four by origin, proved to be the most critical of traditional African beliefs. In contrast, a western influence, facilitated by the mission churches, did not predispose followers towards taking a critical view of African traditions.

Looking back, I consider the quantitative part of the research as an adjunct to the qualitative part. In terms of data, the qualitative component provided much greater insight into what was happening to religion in that society. The survey gave an indication of how significant the trends that came out of nine months of open interviews were. The use of complementary approaches in this instance meant that quantitative research was at the service of the qualitative part, not the other way around.

This example points to an urgent need for the rehabilitation of qualitative research. There are insights that cannot be put into numbers and therefore escape quantitative verification. Qualitative methods are more than just part of the empirical cycle dominated by the interests of the quantitative researchers that they serve. Anthropologists have a long tradition of producing non-quantitative data and monographs, in urban settings as well as rural, which show how this type of research can be done.

The same suggestion can be heard among critics of the empirical cycle. They also assert the relevance of symmetry and complementarity between numbers and narratives. The effect of the presumption of the importance of numbers is that the empirical cycle is accepted as the ultimate research model and as the only means for deriving reliable knowledge. Especially among those scholars with constructivist sympathies, this type of complementarity may not meet with their approval. They would regard quantitative results as being of limited relevance and will point to the blind spots that remain. In addition they would suggest that sound and plausible knowledge can also be obtained in a different manner.

The example of the relation between education and secularization may serve again to illustrate what the defenders mean (and me among them) when they speak of this radical rehabilitation. Suppose the fieldworker visits an interviewee and they engage in a meaningful conversation. The researcher pays attention to any signs conveyed in words, through silences, or body language, that seem to point to deeper layers of signification. The interviewee will, for example, tell the story of his or her life, if only to make clear in what larger framework his or her discourse must be understood. The researcher may interrupt to seek further details. Initial contact may lead the researcher to return regularly to this interviewee because in every session something new is uncovered. The researcher will seek rapport with his or her interviewee and will take any opportunity, not only to hear what that person says, but also to see how he or she lives, studying both reflection and action. This may result in a friendship that lasts for a long time. By proceeding in this manner, the researcher will be able to show the richness of the case that emerges. It may be richer than neo-positivist constraints could allow, but it need not be less relevant.

If our researcher does his/her work in preparation of quantitative work, recommendations for a survey design that would follow from his conversations may cover half a page, whereas the collected data might justify a whole book. If the researcher had literary ambitions, he or she might even consider writing a novel on the basis of what he or she had been told by the interviewee. In fact, there are many novels that amplify anthropological insights into a given situation. With regard to education and secularization, for example, Chaim Potok's novels are illustrative. Having myself worked for five years in Kisangani, Congo, on reading V.S. Naipaul's "*A Bend in the River*" (1979), I had to admit that I had overlooked a few essential things, despite consciously having kept my eyes and ears open during the time I lived there. True fiction exists (Kloos 1990).

But even outside the realm of literary fiction, aspects of any situation may come into view even though they cannot be expressed in statistical form. In the instance that a correlation is established between higher education and secularization, the question still remains regarding how this correlation in fact works, and whether there is causality. It might be that the children of secularized parents have easier access to higher education and that causality works the other way around, or has already taken place in the parents' generation. But whatever the direction of the causal chain, statistics do not convey precisely what happens with regard to cause and effect. In quantitative research, the simple establishment of some correlation is often sufficient to suggest a causal relation. The funniest example warning aginst this is that of the co-occurrence, in Hamburg, in the 30s of the last century, of a plague of storks and a high birth rate.

The metaphor of the black box is worth exploring. One variable, higher education, or perhaps secularization, goes into the box and produces an effect as the outcome in some hidden way. If the input is higher education, is secularization the outcome? Or can it be that higher education is what comes out of the box? Qualitative methods may help uncover what happens between cause and effect, and in so doing, play a significant role in unravelling what is cause and what is effect.

There is more to this. Surveys are sometimes repeated at certain intervals, in order to discover change through time. It may even be that the same group of interviewees is reinterviewed. In other cases a comparable random sample is drawn. The comparison of the results may point to certain trends. In our example, it may be that all of a sudden, natural science students are less prone to secularization than they had been at the time of the previous survey. Again the question is one of the black box kind. What exactly transpired between those two moments in time? What meaning-making processes took place that may help to explain why the new trend occurred? It may be that a new insight from the natural sciences, that observations are always mediated through the human observer and that they therefore have a certain degree of subjectivity, has exerted some influence. This kind of nuanced understanding can only be discovered through the use of open interviews, that is, by asking interviewees why they answered the survey questions the way they did. What was behind their yes or no, or what did they mean by their four on a scale of five? Qualitative methods are able to uncover data that cannot be quantified and yet remain central to understanding what is happening.

CONCLUSIONS

As I argued in Chapter 2, the current global worldview situation is changing rapidly and in ways that are so new that qualitative work is urgently needed. Now, more than ever, important personal aspects of varied and fragmented worldviews cannot be expressed in numbers. The efforts undertaken thus far to rehabilitate qualitative methods highlight their intrinsic value. It would seem that the natural sciences model of the empirical cycle has lost its monopoly on meaning-making.

Besides, the practice of research on worldview offers an important opportunity to combine views and methods that for a long time have been regarded as being mutually exclusive. Instead of the either/or approach taken in the past, I suggest the need for an and/and approach for today. In combining quantitative and qualitative work, the best of the two perspectives can be put to good use and the shortcomings of each can be compensated for by the other.

Chapter 4

Playing with Perspectives

ANDRÉ DROOGERS*

In the preceding chapters, the researcher in the field of the study of religion was introduced to you the reader, as a meaning-maker who studies other meaning-makers. One notable characteristic of human meaning-making is the abundant use of dualities. Academic meaning-making, regardless of the object of investigation, complies with this tendency. Nature provides several of these contrasts, which in turn become invested with a metaphorical status, as though representing cultural phenomena. Thus day and night, light and dark, young and old, male and female, hot and cold, left and right, obtain extra meanings when invoked metaphorically. Oppositions also form the basis of much scientific reflection. In instances where options have to be worked through and people, whether in religion or in academia, make choices that are unlike the choices made by others, the issue of how to reach a considered, sensible and valid position comes to the fore.

The choice discussed in Chapter 3, to accept either quantitative or qualitative methods, illustrates the dualistic nature of scholarly worldview. When addressing this seemingly technical question, we are immediately confronted with multiple pairs of opposites, such as objectivity and subjectivity, researcher and researched, rule and deviation, empirical and non-empirical and social and individual. Then we also encounter the imaginary divide between reality "out there" and "in here," or mind and matter. Making any choice has consequences. The implications of accepting this dualistic way of thinking in the study of religion should not be underestimated. The consequences influence not just methods, as techniques, but methodology in the wider sense, guiding our behaviour as we design and undertake our research projects, or when we report our findings. Moreover, in the worldview field,

* André Droogers is Emeritus Professor of Cultural Anthropology, especially the Anthropology of Religion and Symbolic Anthropology, at VU University, Amsterdam. He is co-editor of *"Studying Global Pentecostalism: Theories and Methods"* (University of California Press, 2010). A selection from the articles that he has written over the last 30 years was reprinted, together with an autobiographical Introduction, in *"Play and Power in Religion: Collected Essays"* (De Gruyter, 2012).

dualities abound, even at the very moments when they are denied or suppressed. For example, monotheistic religions are inherently dualistic (God's reality versus human reality), whereas within Asian religions reality is seen as being one, not two, as singular rather than dualistic.

Examples of the oppositions flourishing across the field of worldview studies are plentiful. As we saw, we have the choice between neo-positivist and constructivist positions, both organized around other binary sets of options. Neo-positivists emphasize the stark contrast between researcher and researched. Constructivists, however, view both parties as having cooperated in producing knowledge, albeit by playing different roles, and thereby tone down the sharpness of the distinction that they nevertheless recognize to exist. Scholars also have to decide how to move along the spectrum between objectivity and subjectivity. Moreover, in explaining religion, many models are put forward, all with their own sets of contrasts, often expressing a strong predilection towards one of the poles of a spectrum. They may, for example, choose between individual agency and imposed structures, or between external conditions and inner predispositions. Sometimes predilections towards particular ideologies, such as liberalism or Marxism, play a role.

An awareness of the manner in which one deals with dichotomies is needed. Whether one opts for a distant objective approach, sought via quantitative means, or for a participatory subjective role, often sought via qualitative methods, in either case the researcher's own views and position are important in drawing a roadmap through the landscape of the many options. This includes the way he or she handles the possible influence of his or her own worldview, whether religious, secular or ideological. It also involves taking a personal stand on other worldviews. It may be that personally held views on "scientism," that is, the view that empirical science produces the most reliable form of knowledge, implicitly or explicitly also play a role in making choices.

Whether one is a champion of objectivity or intent upon the responsible uses of subjectivity, in either case, the researcher's role and views need to be made explicit. These views may be considered a handicap, especially if objectivity is a primary goal. On the other hand, they may come to be viewed as an asset that locates and anchors the researcher who is comfortable with the idea of subjectivity firmly within the context of his/her research. In both the distant objective and the more engaged approaches, personal locatedness is at issue.

I offer a rather idiosyncratic solution to the problem of the exclusivity of competing perspectives, whether paradigms, methodologies or worldviews. My solution, tentatively developed here, is that even competing views, regardless of their mutually exclusive characteristics, can be combined and used simultaneously. However, this is only possible if the human gift for play can be fully recovered for methodological use. One should learn to play with oppositions. I have called my contribution to worldview research "methodological ludism," ludism being a neologism, after homo ludens, the playful human (Droogers 1996, 1999, 2012, Huizinga 1952, Turner 1982, 1988). As I will show, this approach is useful where theoretical or methodological discourses collide within academia, but it is also relevant in relation to inter-religious conflicts and dialogue. Methodological ludism can be helpful in handling options and contrasts. It provides a means to avoid the pitfalls of unilateral positions. Taking an eclectic position is possible.

My test case in this instance is the following: Does the believers' conviction that the sacred (or the divine, supernatural, or transcendental) can be experienced and is open to communication, play a role in the study and explanation of religion? If so, what role does it play? If not, why not? These questions are loaded with dichotomies. First, I will sketch the problem of scholarly understanding in more detail, mapping the alternatives. Then I describe the human gift for play and elaborate on its application to methodological ludism. I then provide an example of fieldwork experience in which methodological ludism was applied. In conclusion, I explore the relevance of this approach when dealing with the other dilemmas outlined.

TRUE KNOWLEDGE

The problem of the search for true knowledge tends to present science and religion as different camps. Science is frequently acknowledged as being critical of religious views. This leads to the question of whether believers' manifest experience of supernatural entities or forces can be admitted as evidence in the explanation of religion. Two ways of meaning-making, one religious and one scientific, collide in this confrontation. The position taken in this debate depends on yet another methodological problem. In order to understand a particular worldview, how far can and must one identify with it and participate in it? Here the researcher's role can be decisive.

What complicates all of this, is that the worldview field itself is hopelessly divided. Religious spokespersons often make exclusive claims regarding truth, condemning the ideas and practices of other religions, and criticizing secular worldviews, thereby strengthening oppositions and antithetical positions. Both secular and religious worldviews tend to condemn and exclude each other.

Dualistic thinking is common to both science and religion, even though different sets of oppositions appear to be at issue. If this divisiveness is by definition part of the scientific study of religion, how can we handle this opposition in such a way that our understanding of religion is enlarged and not hampered? Contrast should not obstruct comprehension.

The case is more complicated still. The scientific and the religious fields are not just opposed, but also intertwined, even when strict objectivity is the rule. Since our intention is to study religion via scientific methods, we directly stumble into the peculiar circumstance where the scholarly method and worldview are already part of the field we study. This is the case simply because the demarcation of the field, as we saw in Chapter 2, is the result of the application of these methods, and is therefore influenced by implicit and explicit choices. There are therefore multiple maps of the field available, each offering differing interpretations of the boundaries. Though religion is a common sense category, taken from everyday vocabulary, students of religion have their own ways of defining the term and the boundaries of the field, and may even boycott the term completely (Asad 1993, see also Droogers 2009). Inevitably we look at religion through science's spectacles, every scholar having his or her own lenses. The fact that secular worldviews were usually not viewed as part of the field of religion shows that the opposition has drastic consequences, depriving scholars of opportunities to study interesting worldviews and draw fruitful comparisons. The label "religion" remains dominant, whereas the term "worldview" has gained only limited acceptance.

This leaves us confronted with a problem that would seem less difficult if our field of study focused on secular phenomena, such as kinship systems or youth culture. Though we would be involved to some extent with these matters (kinship and youth being part of our own experience), the study of religion is very much a worldview in and of itself. The study of religion, from its very origins, is marked by its object and could itself be approached as an integral part of the field it explores, precisely because it called it forth and determines its limits. Both researchers and the researched are finding their way through their own repertoires of dualities (Droogers 2009: 277). Accordingly, in discussing the methodology of the study of contemporary religion, we will have to find a way to deal with the consequences of this similarity between researchers and researched. Aside from an obvious and deeply embedded contrast, there is also similarity between meaning-makers, and this may offer a solution to the problem.

So far the focus has been on the contrast between religion and science. Let us now turn to look more closely at secular worldviews. Even though secular worldviews themselves tend to identify with science because they result from the scientific critique of the religious worldview, their study can nevertheless be viewed in the same way as research on religious worldviews, as a way of meaning-making about meaning-making. Precisely because science inspired the secular worldview, the contrast between science and religion plays a role here as well, albeit in an indirect way. Moreover, although empirical verification is viewed as crucial to secular worldviews, there are always axiomatic presuppositions that usually remain implicit, as with science. These may include altruistic expectations, but also basic ideas such as the supposed moral goodness of human beings.

Personal experiences concerning worldviews may influence the scholar's perception of religious and secular worldviews. In the study of worldviews this must be taken into account, even when researching secular worldviews, and despite the claim that these worldviews share a scientific status. The constructivist critique of neo-positivism applies here as well.

OBJECTIVITY AND SUBJECTIVITY

In the 1970s, in the Congo, while conducting Wagenia fieldwork on religious change, I studied the local Kimbanguist church, as mentioned in the previous chapter. It was a church that came from an African initiative, having started in 1921 in the Bakongo area as a prophetic movement around the person of Simon Kimbangu. Having developed my own set of preferences, I must admit that at the time, as a young anthropologist, wishing to see African cultures spared from drastic modern influences, I sympathized with the aims of this church because it sought explicitly to be African. Knowing what missions had done to cultures, the case seemed particularly interesting to me since no missionary effort was involved. During that first period of fieldwork I very much enjoyed my visits to this church. However, when I returned after a few years, the national leadership of the church had begun to raise funds for a huge church building near the capital. I cringed at what I saw as the exploitation of the low-income members, who from Sunday to Sunday were urged to pay for a building that they probably would never see. In addition, the hierarchies in the church had been strengthened and the leadership had gained power. Aware of my own subjective perception, and even though I was trying to be as objective as humanly possible, I had developed a clear sense of antipathy, my subjective view adapting to changing circumstances.

One of the explicit methodological decisions that we need to make when we study worldviews, is that some form of objectivity is needed. This speaks for itself in neo-positivist approaches, in which objectivity is a central norm. But even in adopting a constructivist perspective, one has to define a position, perhaps even more so because of the stronger awareness of the working of subjective factors and of cognitive constructions. Besides, the emphasis on worldviews as constructions can lead to a reductionist critique of religion that is not very different from the (neo-)positivist rejection of religious worldviews. The conditions under which a worldview emerges receive attention in constructivist methodology as well. In any case, the researcher's own worldview presents a possible challenge to objectivity. It may also be that he or she has an opinion about worldviews other than his or her own, whether religious or secular, either sympathetic or critical, which directly or indirectly influences the results of his or her research.

As relevant as the objectivity ideal is the role that subjectivity may play in the study of worldviews. This is true not only in the negative sense, as a sin against objectivity in a neo-positivist framework. As we saw already, subjectivity can be an asset and a research tool, especially in a constructivist perspective where knowledge is the result of the encounter between researcher and researched. An awareness of the role of subjectivity in that process will help to determine the validity of the results that are obtained. If subjectivity need not hinder the task of seeking objective results, to what extent can it be useful, and how can objectivity be guaranteed?

In the matter of the study of religious worldviews, the tension between objective and subjective factors may be more obvious than when a secular worldview is the object of research. The question is a consequence of the fact that religions do not obey the scientific rule that only what can be proven to exist empirically does exist and can therefore be considered as true. However, even a secular ideological utopia, whether Marxist, liberal or some third way, may not stand the test of empirical verification either. Yet, the question is more perplexing in the case of religion.

Scientific efforts to understand religion have to find a way to handle the fact that the perception that is essential to the believer's experience is denied by science. In the study of profane topics, science presupposes the validity of the perception of the reality it claims to examine. In the case of religious themes it denies, or at least abstains from providing an opinion on the existence of super-natural reality (which is why this reality is called supernatural or non-empirical). The understanding of religious worldviews is put at risk by denial.

BERGER'S THREE METHODOLOGICAL POSITIONS

The most common way that the scientific study of religion has tried to overcome this problem is by taking into account what people say about their religious experience and observing how they act. At the same time, the strategy is to abstain from venturing an opinion on the question of whether the other reality "really" exists, simply because its existence cannot be proven empirically. Peter Berger (1967) has labelled the latter position "methodological agnosticism," the adjective "methodological" suggesting that the researcher may hold a different opinion in private, but that in his or her research, for methodological purposes, he or she avoids expressing any opinions on that matter. In his typology, Berger includes two more possibilities. "Methodological atheism" denies the existence of the supernatural reality on empirical grounds. "Methodological theism" accepts the existence of a supernatural reality that manifests itself, even though it cannot be known fully by humans.

In fact the three positions reflect the discussion that started with modernization, the process by which the results of science and technology are applied in society. Viewed from some distance, the debate is part of modern culture's quest for a corresponding worldview. Students of religion are the children of their times. They are challenged by the subject of their study, simply because religion, just like secularization, is at issue in their own culture.

Berger's tripartite typology refers to researcher's positions, not to the field or followers. The standard methods of a given discipline will influence the degree to which the scholar comes up against the problem of distance or nearness, as we saw when quantitative and qualitative methods were discussed. Anthropologists of religion working principally with participant observation (and not all do) will differ from sociologists of religion who work principally with surveys (and again, not all do). Moreover, the question of the researcher's views on the believer's claims can be avoided by shifting the emphasis to the question of how the believer's faith experience can best be described. In that case Berger's three positions become less urgent. A follower of scientism, on the other hand, will give much more attention to the contrast between the truth claims of science and religion, since science is thought to produce the best "conceivable" knowledge.

To relativize the question, it should also be mentioned that not all believers are preoccupied with the absolute nature of religious truth. The stereotype of a believer cognitively defending the truth of his or her faith may be the invention of the academic atheist critic of religious truth, who draws a stark contrast between the believers' view and his or her own position. The recent attention given to fundamentalism certainly nourishes that image. Besides, if religion is viewed primarily as experience, then the cognitive side becomes less important and is often limited to the person's interpretation of his or own reality, not the supernatural reality.

In my view, methodological agnosticism and atheism do not differ much in practice, because both (though admitting the believers' views on the supernatural to their description) refuse to give the believer's conviction a place within the explanations that they offer. The first refuses it because nothing can be said about it with certainty, the second because it can be said with scientific certainty that the presumed supernatural reality, already super-natural, is not real at all. Since the believer experiences that denied reality, the question that remains is whether the researcher can permit him or herself to deny or ignore the existence of such an essential part of the study field without losing insight into the matter. This means we should look for a way to enable methodological atheists and agnostics, as researchers, to be able to stick to their view on the presumed reality of the supernatural, and yet do justice to what the believer considers to be the core of his or her convictions. How can a position that solves the researcher's problem be reached in such a way that the research is not compromised and the person being researched feels understood?

The case of methodological theism is not without questions either, even though it appears to give the supernatural a central place. Which supernatural notion is defended, of which religion? The supernatural force or entity may be thought to manifest itself, but it does so in as many different ways as there are religions. Even within one religion there may be striking differences. The methodological theist who, in private life, is a follower of a particular religion, will have to find a way of qualifying the manifestations of the divine or supernatural beyond his or her own religion. This would demand a theology of religions. Theoretically several positions are then possible, from the exclusive claim of one religion, to the acceptance of the presence of the minimal supernatural or divine in all religions, each in its own way.

In the latter case, the perception of the supernatural, as a universal notion, inevitably has to pass through the sieve of the human experience. Then the cultural context intervenes, creating diversity from a source that is viewed as homogeneous. Within this cultural perspective the supernatural is thought to be less concrete and less personal in origin, a vague and relatively empty notion, to be filled in by concrete religions. It is the minimum that a maximal number of religions have in common. In most cases, however, religious heterogeneity does not combine easily with the general view of the methodological theist. Scholars of the phenomenology of religion in particular, have pointed to similarities between seemingly diverse religions (Sharpe 1975: 224). In the religious field, some of the newer religions seek to bring together what they consider to be the best elements of existing religions. Yet there remains a tension between the supposedly universal supernatural and the elaborate forms it takes in concrete religions.

REDUCTIONIST EXPLANATIONS?

Agnostic, atheist and theist methodological positions are not just about religions' truth claims. They also have consequences for the way religion is explained. The basic question is whether religion can be sufficiently explained, in a reductionist manner, in non-religious terms (psychic, social, economic etc.), as methodological atheists and agnostics would. By contrast, according to the methodological theist view, an explanation must include the notion that supernatural reality manifests itself as believers affirm from their experience. If believers' statements are to be taken seriously, the question arises as to how seriously. Should they be accepted only to the extent that they help to explain the religious in a reductionist manner, that is, by how they were derived from, or stemmed from the non-religious? Or is it conceivable that the believers' explanation of religion provides evidence of the existence of the supernatural?

The problem is familiar to anthropologists who study cultures, usually a culture other than their own. The method of participant observation is meant to give voice to the practices and views of the people studied. Here too the question arises regarding how insiders' views can best be appreciated, in comparison with the fieldworker's views. Anthropologists use the terms emic and etic (derived from phonemic and phonetic), as shorthand for the subject's and the fieldworker's positions and perspectives. The distinction does not prevent overlap between the two points of view, but shows where indigenous and exogenous data and interpretations come from.

It should be mentioned that methodological agnostics and atheists generally do not find the question of the value of informants' truth claims very interesting or important, since they view the reductionist position as the only viable one. Their position has often been nourished by the conviction, now maintained only by a minority of scholars, that religion will not survive the secularization process. Science is thought to have contributed to this predicted effect by suggesting that the existence of the supernatural cannot be proven empirically.

Some of the main theories that explain religion in a reductionist manner, like those coined by Marx (religion as a way to survive oppression) and Durkheim (the real object of religion is the group, society), stemmed from the bewilderment experienced by their authors when forced to recognize that religion was so resilient. Since, in their view, this resilience could not be the consequence of the existence of the supernatural, to them it was obvious that such an illusion could only survive because it served important non-religious purposes.

Modernization has not put an end to religion and on the contrary seems to have stimulated its continued existence. Religion plays a functional role for the very people that are subjected to the negative effects of modernization. And even those who have prospered within the context of modernization may trace their wealth to divine blessing. This means that the supernatural continues to seem real to many people, justifying the search for an answer to the question of how the views of both sceptics and faithful can be part of the study of religion.

PLAY

Participant observation involves a double perspective, combining involvement and distance, inside and outside. The same can be said of play, an important ingredient of methodological ludism. Much has been written about the subject, and in very diverse ways (e.g. Caillois 1958, Handelman 1987, Kolb 1989, Norbeck 1974). This variety seems to leave room for a perspective on play that offers a solution to the problems we are discussing. I define play as "the capacity to deal simultaneously and subjunctively with two or more ways of classifying reality" (Droogers 1996: 53). In the spirit of this definition, the qualitative method of participant observation can be characterized as playful, even though not all fieldworkers are aware of the fact that they are playing, or at least playing with *emic* and *etic* roles. The adjective "subjunctively" in the above definition is borrowed from Turner (1988: 169), who introduced the contrast, yes, yet another one, between the indicative "as is" and the subjunctive "as if." The liminal phase of ritual, with its inversions of hierarchy and symbolism, and its experiments with the normal, is characterized by this subjunctivity. Turner (1988: 169) also points to the political dimension of play. In suggesting alternatives, play can be a threat to vested authority. Its subjunctivity makes it subversive.

Furthermore it should be noted that the emphasis in the definition I suggest is on a human capacity. Bellah (2011: 74–83) traces the origins of the capacity for play in human evolution. The emphasis on human capacity is also present in my definitions of culture (roughly the capacity for meaning-making), as are worldview (the capacity to raise and answer the five basic questions, expressed in the seven dimensions), and power (the capacity to influence other people's behaviour). Each of these was discussed in Chapter 2. In all cases both the capacity and its product are taken into account. The emphasis on human capacity therefore allows for the making of a perspective on the dynamics of processes and avoids static descriptions of the concrete results of these processes: culture and not just cultures; worldview and not only worldviews; power and not just the powers that be. In play, even the "as if" and the "as is" can be combined, parallel to capacity and what it brings forth.

Simultaneity is essential to the definition of play in that it suggests the possibility of combining contrasting views. The primary connotation of play is that it is the exception from the normal, the wink, the double entendre. It suggests a stereophonic environment, an inner dialogue of different orders, of contrasting sets of rules.

Play is not necessarily the opposite of seriousness, because once a playful situation exists, it is taken seriously and is no longer "just a game." That is the reason why play is not always recognized as such. Any form of play demands a serious attitude. If you do not take the game seriously, you are a spoilsport.

In Western society work appears to have gained the monopoly on seriousness, and play has virtually been exiled to the domain of leisure and sports, where it has been commodified. Paradoxically play generates serious work and income for some, but remains a relegated separate sphere to others. Yet, this hijacking of play should not prevent us from returning it to the legitimate place it occupied for a long time, even in the West.

Play can be discerned in a number of human phenomena. Religion is the most obvious example (see also Bellah 2011: 91–116). Natural and supernatural realities are combined, subjunctively and simultaneously. The supernatural becomes a possibility, different from human reality, separate and extraordinary. The "as is" finds its complement in "as if" and the other way around. Religion has been viewed by several authors (Fernandez 1986, Van Baal 1972, Winnicott 1971) as dealing with the paradox of humans being, at once, part of nature or society, and yet autonomous, reflecting on the world, including nature and society, from a distance. Play is a way of both being part and yet standing apart.

Another common practice that is facilitated by play is the use of metaphors. Metaphors happen thanks to a playful exchange between separate domains. Every time a metaphor is used, a clear image from one domain is combined with another domain that needs clarification. When somebody suggests that life is like a wheel, he or she is playing with two domains that together represent an experienced reality. Religion makes intensive use of metaphors and tends to reify them to the "as is" sphere.

METHODOLOGICAL LUDISM

Play can serve to solve some of the problems at issue here. In my view, Berger's three alternatives do not exhaust all of the options. There is a fourth possibility, that I call "methodological ludism." It does not suffer from the limitations that are part of the three positions that Berger put forward. In a way it also elimi-

nates a core problem. Methodological ludism is in part inspired by constructivist arguments. The human capacity for play, "to deal simultaneously and
subjunctively with two or more ways of classifying reality," is used to gain access
to the best of two worlds. The researcher assumes the role of homo ludens. He
or she makes an effective use of play by occupying varying positions, if only for
as long as is necessary to understand what the seemingly contrasting positions
look like, whether of science and religion, researcher and researched, outsider
and insider or *emic* and *etic*. He and she might situate themselves as part and
apart, subject and object, believer and atheist, faithful and faithless, body and
soul, religion B (or C) and religion H (or I, or J), or, even neo-positivist and constructivist. That being the case, truth claims can be studied closely. The emphasis on strong oppositions can be mitigated and gaps can be bridged, if only as a
thought experiment and for a short while. Since play is not instrumental and
has no function to which it can be reduced (Huizinga 1952: 14), it is a perfect
and impartial tool to explore a field beyond the commonly drawn boundaries
of scientific knowledge. Methodological ludism launches the academic carnival.

The scholar of religion could acknowledge moreover that the believer is
of the same homo ludens genus. Several of the dualities just mentioned can
also be found in the believers' experience. The scholar and the believer have
more in common than the established contrasts suggest. The believer is also
gripped by the tension of being a part of and standing apart, of being both
subject and object, of having to combine body and soul, and of having certainties as well as doubts (Horton 1993: ch. 7). Although believers generally
tend to be too serious to admit that they are playing with reality, in fact it is
what they do. The need for a transparent worldview, plus the role that power
plays in maintaining and promoting that way of looking at things, buttress
the absoluteness of the perspective taken. Especially from the margins of the
religious power centres, religious innovators seek out and test alternatives to
official views and practices. Not only magic (the production of religious views
and practices that are considered illegitimate by the leadership), but also new
prophetic movements or other revivals, renewals and reforms, belong to this
category in the margins. If religion is counted as a way of playing seriously
with the possibilities that a supernatural reality offers, the truth claim suddenly becomes less compelling. Yet, it is not just a game, since seriousness is
essential to play. It is this exaggerated seriousness that is the pitfall of any
exclusivist religion, causing external strife and internal oppression. Here too
the dualistic straitjacket can be shed. Like scholars, believers would be liberated. World peace would be served. But let us return to the study of religion.

The scholar's playful shift from one perspective to another need not
demand a final farewell to one position and the permanent embrace of the
other, just as the believer need not abandon the supernatural when accepting
that religion is play. The basic intention is to understand, by experience, what
the opposite pole is like. Afterwards one may continue on the course of the
objective outsider, the convinced neo-positivist, the orthodox believer, or the
staunch atheist. But by playing this game, one may have gained understand-

ing. Methodological ludism makes it possible to move successively through the three positions that Berger defined, and go beyond them, ignoring the influence of unilateral researchers' and science's standpoints. The sedentary scholar can become nomadic again, the hedgehog may turn into a fox, if only for as long as it seems useful to do so.

One should ask whether the researcher's prescribed objective distance from the reality experienced by the believer does not stand in the way of insight. Especially in relation to qualitative fieldwork on religious world-views, such a question cannot be avoided. Since constructivists view the interaction between researcher and researched as the source of knowledge, this includes participation in the religious experience of the respondent. As shown in Chapter 8, participation may even mean sharing gossip, including feelings of guilt and betrayal in the researcher, yet delivering new information and insight. Constructivist arguments could be advanced to suggest that it is important to get as close as possible to the thought processes, religious or secular, that people employ to interpret reality. Equally, the researcher's thought processes, as part of the enterprise, should be made explicit and not excluded from the research context.

Ironically constructivist scepticism about the empirical reality that most neo-positivists say exists autonomously out there leads constructivists to pay special attention to religious reality, the existence of which neo-positivists in turn are very sceptical about. The critique against the dominance of the neo-positivist tradition makes scientific knowledge a relative form of knowledge. Consequently the step towards the appreciation of religious views as relevant knowledge is a small one. Though marginalized by the secularization process, they can be rehabilitated. Again methodological ludism may serve as the effective means by which to do this.

For anthropologists, participant observation is the method that almost defines their trade. The term itself contains a paradox. Anthropologists have to find a way to overcome the opposition between participation, with its subjective rapport and close contact, and observation, suggesting the need for distance and objectivity. Somewhere on the spectrum between the poles of participation and observation they will have to situate themselves, making a simultaneous use of two roles, participant and observer. Some form of identification is implied, but at the same time distance is necessary. This seemingly schizophrenic method has been applied now for more than a century and there is sufficient evidence to accept that it works and that its internal contradiction is not its weakness but its strength.

> I became a strange hybrid, caught in a no-man's-land betwixt and between cultures, learning something of a visited way of life yet relying heavily on my own. But perhaps it is precisely in the clash between world-views, in the tension between symbolic systems (how reality is defined, the body held, experience articulated) that some anthropological insights emerge. (Desjarlais 1992: 19)

This model can be put to good use in the service of methodological ludism.

EARLIER EFFORTS TO BRIDGE THE GAP

Play allows for a double perspective and can help bridge the gap between researcher and researched. This effort is not new. In the history of the study of religion, the philosophical phenomenology of Edmund Husserl has inspired scholars in the field of the phenomenology of religion (Eliade 1969, Van der Leeuw 1956, Widengren 1969, see also Cox 2010, Momen 1999) to get as close as possible to phenomena and to describe them without prejudice. The subject's experience is the important source of knowledge, for example about religious phenomena, and should be studied through empathy. The scholars within this tradition have been criticized because the boundary between their professed objectivity and practical subjectivity was not always clearly delineated. Their Christian background, if applicable, was thought to frustrate understanding from within. Yet their serious effort to move inside a worldview should be seen to be an early example of a playful method at work.

Similarly Max Weber's interpretative sociology, centred on the concept of Verstehen, offers a way of understanding the meaning that the actor, consciously or unconsciously, gives to his or her actions, within a context of mutual understanding, and drawing from a "world of meanings" (Käsler 1988: 178). The method has both quantitative and qualitative traits. Weber saw this approach as an empirical sociology that aimed at the understanding of meaning through the construction of pure "ideal" types (Käsler 1988: 176, 177). Weber did not go so far as to opt for a method that was applicable to the "human sciences" (Geisteswissenschaften). Dilthey and his school did however, and invested empathy and intuition with great significance. To Weber, causal explanation and the statistical verification of a hypothesis remained essential for interpretation (Käsler 1988: 178). In contemporary terms, Weber was more a neo-positivist than a constructivist. Yet, though he put much emphasis on the role of instrumentality in people's meaningful behaviour, this certainly was not the only type of meaning he looked for (Käsler 1988: 179). In summary, though not in a radical manner, Weber's interpretative sociology paid close attention to the method of understanding the actor's meaning making. Weber obliges the researcher to take the position of the researched and Verstehen can be understood as a form of methodological play in the sense outlined above.

Turner's contribution to the understanding of play in ritual has been mentioned already, but he had more to say about the concept that is of interest to us (Turner 1988, see also McGilchrist 2010). According to Turner, play is presented as the interface between the right and the left brain hemispheres. These halves differ in function. The right hemisphere enables synthetic and holistic thought. It mediates the perception of space and houses information that is organized in patterns. The left half is more analytic, enabling linear thought and assessment of time, the latter especially important in the analysis of causality. It also makes speech possible and houses any sequentially organized information. Where the right half sustains the idea of the whole, the left half is the seat of dichotomous thinking. The two are therefore very complementary. Play assures the link between the two halves. Ritual, understood as a form of play, stimulates both hemispheres and creates a sense of wellbeing, even ecstasy and mysticism, in an experience of unity, above fragmentation, contradiction and paradox.

The idea that play is grounded in the abilities of the human brain can also be found in so-called connectionism, inspired by cognitive studies. It defends the idea that human knowledge is not only organized in a sentential verbalized form, the prerogative of the left hemisphere, but is also stored in the right hemisphere as "non-linguistic chunked mental models" (Bloch 1991: 194). People are able to consult the information available in these models in a parallel nonlinear way, carrying out "thousands of tiny computations simultaneously" (D'Andrade 1992: 29). The phenomenon connectionism is focusing on is therefore also called Parallel Distributed Processing (PDP) (D'Andrade 1992: 29). Parallel processors that are connected with each other in networks are supposed to be able to handle lots of information simultaneously and in a very short time. Once a conclusion is reached, it can be verbalized in the familiar sentential manner. Viewed in relation to the neurobiological information that Turner used in the early 1980s, the right brain hemisphere is the locus of the PDP, whereas verbalization takes place in the left half. An interesting aspect of this model of human knowledge organization is that the scholarly habit of thinking in dichotomies can be put into context as a manifestation of the analytic left brain hemisphere, whereas overview and synthesis are much more connected with the simultaneity that is typical of the right half. Multivocal symbols, with their rich patterns of meanings, can also be situated there. Play, as the simultaneous reference to different orders, combines synthesis and analysis, and functions as an interface.

Finally, another approach that is of interest to us is phenomenological anthropology, or perhaps phenomenological ethnography (Jackson 1996, 1998). Notions such as embodiment, experience, narrative and reflexivity are central in this approach. "Direct understanding and in-depth description" are the goals of this approach, and phenomenology is presented as "the scientific study of experience. It is an attempt to describe human consciousness in its lived immediacy, before it is subject to theoretical elaboration or conceptual systematizing" (Jackson 1996: 2). Reification of concepts, including dichotomous terms such as subjective and objective, and the subsequent "certification" (Dewey in Jackson 1996: 8) of the world through previously legitimated words, including the term culture (Jackson 1996: 18), is condemned as a hindrance to internally derived knowledge. Humans "live their lives independently of the intellectual schemes dreamed up in academe" (Jackson 1996: 4). Moreover, this approach suggests that pre-established schemas represent power interests that impede engaged scholars' efforts to improve the world and the quality of life. A worldview in Husserl's terms is primarily a life-world (Lebenswelt), or in Pierre Bourdieu's terms a habitus, more than a system of thought (Jackson 1996: 6, 13). In a constructivist manner, the communication between subjects replaces the us/them, the universal/particular and the objective/subjective dichotomies. This does not mean that the researcher lacks awareness of the influence of his or her own situation. On the contrary, this awareness nourishes the wish to look at the world from the vantage point and with the metaphors of the researched (Jackson 1996: 9). Interestingly Jackson (1998: 28–32) includes play within his vocabulary of phenomenological anthropology. In his view simultaneity and the subjunctive also form part of an approach: "Play enables us to renegotiate the given, experiment with alternatives, imagine how things might be otherwise" (Jackson 1998: 28, 29). "Mastery play" gives people the feeling that they control their world and make existential choices, even though nothing really changes (Jackson 1998: 30).

THE PRACTICE OF METHODOLOGICAL LUDISM

Methodological ludism is easier to formulate than it is to put into concrete practice. Though the mindset needed to apply it can be assimilated, the experience of implementing it in fieldwork settings is not so easy. Only recently, an effort has been made to map the methodological difficulties and challenges (Knibbe and Droogers 2011).

Several problems present themselves when translating methodological ludism into a research tool, as Knibbe's experiences illustrate. She completed her MA fieldwork within the context surrounding the Dutch spiritualist medium and healer, Jomanda. Interestingly Jomanda presented her approach as a new science, thereby making the tension between science and religion part of the fieldwork that Knibbe had to work within. Medical "intelligences" from "the other side" performed operations on patients, using sophisticated methods that were as yet not available to earthly medical science. Jomanda encouraged people to collect proof, including pictures, of the effect of the work of these intelligences. Truth claims came to the fore, in an almost positivist sense. Though ideas were part of Jomanda's package, the basic experience was corporeal, inevitably so, the goal itself, healing.

In her fieldwork Knibbe adopted the attitude of methodological ludism, as suggested by me as her supervisor. And yet she soon discovered that the simultaneity that was presupposed proved difficult to implement. Adopting Jomanda's viewpoint and seeking to experience the effect of the healing intelligences, she discovered that it had become impossible to keep sufficient distance, in the fieldworker's usual observing way. Even between participation and observation it was difficult to commute, once the participation became total. Containing her own sceptical frame of reference within parentheses, Knibbe "religiously" followed all the instructions that Jomanda gave to her audience, for example when seeking a solution to a personal problem. Participation in the ludist manner meant that Jomanda's worldview was learned, substituting previous frames of reference, such as the safe scientific worldview that Knibbe was used to applying both professionally and in her personal life. Learning a new frame of reference meant learning new ways of experiencing and perceiving what happens during the healing services but also in everyday life. She moved beyond the bounds that the three methodological postures coined by Berger share, between science and religion, and fully into the religious area. Thus she understood the "economy of hopes and fears" (Knibbe and Droogers 2001: 292) that predominated in Jomanda's healing sessions. This was much more than an intellectual exercise. It was a bodily experience. She learned to interpret the signs that the "other side" gave off through Jomanda, trusting that in the end all would be well. The seriousness of play led her to behave as she did. The "as if" became "as is."

Since the simultaneity was not possible in practice, Knibbe came to the conclusion that there should be an end to the game, unless she intended to continue being Jomanda's follower, never to return to academia. The method of ludism therefore proved to contain an existential risk: after learning Jomanda's worldview, Knibbe also had to unlearn it. The simultaneity of the theoretical model of methodological ludism requires a commitment to a linear set of timeframes. After being part of the context, she had to move on consciously, to stand apart again, to be de-conditioned. In terminating her fieldwork and in writing her thesis, she succeeded in unlearning. Having gone to the opposite extreme, she acquired insights that would have remained undiscovered were she to have adopted an attitude of methodological agnosticism or atheism. In hindsight she also discovered the risk that methodological ludism involved. Only then was she aware that the experience served as her rite of initiation into the trade of anthropology. In subsequent fieldwork she found it much easier to enter into the life-world and experiences of the believers that she studied.

In hindsight, Knibbe also realized that during her initial fieldwork she had exaggerated the engagement of Jomanda's visitors, and downplayed the scepticism that had been expressed among them as well. They too had to find a way to change their frame of reference, at first standing apart and then becoming a part, in order for some of them to stand apart again afterwards. The basic playful attitude to religion, usually hidden behind the exclusive claims and absolute certainties, allows for doubt and uncertainty. If religion is fundamentally a testing of possibilities, then criticism and rejection are a substantial part of it. For one can imagine that where the study of religion basically entails the meeting of two or more worldviews, a movement towards identification and a movement towards detachment may occur. The logic behind these two movements is indicated in Chapter 11 in which religion is interpreted as being simultaneously intimate and strange for the student of religion: religion is "our intimate stranger."

Students of religion might also consider playing the role that theologians, though not always going by this name, have played so far in particular religions, in this case for religions in their totality. This applied side of the trade will be discussed in Chapter 10.

When proposing methodological ludism, I had not foreseen what it might do to the fieldworker. Knibbe's experience serves as a warning that ludism may provide unexpected outcomes, especially in initial fieldwork contexts. I should, for example, have recalled the stories about fieldworkers who went into the field, never to emerge again, along with the reports on fieldworkers who were converted permanently into the religion they were to study.

Religious and secular worldviews alike may moreover be totalitarian and anti-human in their demands, as history has sadly shown. Participation along ludist lines can then become impossible. What German Nazis or the South African apartheid regime did on the basis of their worldviews cannot be easily studied in a ludist way. Yet, these worldviews should be studied, but by other means. Empathy has its limits.

Methodological ludism is also engaged scholarship. It obeys the ethical code that the quality of human life and the freedom of human meaning-making should be respected. Participation certainly has its risks and limits. In such situations the researcher may choose to study a morally malign worldview from the perspective of its opponents, taking sides in the conflict, especially in view of the ethical code just mentioned. Meaning-making can be lethal and worldviews can be destructive.

When all is said and done, the risks inherent in undertaking ludist fieldwork are part and parcel of constructivist presuppositions regarding the interaction between researcher and researched, producing insight and knowledge. This indeed means bidding farewell to the safety of the neo-positivist methodological positions that Berger offers, conditioned as they are by the contrast between science and religion and between researcher and researched. The playfulness of methodological ludism opens up a different perspective, riskier and having its limits, but also more promising. It challenges the fieldworker to be initiated as a meaning-maker among the meaning-makers.

IN CONCLUSION

The playful approach provides the opportunity to rethink a number of problems that accompany dualist thinking. The oppositions that serve as signposts in the landscape of academia facilitate mapping, but tend to impose mutually exclusive options. Especially when these are institutionalized, they limit academic priorities, restrict the allocation of scarce resources such as research funding, academic posts or publication opportunities, and they frustrate scholarly progress more than they stimulate it. The academic landscape is parcelled out.

In the study of religion, and especially of worldview changes in the moving target context of modernization and globalization, going beyond established dichotomies will open new perspectives and provide new insights. A ludist approach serves this goal. Instead of being seduced into opting for one position over an alternative, scholars could adopt the playful approach in order to access the best that two worlds can offer. The universal human capacity to deal simultaneously with two ways of categorizing reality can be applied to the sets of contrasts that have haunted the study of religion since its inception. The basic goal is that the scholar adopts each alternative position successively, if only for the amount of time required to understand it. To understand one's own position is rather easy, but to get the feel of an alternative view may be much more difficult. Yet it will be worthwhile if our aim is to rethink the old and worn-out categories imparted by one generation on other. Even if a conclusion returns the researcher to the position where he or she began, the exercise will have been valuable. This effort will produce a better map of the field of study and result in improved scholarly debate.

Though it may seem ambitious, the playful approach can be of use in at least three areas that form part of the study of religion. These three areas include the theoretical framework used, the methodology adopted, and the applications available. Though this volume is primarily about methodology, theory and their applications also relate to the methodological debate.

With regard to the theoretical framework, the contrast between science and religion must be rethought, including the way religious and secular worldviews oppose each other. This includes the question, dear to believers, of whether the experience of the supernatural is relevant to the understanding of religion. Explanations of religion can be reappraised. A playful approach opens a new perspective for understanding religion. The seriousness with which religions present themselves has misled scholars of religion. They failed to recognize the less knowable aspects of the playful believer. In both religion and academia, the unilateral options that govern most of the existing paradigms may be cast in a different light. The epistemological problem posed by the neo-positivist and constructivist approaches can be appreciated anew. The problem of exclusive truth can be relativized, while still maintaining the right of any believer to take his or her conviction seriously. The only requirement is that he or she must give an occasional knowing wink.

As far as method is concerned, the relationship between quantitative and qualitative methods and all the theoretical implications that stem from that relationship, can be reconsidered in a playful manner. I propose that it is necessary to experiment with methodological ludism as a way of going beyond the three positions that Berger suggested. Knibbe's research experience shows how the ludist position, though not free of risk, can significantly increase insight into the contexts we study. Part of the risk seems to stem from the existential need for certainty and from guarding personal parameters. Here too, play can be taken too seriously and thus begin to operate in disguise. Yet once this is understood, the path to new understanding lies open.

When applying the knowledge obtained in the study of religion to the problems that humanity is currently faced with (Droogers 2010), the playful method may prove to be enormously useful. Conflicts abound, between and within religions, often leading to violence and killing. The principles that inspire the playful method can be tested when believers – or scholars! –

defend exclusive views. The variety of religious forms currently in existence may be the cause of problems, since living among differences is demanding. The need for inter-religious dialogue becomes more compelling each day. Though it may sound utopian to suggest that the playful approach may serve to assist in solving these problems, I see genuine potential here. I return to this theme in Chapter 10.

Part II

Beyond Dichotomies: Studying Religious Change in Ritual, Experience, Language, Morals and Identity

Introduction to Part II

ANTON VAN HARSKAMP*

Going out to study real religion in the field is embarking on an intersubjective journey. It is a journey in which the researcher has to deal with many dichotomies and tensions, which emerge during the ever dynamic encounter of "the self" (the researcher) and "the other" (the religious believer). Just because of the intersubjective character of qualitative fieldwork research (Chapter 3) one may imagine that this type of research is a form of intellectual and mental playing by the researcher with distinct positions and perspectives (Chapter 4). The researcher plays with, among other things, social science and religion, with views on "the secular" and "the sacred" in religion, with being almost inside and being altogether outside religion, with different scholarly methods, with multiple identities of both the researcher's "self" and the researched "other" and so on.

In Part II of this volume on the methodology of studying religion, we find five case studies in which such dealing with dichotomies and tensions in the field is illustrated. In each of the case studies one aspect of a form of modern religion is highlighted. The distinct aspects are presented in this order: first the aspect of "ritual" (in a pentecostal Christian community and in a spiritual society in the Netherlands, Chapter 5), second "experience" (in a religious meditation centre in Amsterdam, Chapter 6), third spiritual "language" (in the life stories of a number of Dutch artists, Chapter 7), fourthly "morality" (in a group of Catholics in Limburg, a once deeply "Catholic" province in the Netherlands, Chapter 8) and finally the aspect of "identity" (of Muslims in the Netherlands, Chapter 9). In each chapter the methodological consequences of the qualitative encounter of the researcher's self and the researched other are discussed.

In Chapter 5 on *ritual* the central methodological question is: what happens when a researcher of religion wishes to observe religious practices while participating fully in religious rituals? So, what happens when a researcher "plays" in her fieldwork between the role of a researcher and the role of a

* Anton van Harskamp is a philosopher of religion, and Emeritus Professor of Religion, Identity and Civil Society at VU University, Amsterdam. He is the co-editor of *Playful Religion: Challenges for the Study of Religion* (Oberon, 2006) and the author of books on new religions and civil society. He is the co-editor of volumes on conflicts in social science, on individualism and on moral philosophy. His main research interest is the social theory of the impact of new religions on civil society.

practising believer? Is participation in a religious ritual, that is, is experiencing ritual in affective ways, an adequate strategy to reach for a deeper understanding of religion? The researchers in this chapter demonstrate that by reflection on the self's participation in religious rituals, as well as on the reactions of the others in this participation, one can arrive at a deeper understanding indeed of the ways rituals are significant for the believers' ways of giving meaning to their world.

In Chapter 6 on religious *experience* the central methodological question is: how to approach religious *experience* in modern forms of religion? It is often thought that religious experiences in our era of individualization and subjectivation are purely personal, and that the content of an experience can only be found in the singular mind of the individual believer. This chapter even signals that a "dogma" in the academic literature on contemporary spirituality is that reaching for unique and authentic experiences is a prime and fundamental epistemological principle for understanding modern religion. The religion researchers in this chapter argue on the basis of their participation in a new-religious meditation course, that this "dogma" has to be nuanced. Their method of participant observation is the main instrument by which they detect that in a spiritual atmosphere in which personal, unique and authentic experiences are stressed indeed, these experiences are at the same time incited, approved and even pre-constructed by new-religious authority. Precisely by participant observation, so by being social outsider and social insider in new spiritual worlds, one may find that individual, unique and authentic experiences are at the same time socially "constructed."

In Chapter 7 on spiritual *language* the central methodological question is: how to study forms of secular and spiritual worldview-making? In this chapter the worldview-making of a few dozen Dutch artists is the central issue. The researcher demonstrates in this chapter that a (playful) combination of ethnography and literary analysis of the language in life narratives of the research "objects" can be a fruitful methodology for arriving at two remarkable observations: first that many de-churched artists are searching for worldviews which apparently replace traditional religious worldviews; second that the seemingly unique and singular life stories of the artists can be modelled in "only" five patterns of worldview-making.

In Chapter 8 on *morality* the central methodological question is: how has the self of the fieldworker/ethnographer to deal with moral dilemmas when this self participates in the moral universe of the other? In this chapter the researcher demonstrates that insight into the deeper layers of morality in religion can be gained by opening up culturally repressed genres of speech, like gossip. By gossip people create a shared moral universe. The problem with which one has to deal (= to play seriously) is that, when the fieldworker participates in gossip, she as a researcher seems almost simultaneously to break the trust generated through complicity in gossip: research seems to be inevitably a betrayal. The researcher argues that deep reflection on the inevitable involvement in doing qualitative fieldwork and on the equally inevitable betrayal of intersubjectivity is a major condition for doing honest, that is, non-judgmental fieldwork.

In Chapter 9 on *identity* the central methodological question is: how has the fieldworker on religion to deal with (to play seriously) with contested identities (of herself and of the others?). In this chapter three cases are discussed in which fieldworkers entered the politicized field of Western Islam in the Netherlands. The researchers in this chapter demonstrate that in order to understand Western Islam from person to person, one has to make shifts in the traditional insider/outsider positioning, in particular by searching for a (partial) physical or mental inclusion in the cultural spheres of Western Islam.

In each of these chapters it is made clear that doing fieldwork on religion is basically an involving enterprise. In Chapter 11 of this volume the reader may find more reflections on the intersubjectivity of qualitative religion research.

Chapter 5

Fieldwork on Ritual: Understanding through Participation

KIM KNIBBE,* MARTEN VAN DER MEULEN,**
AND PETER VERSTEEG***

INTRODUCTION

During his research in a new suburb in the centre of the Netherlands, where he studied the role of churches in civil society, Marten van der Meulen participated in an Alpha course (Van der Meulen 2006). The Alpha course is a missionary activity with a strong evangelical outlook that has become popular in many different churches worldwide. This particular Alpha course was organized by a conservative-reformed church plant, which was the subject of one

* Kim Knibbe is a University Lecturer at the Department of the Comparative Study of Religion, Groningen University. She has recently published a monograph entitled *Faith in the Familiar: Religion, Spirituality and Place in the South of the Netherlands* (Brill 2013), based on her research into Catholicism and contemporary spirituality in the Netherlands. Furthermore, she has co-edited with Anna Fedele the volume *Gender and Power in Contemporary Spirituality* (Routledge 2013). Alone and with Peter Versteeg and with Andre Droogers she has written reflective articles on the practice of doing ethnographic research on religion. In addition, she has carried out research on Nigerian Pentecostalism in Europe and published widely on this topic.

** Marten van der Meulen is University Lecturer in the sociology of religion at the Protestant Theological University, Groningen. His research focuses on Christian congregations, civic participation and migration. Publications of note are "Civic Engagement Measured in Square Meters," Social Compass, 2012, and "The Continuing Importance of the Local. African Churches and the Search for Worship Space in Amsterdam," African Diaspora, 2009.

*** Peter Versteeg is a cultural anthropologist and independent researcher. He worked as a project coordinator at the VU Institute for the Study of Religion, Culture, and Society (VISOR), VU University of Amsterdam. In 2008 Versteeg was guest editor of a special issue on secularization and existential security in the Netherlands for *Social Compass* (55 [1]). In 2011 he published with Mellen Press *The Ethnography of a Dutch Pentecostal Church: Vineyard Utrecht and the International Charismatic Movement*. With Katya Tolstaya he published in 2014 "Inventing a Saint: Religious Fiction in Post-Communist Russia" in the *Journal of the American Academy of Religion*. Versteeg's research interests include identity formation, fiction and worldview, and the philosophy of the empirical study of religion.

of the case studies in his research. In his field notes Van der Meulen describes an event of this group after the so-called Holy Spirit weekend.[1] This weekend, in which there is a lot of emphasis on praying and being filled with the Spirit, is often seen as the central event of the Alpha course. Van der Meulen could not attend this meeting and hooked up with the group after the weekend. To his surprise he noticed some important changes in the group and his place in it. He describes himself as a "regular member of a group that was cosy, but not very close." After the Holy Spirit weekend he noticed how he felt sometimes like a "spectator of a group that had experienced something together." That same evening, spectator Van der Meulen was invited to assume closeness with the group through helping and praying with laying on of hands for a group member with cancer.

Another co-author, Knibbe, through her fieldwork in a spiritual society, unintentionally became subject to the bodily sensations that are expected to occur during ritual practices such as group meditations and energy-work. However, it was not at all clear to her what these bodily sensations meant nor whether they were common. Asking the other participants led to long discussions, but no unambiguous answers.

These incidents related to ritual acts call into question the role of the researcher in understanding ritual, the question of the meaning of ritual, as well as the relationship of the researcher with the other participants. Is a researcher inherently "different" from the other participants because of his or her agenda? To what extent is he or she the same through the fact of embodiment, going through the same ritual motions? Doing qualitative research, and in particular fieldwork, is often referred to as not so much a quest for gathering objective facts, but as establishing a field of intersubjectivity, a hermeneutic merging of horizons. How can we speak of common involvement in the context of ritual, when much of what is going on is nonverbal, shared through gestures, bodily sensations and emotions? Yet, as Van der Meulen and Knibbe both experienced, these same ritual acts can create irrevocable changes in people's subjectivities as well as in the shared field of meanings and gestures.

In this article we will explore this issue through examining two examples. The first is an elaboration of what happened after the Holy Spirit weekend, and how Van der Meulen came to understand and share in what was happening via ritual gestures such as praying. The second example concerns Knibbe's fieldwork in a spiritual society where people practise their paranormal skills. Before going into these examples we will summarize some of the vast literature on ritual as it has influenced our understanding of ritual and to the extent that it is relevant to the questions we wish to examine here.

---

1. Fieldnotes, Van der Meulen (2002–2005).

STUDYING RITUAL

In studying ritual, questions of methodology and epistemology are of great importance, that is, *what is the nature of ritual* and *how can we know anything about ritual?* Like the concept of culture, ritual seems to be a concept with an endless supply of definitions.

Boudewijnse (1995) argues that there are two major trends in the history of constituting ritual as a field of study. One trend has been that from the middle ages onwards, as the distinction between mind and body became more pronounced, behaviour evolved from a clear indicator of the state of mind and intentions of a person, indeed as one and the same thing, to something that could be divorced from the inner processes. Subsequently behaviour had to be interpreted, and it became feasible that it could lie about inner feelings. In short, behaviour became *representative* of something else unseen, requiring the efforts of scientists and philosophers to understand it. Behaviour and intentions became separated as well, so behaviour that was not directly serving a practical purpose had to be "symbolic." This has been reinforced by the second trend emerging in the nineteenth century, when religion in philosophy and scientific thinking was replaced by ethics, because the validity of religious beliefs seemed to evaporate under the scrutiny of reason. The only thing resisting this "solvent" was ritual, which has earned it the status of a separate category of human behaviour (see Goody 1977).

One of the most influential authors on the subject of ritual, both within anthropology and beyond, is Victor Turner. In *The Forest of Symbols*, when he tries to distinguish ritual from ceremony, Turner makes his briefest statement on the nature of ritual: "Ritual is transformative, ceremony confirmatory" (Turner 1967: 95). In his definition, however, this view is not expressed very clearly, for there he states that ritual is "formal behaviour for occasions not given over to technological routine, having reference to beliefs in mystical beings or powers" (1967: 19).

Ritual in Turner's view has a central role in reconciling and preparing people for society and their position in it. He took society to be a structure of positions, which meant he focused on ritual to tell him about the conflicts within these structures as well as showing him the central values in a society. The central distinction between pre-industrial and post-industrial societies pervades his most important contributions, like his exploration of the liminal, the "betwixt and between" transitional period that especially characterizes initiation rituals. Consequently, he seems to see most rituals as *rites de passage*, a transition between two states, effected in three main steps: separation, transition and reintegration. Generally, rites of passage are associated with life crisis rituals, but in their original sense, the way Arnold van Gennep meant them, they are all rituals that *bring change*, including, for example, seasonal rites.

Turner's view is a decidedly symbolical one. He has clear thoughts as to the effects of ritual on people: they imply the manipulation of symbols in a space away from everyday reality, an inter-structural interlude, in order to align the forces and meanings the symbols represent according to the way they are needed to ensure the general social equilibrium or to adapt to change.

Two other authors who have analysed the nature of ritual in depth are Humphrey and Laidlaw. Their conclusions seem to directly contradict the traditional "anthropological" approach to ritual as exemplified by Turner, who was influenced by both Durkheimian functionalism and Weberian interpretivism. Instead of taking "ritual" as the phenomenon to be explained, they take the more dynamic (and abstract) approach of exploring "ritual" as an adjective, and "ritualize" as a verb, in order to arrive at a generalization of the nature of ritual acts (cf. Bell 1992). In their conclusion they state that "The pivotal transformation which ritual effects is to sever the link, which is present in everyday life, between the actors' intentions and the identity of the acts they perform" (Humphrey and Laidlaw 1994: 260). By this they mean that, during a ritual act, gestures and body movements can be made that are on the outside "normal," as they belong to the repertoire of acts in daily life. However, in ritual, these acts take on a different meaning, a meaning usually very loosely and contradictorily defined. The special thing about ritual is that ritual acts are given an object-like existence by the fact that they are "ontologically constituted beyond individual intentions" (1994: 267). A ritual act seems to have an ontological status like that of natural categories; it is just *there* to be performed, while both its meaning and effects are very variable.

Humphrey and Laidlaw argue that ritual in itself tends to disperse meaning; consensus about its meaning is the result of outside forces, reactions to ritual, to its essential endless meaninglessness, its weird means-end relationship. They point out that the several ways in which they have observed meaning in ritual can be re-appropriated (assuming that "originally" it arose out of meaningful activity): by "meaning to mean," that is, by consciously ascribing certain meanings to the ritual acts performed and assembling them in the overall meaning-making in life, or by psychologically responding to the ritual act, generating culturally patterned emotions.

They quote Wittgenstein, who suggests that the very pointlessness of ritual evokes a psychological reaction which attributes "depth" and "ancestry" to it. Its "depth" is not dependent on its ancestry, but on the experience in ourselves (Humphrey and Laidlaw 1994: 266). The ritual act is as disquieting as what it may be thought to represent, provoking a "rushing in of meaning." But they maintain that the ontological "object-like" status of ritual should be separated from this "rushing in" of personal and conventional symbolism.

However, there are other approaches to ritual, to the problem of meaning and to the relationship of the individual subjectivities with regard to ritual acts that are of importance. Bell (1992) argues that the distinction between act and meaning, central to the analysis of ritual, obscures the fact that rituals produce and reproduce relationships of power, as well as provide the basis for researchers to establish their authority, since they can provide insight into the meaning of a ritual. The view of Michael Jackson speaks directly to this criticism (although chronologically it was formulated before Bell's book was published) as the writings of Jackson are exemplary of a steady stream of literature emerging during the last few decades that has concerned itself with rediscovering the body and sensations, not as simply discursively constituted, as a Foucauldian approach would have it, but as of fundamental ontological importance for our being in the world and thus for our understanding of it as social scientists (see also Knibbe and Versteeg 2008). Central to this conceptualization, which revolves around Bourdieu's concept of habitus, is Jackson's assertion that "the body" should be considered as a subject, not as an object. With this assertion he defies the Cartesian division between subjects and objects, which causes the body to fall into the category of objects, the "accidental vessel of flesh for a subject." Habitus, then, is the interplay between bodily habit, on the one hand, and intentions, on the other hand; the dynamics between patterns of habitual practical activity and forms of consciousness (Jackson 1989: 119).

In his view, thinking and communicating through the body precede and remain beyond speech, human movement does not symbolize reality, it is reality: "The subjugation of the bodily to the semantic is empirically untenable" (Jackson 1989: 122). In trying to explain why ritual seems to defy explanation to the extent that any interpretation may seem correct and plausible, he quotes Bourdieu:

> Rites, more than any other type of practice, serve to underline the mistake of enclosing in concepts a logic made to dispense with concepts; of treating movements of the body and practical manipulations as purely logical operations; of speaking of analogies and homologies (as one sometimes has to, in order to understand and to convey that understanding) when all that is involved is the practical transference of incorporated, quasi-postural schemes (Bourdieu 1977: 116, cited in Jackson 1989: 126).

Therefore, in ritual the body use should not be explained as symbolic behaviour but taken at face value and analysed as what it is: a particular way of moving, of thinking and communicating with the body.

In ritual, the habitual relations between ideas, experiences and body practices may be broken, for example, by letting women perform as men, men as women or humans as monkeys. In this way, new ideas and experiences can be provoked. Consequently, Jackson defines ritual as the "Disruption of bodily habitus during which people can act out the possibilities of behaviour they embody but normally cannot express" (Jackson 1989: 129). The relation of the body movements in ritual with those in daily life is different, simply because they are performed by different people and for their own sake. In this way, "mimeticism, which is based upon a bodily awareness of the other in oneself...assists in bringing into relief a reciprocity of viewpoints" (1989: 130).

Ritual can be seen as consisting of bodily techniques that move people to a world where boundaries are blurred and experience can be transformed.

Their meaning is indeterminate and ambiguous, and allows for individuality. Words limit the range of meaning they can express, and lead to falsifiable truths, truths that can be contradicted, whereas bodily techniques lead to experiential truths.

In Jackson's view, being embodied can be the common ground on which to base anthropological findings:

> for by using one's body in the same way as others in the same environment one finds oneself informed by an understanding which may then be interpreted according to one's own custom or bent, yet remains grounded in a field of practical activity and thereby remains consonant with the experience of those among whom one has lived (Jackson 1989: 135).

Naturally, this has great consequences for what we have proposed as our subject here, namely the processes of intersubjectivity established through ritual and the ways a researcher participates in these processes. To get a grip on the relative merit of the approaches presented here, we should first illuminate the points where they most contradict each other. Humphrey and Laidlaw rigorously separate the nature of ritual from the meaning it is supposed to have. They see ritual as consisting of acts which have somehow become separated from meaning. According to traditional approaches in anthropology, as exemplified by Turner, ritual is *about* meaning and symbols and little else, symbols and meaning justify their existence and reveal the deepest values of a society, whereas Humphrey and Laidlaw identify these processes of "meaning-making" as the re-appropriation of ritual acts, and *not intrinsic* to them. Coming from a very different angle, Jackson maintains that no physical act or gesture is meaningless, but has to be understood through its relation to other acts and gestures and through the embodied "reciprocity of viewpoints," established by participant observation.

We suggest the following characterization of the ritual mode. Physical acts in ritual assume the character of being ends in themselves, but their meaning and value remain dependent on Jackson's version of Bourdieu's habitus and the cultural categorization constituting experience. Therefore, understanding the meaning and rationality of ritual acts means exploring the relationship between bodily, empirically observable acts and meaning; the relationship between the seen and the implied among the people who perform them.

All these considerations of the nature of ritual have in common that the meaning of ritual is quite unstable and variable, but also that ritual acts can provoke profound reactions and transformations that escape any attempt to pin them down verbally. What does this mean for the researcher attempting to study ritual? The introductory examples show a certain irony where the study of ritual is concerned, an irony which is at the heart of a recurring debate on the meaning of ritual practice. Although many students of ritual nowadays favour a subjectivist method of studying ritual, which means that they really make an effort to become a ritual participant, it seems hard to move beyond an objective stance and draw interpretive consequences from a methodologically acknowledged subjective position. Apparently it is very difficult to say something about the meaning of ritual practices when the viewpoint is primarily emic.[2] On the other hand, we may ask whether there are interpretations of ritual that are true to methodological subjectivism in their interpretation or whether this leads to a variety of *theologies* of ritual which have neither comparative salience nor academic scope.

We argue that a subjectivist position is possible as an analytical approach in the study of ritual. This means that we have to fully take into account the fact that ritual has no intrinsic meaning. Meanings become attached in a constant process of prefiguration within a particular tradition, within the actual practice in a ritual context, and through the refiguration of the people involved in the actual practice or reflecting on it (Ricoeur 1984). The emphasis in research should therefore be on this signifying capacity in relation to the objective and temporal nature of ritual practice. Through participation the researcher becomes part of this reciprocal process in ways that are not always distinguishable from the researched and that go beyond the semantic. In the following, we will explore in more detail how this happens.

INCLUDING THE RESEARCHER

A TUESDAY EVENING IN 2004, A PRIVATE HOME IN LEIDSCHE RIJN (UTRECHT)

The theme of the night is prayer. On a DVD, Nicky Gumbel, Anglican vicar and Alpha inspirator, tells passionately some stories on the topic of how prayer has changed the lives of people. The group seems impressed by what they hear, because when the tape stops they are quiet for a few moments. Then the group disperses in small groups to pray for different personal issues that people may come up with. Van der Meulen is part of one of the groups that is led by Patrick and Lois. People are a bit shy; they are obviously not used to this form of praying. It is quiet for some time. Then Paul, who is an elder in the church, says that he wants to request prayer for two things. The first thing is that he finds it difficult as an elder to be open about his faith. The second thing is more important. He is clearly nervous, looks up and strokes his chin with his hand. He and his wife cannot have children, he says. "That is rather difficult." Louis and Patrick pray for Paul. Louis starts. He prays for a long time. He prays in a low voice, articulating his words carefully. He asks for blessing and openness in this situation. Patrick does not pray but only says "amen" to Louis' prayer. Louis has tears in his eyes when he has finished praying. It is quiet again for some time. Louis asks whether there are other topics

---

2. Everson (1991) states that the position that ritual is meaningless, advocated by Frits Staal, is a form of objectivism, in which meaning is submitted to language. On a different note, Stringer (1999) suggests to talk of "significance" instead of meaning to separate the latter from a self-evident semantic context.

for prayer. There is prayer for the father of one of the members. It is quiet again. Nobody seems to want to mention another topic. Then Van der Meulen asks whether Patrick and Lois want prayer. Patrick hesitates but then says that he is seriously ill; he has a form of leukemia. The group is taken aback. Patrick: "Well, I didn't think it necessary to tell a lot of people. My family knows it, though." Louis starts praying for Patrick but then invites Van der Meulen: "You are welcome to pray for him too." Van der Meulen nods. Louis puts his hand on the left shoulder of Patrick, Van der Meulen puts his hand on the other shoulder. Louis prays, for a short time. Van der Meulen prays too: "Lord, please heal Patrick in heart and soul, spirit and body, in Jesus' name." Patrick is rather moved after the prayer. One of the women pats him on the shoulder. He says: "this old man should sit down for a while."

After some talking, Patrick says he'd better check his watch to see what time it is. It is time to close the night indeed, but the other group is not ready yet. While they are still sitting in the circle, Louis says that it was good of Van der Meulen to ask whether they wanted prayer. It appears that Louis wants prayer too, asking specifically to be filled with the Spirit. The group stands up again. Patrick prays for Louis. After being prayed for, Louis checks with the other group. They have finished as well. The group moves to the living room. It is very quiet there. One of the women has red eyes and unkempt hair. She is very peaceful. Apparently the moment of prayer has also been intense in the other group.

Van der Meulen's research objective was to study forms of civil society in Christian congregations in a new suburb. This meant he was first of all interested in the ways a ritual practice such as this prayer event could constitute bonds between group members. A significant conclusion was that ritual creates and enhances closeness and that this cumulates the social capital of this group.[3] But does this mean that the researcher in this example arrived at that conclusion through participation? Van der Meulen describes himself as a spectator who clearly missed an important change in the group. He "saw" a change in the intimate nature of the evening after the Holy Spirit weekend, but this impression was only confirmed at the moment that he responded to the question to pray for somebody in the group. It seems as if he became aware of having been a spectator at the moment when this distance was reduced. For the group the emotional and physical closeness, growing openness and the personal change that group members experienced, were signs that God actually was doing something in and through the Alpha course. Because of his research objective the researcher could not just appropriate this religious experience, but by being conscious of the disparate interpretations, some of them as a researcher and others as a believer, could look more closely at what was going on.

---

3. We may note, as Van der Meulen does, that we are dealing here with a particular kind of social capital, namely a form that is seen by the group as being a direct effect of divine involvement.

This is one example of how the researcher's participation in ritual practice can become part of social hermeneutics. We might wonder, however, whether it mattered for Van der Meulen's analysis had he kept his distance as a spectator. Apparently it did matter, because had he not participated in this way, that is, as a believer praying for a group member, he would not have felt what it was like to become part of the transformation in this group. The fact that Van der Meulen was recognized as a believer was perhaps even more critical for the course of events. We might ask whether this fact is also of importance for his theory of social capital. Could he sense what was developing socially because he was part of the process?

In the next section we will discuss another example of fieldwork where the researcher explicitly made her own experience the subject of conversation.

A PROBLEM OF MEANING

A WEDNESDAY EVENING IN 2002, VILLAGE HALL WELDEN

Every two weeks at eight o'clock the Spiritual Association of the Hills gathers in the village hall, somewhere in the South of the Netherlands.[4] There are about 40 people present, men and women; many couples. In a low and calm voice, the leader of the night's event tells the audience how he became a medium, how he, after having been a successful businessman "lost almost everything." When he went to a medium for help she recognized him as a "colleague." He explains what he is going to do: some people will be invited to sit on a chair in front of the audience. What the group will see, he warns, "will not be spectacular. I pass my hands around their bodies to unblock their energies. Sometimes I whisper something in their ears." But he expects that when these people share what they have experienced during this time, the audience will understand that it goes very deep.

Before inviting anyone to come forward, the medium leads a meditation accompanied by soft music, urging the audience to open themselves to the divine energies, to feel oneself and to love oneself. Later into the healing he compliments the group: "You see, I am sweating, that does not always happen. I get so warm because you are a very good public, creating a good atmosphere."

During this meditation everybody in the audience is holding hands. On the left the researcher is holding the hand of a woman she knows, holding her right hand is a man she has seen earlier but has not yet spoken. While soft music plays, she follows the instructions for meditation, relaxing. Suddenly, a strange sensation starts up in her right arm. It tingles, and her fingers start moving involuntarily, inside the man's hand. As soon as seems proper she lets go of the man's hand, and puts her own hand on her knee.

---

4. Kim Knibbe has written before about this group and this particular case in her PhD dissertation (Knibbe 2013).

Ignoring the wriggling, Knibbe concentrates on the question of how the people of the spiritual group will explain this phenomenon. It may not be a "deep experience" like the medium had told them to expect, and it had nothing to do with him passing his hands around her body because she is sitting in the middle of the audience. But it is definitely the kind of phenomenon that this group likes to discuss and speculate on. Meanwhile, the healing continues and with it the expectation that more miraculous and unexpected things might occur.

After the meditation, some people are invited to sit in front, on chairs facing the audience. The medium walks around these people, passing his hand around their auras without physically touching them. Most people sit with their palms facing upwards in meditation, receptive to the divine energies. The medium stops to talk to one woman and she opens her eyes. He comments that she probably did not feel so much, because she couldn't let go of her thoughts to "return to herself." She answers: "Yes, it seems to be so simple, but somehow I cannot manage to do it!" He turns to another woman, one of the regular visitors: "You are a very level-headed person but you should learn to love yourself more. You have been raised with a heavy emphasis on doing your duty, but you have to learn to arrange you own priorities. Maybe at first people will be a bit angry when you say no to their requests, but they will not mind later on, and come to understand."

She nods, and confirms his description of how she was raised. But when he tells her she should give more weight to her own priorities, she protests: "I thought I was doing that already!" After this exchange, the woman sits next to Knibbe in the audience. Disappointingly, her only comment to Knibbe and the woman on her other side is: "at least I got rid of that terrible headache I had all day!"

To another of the regular members, Piet, the medium says: "I think you have been able to experience a more tranquil mood than usual." Piet nods. After the healing he tells Knibbe that he felt he was becoming very drowsy and heavy limbed; an unusual state for the energetic person he is.

After the healing, some of the visitors happen to be talking about the man, whom we will call Matt, who was holding Knibbe's right hand. Some of them had gone on a trip with him to England, visiting places where the energies of the earth are supposed to be particularly strong, such as Glastonbury. They noted that he enjoyed showing off his paranormal powers, especially to young women. He claimed to be a psychic, which some people doubted, and a magnetist, which was less controversial.[5] Then Knibbe tells about her wriggling fingers. The group concludes that Matt was probably magnetizing her. On the

---

5. A magnetist is someone who can heal pains or remove energy "blocks" by using his hands to transfer energy to his patients. Many magnetists are now turning themselves into Reiki-masters. Reiki is similar to magnetism, but more organized by courses and degrees. Magnetism is considered not very hard to master, although people are believed to have different "energy levels."

researcher's question why he would do that without her consent, they answer that it was indeed not a very ethical thing of him to do. They suggest that it was probably to arouse Knibbe's interest in him. During the trip to England, when they told him he should not use his powers like that, he denied it and just continued doing it anyway. According to Jacques the young women travelling with them were afraid of him.

Jacqueline, one of the visitors, remembers what a psychic recently told Matt. This medium was invited to the group to read and draw people's auras – it was a meeting Knibbe had attended. The medium told Matt that she saw he was a magnetist and that he liked women. She then told him that he would not listen to other people warning him when he was "going in the wrong direction." According to the medium this would only change when Matt learned it the hard way and she warned him "that the top of your head will start to itch" because of a different kind of energy.

At that time the regular group members agreed that it was a polite but very strong warning to Matt that he was abusing his powers to boost his own ego. Now, they conclude, he still had bettered his life, as was evidenced by the researcher's wriggling fingers. One of the women gives Knibbe the advice that next time she is seated next to Matt, she just should resist inside. Then his powers will not be able to penetrate her protection.

This seemed to be the end of the story. Two weeks later, however, the event is raised again while the group is having a drink at the bar before a meeting. Jim tells the story to Linda, a psychic and a magnetist as well, who was not there when it happened. She has a different view of the event. She asks Knibbe which of his hands she was holding. "The left hand," the researcher replied. "Well, then, he couldn't have been the person giving you the energy." According to Linda, the left hand is the "drawing hand," the one that receives energy. Her explanation for the wriggling fingers is that Matt must have "blocked" himself from receiving the energy of the whole group (everybody had been holding hands) and that meant that all the energy circulating from one hand to another was fed into Knibbe's right arm without finding a way out, causing her fingers to start wriggling. Matt had not been magnetizing her; he had just been protecting himself.

Nevertheless, Jim still found this objectionable. By blocking himself from the group energy, Matt knew that Knibbe would be the end-station, he argued. That's also not very nice, is it? Linda shrugs: she can understand he had wanted to protect himself. Especially psychics and magnetists are sensitive to other people's energy.

ANALYSIS

In analysing the case studies in terms of the participation of the researcher in the ritual, three observations can be made. First, participation enhances the understanding of the significance, if not the exact "meaning" of ritual and the ways it creates shared understandings that go beyond the verbal. For this reason, evocative narrative seems to be the best way to convey what happened, rather than a "cause-effect" factual account. Second, the participation of the researcher triggers interpretations of the practice by the other participants. Third and final, the researchers in both cases more or less induced interpretations during and after the ritual event.

Participation can increase the understanding of what ritual practices mean in a particular context. We see this in the case of Van der Meulen, where the prayer starts as a rather conventional discussion and sharing, but which acquired a different mood and sentiment when the prayers got in motion. The use of touch, the performance of the praying people, the use of space and the actual bodily practice of praying, all added to the fact that the researcher had an experience of prayer in this group. But as has been said before, thanks to this experience Van der Meulen also became aware of the type of change that had taken place in this group. Whereas at first he had felt an unproblematic insider, he was faced with an outsider's feeling after the group had been on the Alpha weekend. He only regained his insider status through his involvement in the praying. His feeling of being included in this intimate and spiritual highlight of this group gave Van der Meulen a clear idea of what had taken place during the weekend. The group had encountered its own capacity for intimacy and closeness. For Van der Meulen the experience of closeness showed him the essential mood and motivation for this group of Christians to be active in their new living environment.

In the event that Knibbe experienced we see how the researcher's wriggling fingers point to the fact that the participants experience these rituals as sensuously powerful, having real consequences. The body is a field of interpretations, onto which known and unknown spiritual changes are being read, and eagerly anticipated. The "healing ritual" creates the temporal space in which things might happen, but just as easily might not happen. The fact that they sometimes do not happen only adds to the credibility and ontological status of bodily sensations when they do occur: these sensations cannot be willed; therefore they must originate from "somewhere" or "someone" else. Exactly from where or from whom is subject to discussion and ongoing "research."

Our second observation concerned the fact that through participation the researcher can trigger interpretations of practices by the participants. This has been seen as a researcher's caveat, an obvious flaw in the method of fieldwork, something to be avoided at all costs by being the fly on the wall. When we look at the examples of Van der Meulen and Knibbe we see, however, that the "flaw" can be made fruitful, by being straightforward and reflexive about the role of the researcher.

With Van der Meulen we see a fieldworker who was recognized as a believer, which made it possible for him to join in prayer with laying on of hands in the Alpha group. Although he was not sure about his role, sensing a difference in the group after the Holy Spirit weekend, he was included in the transformation that was taking place, on his own suggestion to pray for a group member. We see how Van der Meulen takes up an even more active role when he, with a pastoral intent, invites somebody to receive prayer. This position is acknowledged by one of the leaders. The very fact that Van der Meulen prayed affirms the change that the group experienced and as such it reinforced the sense of efficacy of the ritual in the Alpha group.

Knibbe's informants had many things to talk about when she revealed what she had experienced in the circle. The wriggling of her hand, and the setting in which it happened, brought the participants to discuss the abuse of spiritual power, gender roles and normative roles of behaviour for mediums. The event challenged people to test their knowledge and experience of spiritual processes, thus adding to their interpretive framework of the relation between the spiritual world and mediums. As such, the incident made new knowledge possible for researched and researcher alike. By affirming Van der Meulen's offer to pray for the group member, he became included as an insider. At the same time, it demonstrated to the group the transformative power of the Spirit, changing even ambiguous "outsiders" such as the sociological researcher. As such, inviting the researcher to become involved in praying fitted perfectly in the overall goal of the prayer meeting, namely, changing the hearts, bodies and social positions of the participants. In this construed communitas the fieldworker ceased to be a fieldworker.

The intentional character of the creation of meaning is even clearer in the case of the spiritual group. By disclosing the fact that her fingers wriggled, the researcher explicitly and purposely ignited a discussion about the meaning of the ritual. This meaning was not yet present, but was created in the act of discussing. However, it was not a one-way traffic in which the researcher simply distills meaning from a debate among the researched. On the contrary, the participants were interpretation-hungry and actively questioned and engaged the researcher.

CONCLUSION

Taking as a point of departure a conceptualization of fieldwork as the establishing of a mutual encounter, we have explored the epistemology of the participation of the researcher in ritual. In this epistemology of participation, we have paid attention not only to the semantic, but also to gestures and sensations in the fields of intersubjectivity that emerge through ritual acts and the processes of interpretation and attribution of meaning they set in motion. We based this on a discussion of the nature of ritual that problematizes the search for the "meaning" of ritual and instead speaks of ritualization, the ritual mode and rituals acts as possibilities that break open the habitual flow of embodied action but are also dependent on it.

When ritual practices and gestures are seen as prefigured by certain traditions, then the question becomes how they are dependent on the habitus of the participants, including that of the researcher, and how these together create the encounter in which the significant changes expected (by both participants and researchers!) to take place during ritual occur. In this article however, we went beyond this question to single out the *intentional* character of the participation of the researcher in ritual. We argue that it is the recognition of the intentional character of the construction of meaning by the research which makes the difference to earlier discussions of the role of "subjective" knowledge in the interpretation of ritual. This intentionality moves beyond, or at the least moves to the limits of Jackson's "reciprocity of viewpoints." One could also argue that it pushes the limits of methodological ludism as Droogers describes it in this volume (p. 11): "the effective use of play by occupying varying positions, if only for as long as is necessary to understand what the seemingly contrasting positions look like." It is hard play, or maybe even foul play, by taking a shortcut and using your power as a researcher to bring meaning into being.

Both Knibbe and Van der Meulen actively engaged in the formation of the ritual and in the process of creating meanings afterwards. The researchers, in doing this, created a form of ritual and specific meaning that would not have existed without the presence and active intervention of the researchers. Paradoxically, this was done to enhance the researcher's understanding of what was happening. Knibbe's disclosure of her wriggling fingers created new meanings that served to understand the process of meaning-making by the participants. So on a softer note, we could also conceptualize the actions of the researchers as playing together. Droogers (this volume p. 13) suggests that researchers are, like all normal human beings, meaning-makers. They make sense of their field of study. They thus make sense of the religious field, co-creating meaning with the participants. They are like the authentic artists and writers Hummel studied (Chapter 7), although there is still an expectation of objectivity. Researchers should not be over-creative in creating meaning. Maybe they are more like photographers: choosing the setting, directing the persons to be photographed, but still providing an image of an actual situation, instead of inventing one.

It is generally noted in methodology theory that in participant observation researchers are part of the processes they intend to observe. We would add that the researcher is a participant who, just as much as the other participants, induces meaning or is subject to the creation of significance by other participants. By taking account of this position and by being intentional about the possible active role the researcher can play, one can deepen the understanding of the context, as we have shown in the two fieldwork cases. This is not a methodological flaw but it is a participatory method in which misunderstandings, insights and experiences in a ritual setting are taken for what they are: possibilities of meaning and existence created by different participants with different agendas and different intentions, but all investing in their ritual actions to bond, to create understanding and to experience insight. Although the outcome of qualitative research is a form of objectification, the final objectification includes the researcher's own ritual participation in the analysis.

Chapter 6

Fieldwork on Experience: Spirituality, Individuality and Authority

PETER VERSTEEG* AND JOHAN ROELAND**

INTRODUCTION

While for many of the discipline's forerunners religion was understood as a collective endeavour, the sociology of religion has, ever since the 1960s, strongly emphasized the individualized and subjective nature of contemporary religion. To account for the new state of affairs with respect to this field of study, sociologists have enriched the disciplinary jargon with a number of catchy terms, such as "consumer religion" (Possamai 2005), "do-it-yourself religion" (Janssen and Prins 2000; Janssen et al. 2000), "pick-and-mix religion" (Hamilton 2000), "religious bricolage" (Luckmann 1979), "cut-and-paste religion" (De Koning 2008) and "Sheilaism" (Bellah et al. 1985) – terms which have easily been picked up by social scientists, journalists, policymakers and opinion makers alike. A growing body of literature, however, both from sociological and anthropological authors, begins to problematize these concepts and to discuss the underlying analysis of contemporary religion. So, the alleged individualized nature of contemporary religion is discussed by those who describe the new forms of sociality and community by means of which reli-

* Peter Versteeg is a cultural anthropologist and independent researcher. He worked as a project coordinator at the VU Institute for the Study of Religion, Culture, and Society (VISOR), VU University of Amsterdam. In 2008 Versteeg was guest editor of a special issue on secularization and existential security in the Netherlands for *Social Compass* (55 [1]). In 2011 he published with Mellen Press *The Ethnography of a Dutch Pentecostal Church: Vineyard Utrecht and the International Charismatic Movement.* With Katya Tolstaya he published in 2014 "Inventing a Saint: Religious Fiction in Post-Communist Russia" in the *Journal of the American Academy of Religion.* Versteeg's research interests include identity formation, fiction and worldview, and the philosophy of the empirical study of religion.

** Johan Roeland is Assistant Professor in the sociology of media, religion and culture at the Department of Theology, VU University of Amsterdam. His research interests include religious changes in Northwestern Europe, Evangelicalism, popular culture, media and youth. His dissertation on subjectivization tendencies among evangelical youth in the Netherlands, entitled *Selfation: Dutch Evangelical Youth between Subjectivization and Subjection,* was published in 2009 by Amsterdam University Press.

gious individuals organize themselves (Maffesoli 1996; Roeland et al. 2010). While it is admitted that traditional organizations and communities have lost much of their appeal, it is argued as well that those interested in religion and spirituality search for more "tribalized" (cf. Maffesoli 1996) effervescence and networked (cf. Roeland et al. 2010) sociality in, for example, internet communities (Aupers 2006, 2008 [2004]; De Koning 2008), festivals and events (St John 2003), small groups, meditation centres and informal networks. The alleged subjectivized nature of contemporary religion, furthermore, is challenged by those who pay attention to the shared beliefs and dogmas of contemporary religion, which actually exist, although they are often hidden from the scholar's view by a discourse of authenticity and individuality (cf. Aupers and Houtman 2006; Houtman 2008; Knibbe 2013; Roeland et al. 2010).

Although it is widely admitted that the sociology of religion has become much more exciting and effective by widening its scope beyond the once dominant collectivities by means of which religion used to be organized, the discipline's portrayal of modern religion as uncommitted, strictly personal and subjective is increasingly debated. In this contribution, we link up with this sociological debate by offering an anthropological perspective on one – and perhaps the most pivotal – exponent of contemporary religion: spirituality. Spirituality can be described as an experiential oriented religious praxis which aims at individual wellbeing and personal growth. We will, in the first place, discuss a particular case, namely a meditation course, within the scope of the alleged subjectivization of modern religion. We aim to come up with a balanced and nuanced characterization of contemporary spirituality, by discussing on the one hand its tendency of subjectivization, which is in particular visible in its emphasis on (personal) experience, and on the other hand its social nature – which, as we argue, remains an essential aspect of contemporary spirituality. From there we want to discuss the methodological challenges with which the sociology of religion is confronted through the arrival of alleged individualized and subjective forms of religion. Given their eye for difference, irregularity and individuality, qualitative methods – and in particular participant observation – are arguably the customary methods to study such forms. After all, quantitative methods, which are in particular appropriate for studying collective and social patterns, seem to fall short in studying a phenomenon that prides itself on its subjective nature. However, as we will argue further on, by applying qualitative methods, the researcher stumbles exactly upon the social nature of contemporary religion – a sociality which is, moreover, not easy to detect by standard quantitative methods (see Chapter 3).

In the second section, we first discuss how individualization and subjectivization have been theorized in the sociology of religion. In particular the notion of experience will be taken up here, which, after all, is often presented as the prime subjective element of religion. In addition, this section will present some basic assumptions with respect to experience we often find in the sociological literature. The third section describes and analyses our case: a meditation course in an Amsterdam monastery. Our description of this case focuses especially on the way the religious experience is constructed in the setting of this particular case. We will argue that, although the discourse by means of which practitioners themselves frame the genealogy of their experiences is strongly subjectivist, emphasizing the individuality of the experience, the critical observer becomes aware of a number of social dimensions, among which are forms of authority and power, structures of legitimization, standards of authenticity and processes of authenticization. The fourth section offers a number of methodological considerations and "tools" that may be helpful to researchers in the study of contemporary religion. The last section concludes this contribution.

THE TURN TO THE SUBJECT IN THE SOCIAL-SCIENTIFIC STUDY OF RELIGION

Although the concept of subjectivization may have only recently entered the sociology of religion (cf. Heelas and Woodhead 2005), the conviction that modern religion would evolve into a subjective affair dates back much further. Durkheim, for whom religion was essentially "something collective" (Durkheim 2001: 46), already foreshadowed the sociological "turn to the subject" in his *The Elementary Forms of Religious Life* (1912), when he discussed the aspirations of some of his contemporaries "towards a religion that would consist entirely of internal and subjective states and would be freely constructed by each of us" (2001: 45). While Durkheim carefully explored the possibility that "this religious individualism may one day become a fact" (2001: 46), those sociologists writing in the post-60s era were eager to postulate religious individualism as a fact, based on their observations of religious changes that took place in that era. People were indeed moving away from the churches. They turned down traditional Christianity and embraced all sorts of new religiosities, ranging from New Age, paganism and Wicca, to a variety of Eastern religions (cf. Campbell 2007). Most of all, they mastered an ethos of authenticity, personality and individuality, as well as a discourse centring around notions such as "doing your own thing," "finding your own way," "following your own personal path" and "self-realization" (cf. Campbell 2007; Taylor 2007). The observation that religion was turning into something subjective was easily made.

Central to many of the sociological accounts reflecting on this kind of individualized religion has been the notion of "experience." Contemporary forms of religion are, in other words, understood as being "experiential," in contrast to more "traditional" and "conventional" religions that – as the argument goes – were rather characterized by their stress on belief and authority. Such a religion would give way to forms of spirituality that are often labelled as experiential, thus emphasizing some of the main characteristics of these new forms, among which the "rehabilitation of the body" (Taylor 2007: 211), the nurturing of feelings and emotions, the care and attention for the practitioner's inner life, and in particular the positive valuation of subjective religious signification. These trends were seen as different from the disciplining of the body, emotions and religious signification that characterized traditional religion.

The change from belief to experience has in particular been widely discussed with respect to so-called inner-life or holistic (New Age) spirituality. Thus, Heelas, who presents the growth of inner-life spirituality in terms of a "spiritual revolution" (Heelas and Woodhead 2005; Heelas 2007, 2008; cf. Houtman and Aupers 2012), has relentlessly hammered on the New Age notion of inner truth as opposed to the external, discursive truths of traditional religions (see Heelas 1996, 2007, 2008; Heelas and Woodhead 2005). Hanegraaff discussed the return of Gnosticism and the emphasis on subjective, experiential truth in New Age spirituality:

> [T]ruth can only be found by personal, inner revelation, insight or "enlightenment." Truth can only be personally experienced: in contrast with the knowledge of reason or faith, it is in principle not generally accessible. This "inner knowing" cannot be transmitted by discursive language (this would reduce it to rational knowledge). Nor can it be the subject of faith...because there is in the last resort no other authority than personal, inner experience. (Hanegraaff 1996: 519)

Aupers (2012), pointing at the popularity of New Age in popular culture (in particular in the world of gaming), states that New Agers criticize belief: "... they consider the self the locus of *experience* and argue that no truth, beauty or reality exists independently of the self and that reality in all its forms can only be experienced." New Age, in short, seems to be (in the words of Heelas 1996: 23) "beyond belief," beyond what is thought to be a typical feature of religion, namely its emphasis on a system of conceptions (doctrines, dogmas) which is loaded with an authority that comes from outside, be it a Godhead, a holy text, a holy man or woman, an authoritative tradition or the truth of a particular religious community.

These observations highlight an important shared "dogma" of contemporary spirituality: that personal experience is thought to be the prime and fundamental epistemological principle (cf. Aupers and Houtman 2006; Heelas 1996, 2007; Houtman 2008). However, we should not take this experiential bias for granted because it may lead us to a position in which we would all too easily reproduce the emic discourse on subjectivity in our analytical concepts – which is sometimes the case in those sociological accounts which describe contemporary religion as "subjective," "individualist" and disposed of external authority and power. A view on power processes in spirituality is necessary because researchers seem to be satisfied to go along with the presumed free and creative nature of spirituality, without paying attention to the social mechanisms which make this freedom and creativity possible or impossible.

A more critical stance, therefore, would bring some nuance to the discussion, reminding the social sciences of one of its core assumptions, namely that human beings are social beings (cf. Houtman 2008: 23). As we will argue further on, the sociological claim that in contemporary religion the religious subject acts as the prime authority in religious signification is only partly correct. A threesome claim makes up our argument. First, while practitioners of spirituality may formulate their search for meaning as a strictly personal search, they tend to practise this search in groups (cf. Taylor 2007: 215–17). Second, while these groups may be catering for individual seekers, and while the religious repertoires offered in these settings are clearly aimed at the individual seeker, the spiritual practice common in these settings is actually essentially social. Third, while these settings may be "thin" in contrast to more traditional "thick" settings (cf. Zijderveld 2000) in this respect that authority is framed differently ("internal" instead of "external"), external authority is not absent from these settings: authority only takes a different, more subtle and implicit, shape. Let us explain these observations by discussing a particular case in detail: a meditation course that one of the authors visited for his research on Christian spiritual centres in the Netherlands.

THE CONSTRUCTION OF RELIGIOUS EXPERIENCE
AND THE ROLE OF AUTHORITY

The meditation course in the small Capuchin monastery in Amsterdam, in which Versteeg is a participant observer,[1] is one of the many spiritual events and trainings that are offered in this city. This particular course has been organized for a few years by one of the friars, a man in his fifties from a working-class background. Today, in the room next to the chapel, a group of nine people is present, sitting in a circle, including the meditation leader. In the middle of the room is a candle. Before the candle is a text of Meister Eckhart, a well-known medieval mystic. The text reads, in Dutch:

> *Ga dan in je grond,*
> *vandaar uit*
> *worden al je*
> *werken*
> *vruchtbaar*[2]

Before the meditation we start with an exchange of experiences. This group has been meditating together for a few times already as participants in the course. Part of the training is practising meditation at home. Participants tell about their home experiences in the last weeks. Recurring themes are the difficulty to take a regular moment of quietness, doubts about the effect of meditation, but also the experience that indeed things change through the practice. The brother Capuchin addresses all the ques-

---

1. The following description of the meditation session is taken from Versteeg's fieldwork report.
2. Go on, into your ground. From there all your works become fertile.

tions and emphasizes that an attitude of "not expecting" is crucial in meditation. By not expecting things to change but to practise "attention" for the
things that "appear," meditation is a way and a goal at the same time. One
of the group members describes a more specific experience, about something that she took "with her" after the last meeting. The last time we
had practised meditation with a specific word that we had to pick from a
number of words chosen by the meditation leader. Our homework was to
meditate on the same word in the following days. The woman had chosen
the word "sea," and although she felt it was a word that meant something
to her, she says she did not dare to reflect on that word, because it gave
her the feeling that this would cause unrest and sorrow. The meditation
leader adds: "I would indeed be careful with that. Because the sea refers to
the unconscious. The sea can be dangerous and this 'sea' can be dangerous
too. I would say to you, don't do it on your own. Find somebody to talk to.
A friend, a mentor."

This exchange is followed by some teaching on meditation. Meditation,
the brother tells us, has three stages: (1) relaxing, which we can understand
as leaving what keeps us tense, distancing from, letting go; (2) reflect upon,
become aware; and (3) concentration, focusing our attention on one thing.
Letting go means "let it flow away"; by distancing yourself you place something beside you and you don't look at it again. "Wrap it in nice paper and
put it down beside you." Becoming aware means looking at something "without judging." If you feel pain or unease, just become aware of that. Becoming
aware all comes down to the attitude that things are "allowed to be there."[3]
Lastly, meditation is focusing, doing one thing at a time.

We read the text by Eckhart a couple of times. The brother asks to see if
we feel any obstacles when we read the text. Perhaps words we find difficult?
Those are the words we have to focus our attention on. "Say it for yourself,
in chunks. Go into your ground... In your ground... Your ground... Ground."
Then we start meditating. After a short relaxation exercise we are quiet for
15 minutes.

After meditation, another exchange follows. A number of participants say
they found the text very inspiring. A young woman says that the text was an
answer to the word "ground." "Now I get why 'ground' had to have me... It
gives me an autumn feeling: going in the ground, under the ground, so that
fruit will grow again." An older woman says the text means a lot to her: "I feel
it really means something to me because I really want to ground."[4]

A male participant, however, says that he had difficulties with the meditation. "On the one hand I find the text intriguing. On the other hand I think
this is complete nonsense. Your ground. What is that? From there all your

3. "*Het mag er zijn*," a central adagium in this type of spirituality.
4. "To ground," in the sense of "to earthen," is a metaphor referring to the grounding of elec-
trical installations, but in spirituality the expression (*gronden, aarden*) has become self-referential
and it is rarely explained as a metaphor.

works become fertile. What is that? Who says that? Why would that be so?" The brother answers him. He thinks you should not try to *understand* the text. "It has something to say to you. You know what the text has to say to you. I don't have the answer; you give the answer yourself." The text, the meditation leader says, is a condensation, an "essence." It is like an onion. "You can peel the onion and repeatedly think you have reached the core, but then there is another peel." The words of the text are peels, concentrated around an essence. The brother tells the man: "You only look at the outside." I sense a similarity with the experience of the man and I tell the brother that I recognized the question and that I tried to become aware why I was irritated by the words. The brother Capuchin responds again by saying that I should not try to get it. "It has something to say to you. Only you have the answer." Then I ask if it is possible to have answers that exclude other answers: "Suppose you think that this text reveals your deepest self and I think it doesn't, is that possible?" The brother responds: "I find your answer not that important. It's about the way leading to it, not the end goal. It's not about the answer, but about the way you traversed." That road can be "dead boring, empty and dark, what the mystics call the night." "You can't find anything there, but it is a way."

The meditation session described in this vignette is typical for the kind of spirituality that is found on the alternative religious market. The fact that the example is from a Christian monastic setting does not alter that observation (see Versteeg 2007). The basic structure of these kinds of spiritual courses is a form of relaxation and focused reflection. In conjunction with fragments of text (a poem, a guided fantasy, a part from the Bible, or simply practical instructions on how to attend to your breath), these techniques frame what we have called a "hermeneutic space" (Versteeg 2006). The "hermeneutic space" is used as a form of hermeneutics in which individual experience makes sense of itself through a loose assemblage of signs and sensations. The individual participant in a meditation setting is encouraged to take up associations and feelings in order to create meaning, associations and feelings which are often part or become part of a personal narrative.

Striking is that there is hardly any message or viewpoint being communicated other than practical instructions. In this case we see how singular words (the words of Eckhart) cause people to show facets of their self and their life, not very particular but giving a general sense of being in a process of learning to deal with life. As the example shows, for some participants meditation affects experiences of trauma and sorrow and they feel they can share this in a group of relative strangers. Spirituality thus offers a subjectivized route of exploration, placing the individual and her experience at the centre. One of the striking things, furthermore, is that there is almost no reference to God or anything sacred. There is only little input of "traditional" images and when traditional symbols, such as God, are used they are not used in a strongly discursive way. If there is something to be taught, the individual participants will have to find that for themselves. Only they can give the answer, thus underscoring the authority of the individual subject in religious signification.

Our case, however, also suggests that there is actually an implicit yet no less authoritative view of "sacredness" assumed and given in contemporary spirituality. The described example is in particular informative with respect to this, because of the interesting contrast that is created by the critical question of the male group member. The "incident" shows that the practitioners involved in this meditation course, who were invited to freely explore their own sense of sacredness, stumbled upon a number of boundaries which were strongly underscored and sustained by the very same practice. These boundaries become visible at the moment that the spiritual practice, and in particular one of its core elements, the meditation on the basis of a text, is in danger of becoming "profanized": the moment that the words of Eckhart are represented by the critical male group member as being completely relative and the mystic's words are depicted as redundant in the practice of contemplation. This particular moment occasions the meditation leader to correct the critical member, by implicitly stating that this present member has not displayed the "right" approach to such a text.

To be sure, it is not the correctness of a particular belief which is at stake in this case. The meditation leader keeps emphasizing that practitioners need to search for their own answers, and he does not interfere in people's individual narrations of their experiences. What is at stake here is the approach and attitude towards the meditation practice. A particular attitude is assumed to be the right one, to be the appropriate way leading to experience; it is where experience and things coincide. Apparently, there should be an exercise of authority to establish this truth and to lead people away from the suspicion of having entered a vacuum.

Consequently, every experience is allowed but it is always accounted for as something personal, whether it is approved or not. Lack of support or positive feedback does not question the experience – for example, the experience that meditation is not helpful or irrelevant – but, as our example shows, it denotes the spiritual status of the person who shares his experience. So, the meditation leader from our case does not explicitly rule out specific representations. Rather he creates an opposition between acceptance of an experience and the critical reflection on an experience, the latter being a position which defines somebody as observing himself from the outside, not willing or able to submit to a more pre-reflexive inside-experience of meditation. Hence, it is not the acceptance of an authoritative belief which is asked for in this context; it is rather that practitioners are expected to comply with a particular way of attaining and sharing a personal experience. Important in this context, or other forms of temporary and "light" communities, is the desired outcome of becoming an insider.

Notwithstanding its image and practice of experiential exploration, subjective association and personal meaning, this form of alternative spirituality shows some clear mediations of experience through which options of meaning are prescribed and contained. Although there is no institution or explicit ideology to back up this practice of signification and to make meaning a field of power relations, the interaction between meditation leader, individual member and group members clearly monitors experiences. Authority in this case is not doctrinal correctness but correct praxis. A correct praxis is an identity praxis in which individuals demonstrate that they are able to talk about themselves and to expose themselves in a way which reveals spiritual growth.

STUDYING RELIGIOUS EXPERIENCE: METHODOLOGICAL CONSIDERATIONS

Our example shows how researchers in the study of experience should look for the way in which practices become normal and normative, in particular in situations when apparent norms and codes are breached. Describing something that is "deviant" and the way in which this form of disputed difference becomes "normalized" is an important way to understand criteria for authentic experiences, not in the least when it takes place within the seemingly free milieu of alternative spirituality.[5] This approach will lead the researcher to the boundaries of alternative spiritual repertoires, boundaries that are foremost found in ways of expressing and sharing within a group.[6] Participant observation, thus, is not only an appropriate way to do experience-near research, especially in the form of so-called experiencing participation (Lindquist 1995); it is also a way to understand more of the social construction of experience. This layered process is not something that will become visible through a method of surveys and interviews, because this will mainly show a discourse of authenticity and individuality through which people learn to interpret what happens to them. The implicit and hidden nature of this reality construction is covered by a language that claims that what is experienced can be expressed. But by suggesting that stock phrases and discourse are the only access to experience, the experience becomes inaccessible, unless we take into account other, less standard, forms of expression.

5. For example, the command of an authentic language of "depth," which develops into stock phrases (Stringer 1999) is important in these alternative spiritual contexts.

6. Attention for deviance may also demonstrate possible variations within the spectrum of alternative spirituality and as such the relative nature of these boundaries. The critical participant in this case did not lose his interest in spirituality but decided that he would look for a less "narrow" interpretation of meditation experiences. At the time he shared this in an interview, he was participating in group sessions with a Jesuit therapist working with psycho-synthesis, which inspired him very much. Other "deviant" examples from participants in alternative spiritual practices underscore the idea of variation and, a perhaps regained, subjectivity over and against the discursive subjectivity in alternative spiritual practices.

Some participants we interviewed were reluctant to specific textual content (Bible texts, for instance) or what they viewed as "exalted," "vague" or "fluffy" approaches to meditation, while at the same time remaining involved with spirituality. One man in a Christian meditation group had difficulty with the constant referring to images of harmony in meditation by some meditation leaders. Harmony is false and easy, he said. Meditation should not be comfortable. "When I meditate I feel that my back hurts, that my posture doesn't feel comfortable. Meditation is about observing such feelings and accepting them."

The boundaries of alternative spirituality are not easy to detect and quantitative methods are hardly sufficient to analyse these boundaries. Through a quantitative approach the researcher will mainly find the spiritual jargon of inclusiveness, in which tensions, disagreements, restrictions and the subtle mechanisms of authority we distinguished in this contribution, will most probably not be mentioned. To trace these aspects, one needs to immerse oneself in the collectives in which practitioners of spirituality engage themselves. By participating, researchers become aware of the differing interpretations, the competitive discourses, and the frustrations and the disappointments of the participants. Researchers will be faced with the differences in opinion and the way these differences are handled – as in the case discussed above. They will hear the jokes and the gossip by means of which particular conventions are established (cf. Knibbe 2013 and her contribution in this issue). They will become aware of the body language by means of which both acceptance and disapproval is communicated. They will hear and see the customary responses in the group to the words by means of which individuals express their experiences. They will, in short, stumble across what is accepted and what not; what is legitimate and what not; what is normal and what is deviant. Qualitative methods point at the irregularities within a group practice and the processes which try to control these irregularities. By doing participant research one is faced with the question to explore these irregularities and to choose particular positions through an adaptive subjectivity (see Chapter 4).

As we have suggested above, an obvious but often ignored way to get to study these mechanisms is by claiming a more outspoken role for the researcher. While we of course fully understand that this outspokenness poses difficult questions about the production of data in a research process, we feel that this part of participant observation is still largely being kept out of ethnography. At the same time, anthropologists will admit that it is a natural consequence of the viewpoint that the anthropologist is her own research instrument. In this case, the researcher consciously leans towards one side of a dichotomy, taking sides with critical reflection rather than the authoritative position of the meditation leader (cf. Chapter 4). An interventionist approach was disputed but taken for granted in action research (see Huizer 1979), but why is even the slightest form of intervening and playful interfering (Chapter 11) ignored in anthropological research in general? The researcher may – and often does – represent the outside view, the dissenting voice, which can be made hermeneutically useful, as an available position within the group, in particular in the kind of voluntaristic client cults such as those spiritual groups that are consumer-based and lack most of the time an explicit ideological framework.

CONCLUSION

As spirituality is becoming an established field in the study of contemporary religion, scholars need to question the underlying notions of subjectivity and go beyond them. Subjectivization in religion is not the spiritual equivalent of the modern autonomous subject who controls his world through experience and self-discovery. On the contrary, even settings that are as fluid and temporal as Christian spiritual courses, show processes of the authorization of practices and ideas. One could even argue that it is in fact authoritative interpretation and supervision which make such fluid religiosity possible and which safeguards its continuity. The formation of this type of subjectivized religiosity is a social practice and a process of submission to the power of experienced knowledge (Chapter 2); it is a practice in which feelings and thoughts are expressed and shared. It is a practice in a group, in which the group resonates, monitors and authenticates what is being said. Becoming an insider, then, means submitting to practical correctness, that is, learning to appropriate a particular process of individual growth, internalizing an authoritative way of displaying one's emotions. This includes the command of a genre of experience, and the avoidance of other genres – in this case, for example, a critical text inquiry is overruled by pointing at the lack of personal lived experience in relation to the text.

We started our contribution by crediting the value of the current body of studies in contemporary spirituality. We also stated that research into this form of experiential religion generally shows a strong experiential bias in the used methodology. Little attention has been paid to the social processes which produce experiences, and our aim has been to show how a particular qualitative approach can uncover these processes on the level of concrete situations of spiritual practice. More questions need to be asked about how people learn to internalize contextually authentic expressions in religious forms that have little or no institutional backup. We have shown through our case that this will require a qualitative research approach that is both critical and immersive.

Chapter 7

Fieldwork on Language:
Artists Express their Worldviews

RHEA HUMMEL*

INTRODUCTION

The artist's profession speaks to our imagination. We all know the fairy-tale biographies of writers who laboured in splendid isolation for years on end in draughty garrets, who endured the bluntness of publishers, but who eventually triumphed over the bourgeois world when one visionary publisher ventured to publish the artist's unique work. Such stories are not told of other professions. The way we envision the artist is often based on romantic ideas and images. However, artists themselves also propagate romanticism about the artistic life. We will see this shortly, when we analyse some life stories of artists. Analysing these life stories on a deeper level, it will turn out that despite their claims to uniqueness and authenticity, these stories have roots in existing worldview repertoires and copy available life-story models. In this article, some methodological aspects of the search for the artist's life story are described. An important question is how a typology of life stories can be constructed, despite the artists' emphasis on their uniqueness. For a start I will guide the reader through some of the problematic aspects of my type of fieldwork.

"SEARCH-AND-REPLACE" WORLDVIEW

I begin with a specific case. Visual artist Yvonne Struys (1941) lives and works in a remote spot in the northern part of the Netherlands. Anyone who visits her will get the feeling that the more one approaches her destination, the more the end of the world is at hand. In a centuries-old little village church this artist works on her oeuvre which shows up traces of myths, folk tales,

*   Rhea Hummel is Assistant Professor at the Department of Arts, Culture and Media (Faculty of Arts) of Groningen University. She studied Dutch Language and Literature, and Literary Studies. In 2011 her PhD thesis on the way contemporary Dutch visual artists and writers express their worldviews was published. Her research interests include life writing, artists, art, and worldview.

poetry and music. Struys feels herself connected with the desolate place where she lives and works. If one asks her for her worldview, she points to the landscapes and the spaces around her. There she finds inspiration for her work and there she finds "something" that she refers to as "religion." She may speak enthusiastically about impressive banks of clouds, the sheer grandness of the surrounding spaces and the primeval history which can be intuitively sensed everywhere. At first sight Struys' worldview does not display any resemblance to traditional forms of religion in the Netherlands. The artist never attends religious worship, she does not read the Bible, she dislikes pastors and all other kind of clergy. She claims to create herself her very own worldview. Yet, she throws away and uses different religious elements to construct her own worldview. In other words: she is playing with alternatives.

Yet, what is a worldview? Hijmans and Smaling (1997: 15–20) consider worldview to be a specific type of cognitive and affective system for attaching order and meaning to the surrounding world; one may distinguish between collective, cultural meaning systems and individual meaning systems. A meaning system is basically an expression of collective or individual reflexivity. In a meaning system one may find answers to questions such as "What is Truth?" and "What is good or bad?" In short: "What is a good way of life?" Religion may be considered – according to Hijmans and Smaling – a worldview in which answers to these fundamental questions are given by reference to a sacred, otherworldly reality. My research lies in the heart of the worldview studies. Consequently I am opting for the use of "worldview studies" instead of "study of religion." Or in other words: my research is a form of a worldview studies.

This definition of "worldview" offers us a handle on the ways in which artists envision their lives. The artistic worldview may be interpreted by some as a form of "believing without belonging" (Davie 1994), while others may consider the artistic worldview to be a form of atheism. The opposition of many artists to traditional, authoritative religion can be massive. This, of course, has consequences for the ways in which the artists construct their worldview. For instance, the Bible and other established religious writings are rarely sources for the artist's worldview. And yet, very often parts of a religious discourse are used when they try to express their worldview. It turns out that many artists are inclined to use parts of the religion in which they were raised (and which they oppose right now). This use of religion is most of the time implicit. I coined for the underlying mechanism the term "search-and-replace" worldview: artists are apparently searching for a substitute for the religion which they once "received," and while trying to find a completely new worldview, they nevertheless made implicit use of their "old religion." Despite the claim to fully authentic uniqueness, the implicit use of "old religion" is a recurring pattern in the construction of the artistic worldview. The supposed uniqueness of the artists' worldview raises a specific fieldwork problem in that the researcher is contaminated by the claim for idiosyncrasy, as I will show now.

ELOQUENT RESPONDENTS

Most artists are very capable of luring someone into their world of ideas and imaginations. They may be eloquent in discussing their work, life and worldview. Their pronounced expressivity often has a visual component. In order to press home their views, they may make references to their visual work or their own texts: "This painting reflects my search for meaning," they may suggest, or "In this poem one may read back the way I think about the essentials of life." Besides that, artists are constantly striving for innovation. They don't paint the second "Victory Boogie Woogie" of Piet Mondriaan, but instead aim at a painting with a unique, authentic new character, which will get, so they hope, its very own place in the annals of "Culture." Perhaps they wish to be the new Virginia Woolf or the new Philip Roth, but the word "new" has to be stressed. Few people would wish to be seen as "a dime a dozen," but artists in particular would find this unacceptable. This influences the ways in which they seek their customized, individualized worldview.

In the first phases of my research I was dragged into the imaginary conceptual universe of the artist. During my fieldwork I plunged into the artistic universes. Before the interview(s) I studied their work, visited their exhibitions, read or looked at (part of) their oeuvres, researched their backgrounds, and talked to others about them. I then went to the city or village where each artist lived and worked, was shown round their house and atelier, and wrote down their life story. Afterwards I kept in touch with many of my respondents, having sent them the transcripts of the talks and giving them the opportunity to react. At first, these intense meetings clouded my view of the collected material. Fortunately, I did get a clear view on the data by choosing an interdisciplinary methodology for collecting and analysing the collected stories, combining both anthropology and literary studies.

INTERDISCIPLINARY NARRATIVITY

Research of life stories seems to benefit from both an ethnographic and a "literary" approach. Anthropologists are experienced collectors of life stories. Their long tradition in this field has, however, besides many positive also negative consequences for the life story as a method. In my view, anthropological analyses of life stories are often not thorough enough. Although some researchers work with qualitative software programmes such as Kwalitan, Atlas and Nudist, the method of analysing life stories often means intuitively interpreting interview texts. This means that essential information remains hidden in the layers of meaning of a text. That hidden information, the meaning of recurring words for example, can be uncovered by using instruments from literary analysis. After all, for decades literary studies has gained experience with text analysis.[1] Other researchers too use tools from literary analysis to collect and interpret life stories in interview form (see, e.g., Charlton, Pette and Burbaum 2004). I, for example, counted words.[2] This is one of the ways in which a researcher can switch off her own preoccupation with certain terms. It clarifies, on the one hand, the use of words of the interviewee, whilst the researcher, on the other hand, can discover how her own researcher's jargon draws from a specific vocabulary. Thus it occurred to me, after counting words, that it was me and not the writer Eli Brand (1961) who used the terms "ernstig" and "serieus" (both words meaning "serious"). I initially thought that the terms were intrinsically related in Brand's life story.

Through the interdisciplinary nature of my research a new method developed that proved to be very useful for the analysis of interview texts, making it possible to dig up deeper layers of meaning. In this way I could extract a maximum of information from the life stories that I collected.

THE FAILING USE OF SOURCES

On several levels we can retrieve information from life stories. From my research experience it occurred to me that respondents use different – often literary – examples when constructing their life story. Gullestad (1996) discovered in the four autobiographies she analysed various explicit and implicit references: "Popular genres such as speeches, letters, greeting cards, and death announcements have influenced Kari's [name of the respondent – RH] life story in many ways. I see several similarities between the points of view, the subject matter, the words, and the phrasing of these popular genres and the points of view, subject matter, words, and phrasing of Kari's life story" (1996: 182–83). Gullestad also pays attention to the different way in which respondents tell their life stories. Thus she discovered that the fragmented way of narrating of her youngest respondent is rooted in the current "zap" culture and it reminded her of MTV-like television shows and cartoons.

Wuthnow found in the stories of American artists also several cultural references: "Some people model their spiritual journeys on stories of biblical characters; others pick up on themes from medicine, therapy, literature, and music. Whatever their format, these narratives of spiritual journeys remain significant as ways of finding coherence in a tumultuous world" (Wuthnow 2001: 106). In the life stories of the respondents from my research we discover similar references. They too use certain artifices to construct their life story.

1. Literary studies can be divided in three fields of study: theoretical, comparative, and empirical literary studies. In the latter area research into reading and readers is central. The empirical approach is a relatively recent phenomenon (Schram and Steen 2001).

2. In literary studies the analysis of texts often includes counting, for example, to understand what words are deemed important by the author of the text.

I found, however, that something changed in the way of telling, the longer the interview lasted and as the topics became more profound. Informants forgot their artifices and eventually had no more grip on the narrative format they had chosen. One might think that this way of storytelling resembles playing; one looses oneself in the flow of it.

Thus photographer Ruben Groot (1970) used Wagner's Parsifal opera as a blueprint for his life story. Parsifal is seen as a work with mythological, Christian themes. Groot told me the story of the opera, about how a young, somewhat narcissist and self-centred boy grows up to be a man who is capable of being empathetic. Here is a quote from the interview:

> Such a youngling who is very naive at first and kills a swan just like that and who does not realize what he does and abandons his mother and that mother is even called Herzeloyde, you know, and she has kept him guarded in the forest, because she was afraid that he would become a knight too. And then at a certain moment he sees a knight in the forest and he finds that so beautiful and then he runs away from his mother and he wants to become a knight too. And then he shoots that swan to crap and then at a certain moment he arrives, just have to check the sequence, yes, he arrives at the castle of the king and the king has a wound, has an enormous wound and that can only heal in one way and that is by asking the *Mitleidsfrage* and that has to be asked by a stranger and then he comes there and he is so naïve and egocentric and he does not ask the question, so then he is really kicked from there and he does not understand why and then he has to learn a lot. And he travels for a very long time and at a certain moment he returns there and then he is capable to raise the *Mitleidsfrage*. Well, now that I tell you I get goose bumps again, really, then he is capable of sympathy and can pose the *Mitleidsfrage* and yes, that I find so splendid and that has a lot to do with...in one way or another with my religious experience or something like that.[3]

In his summary of the Parsifal-story Groot only has attention for the growing up of the youngling. At first, Parsifal is not capable of asking the king the *Mitleidsfrage*; he is too much focused on himself and his own life, but when he is able to show sincere interest for another person, without expecting

---

3. Zo'n jongeling die eerst heel naïef is en zomaar een zwaan doodschiet en zich niet realiseert wat-ie doet en zijn moeder in de steek laat en die moeder heet dan ook nog Herzeloyde, weet je wel, en die heeft hem altijd in het bos beschermd gehouden, omdat ze bang was dat hij ook ridder zou worden en dan op een gegeven moment ziet hij een ridder in het bos en dat vindt hij zo mooi en dan loopt hij weg bij zijn moeder en wil hij ook ridder worden en dan schiet hij die zwaan aan gort en dan op een gegeven moment dan komt-ie, moet ik even kijken hoe de volgorde gaat, ja, hij komt aan bij het kasteel van de koning en de koning heeft een wond, heeft een enorme wond en die kan maar op één manier worden genezen en dat is door die *Mitleidsfrage* en die moet door een vreemdeling gesteld worden en dan komt hij daar en hij is zo naïef en egocentrisch en hij stelt die vraag niet, dus dan wordt hij echt eraf geschopt en hij begrijpt niet waarom en dan moet hij dus nog heel veel leren en hij reist heel lang en op een gegeven moment komt hij daar weer en dan is hij in staat om die *Mitleidsfrage*. Nou, nu ik het je vertel krijg ik al weer kippenvel, gewoon, dan is hij dus in staat om dat medeleven en die *Mitleidsfrage* te stellen en ja, dat vind ik zo prachtig en dat heeft veel te maken met... op de één of andere manier met mijn religieuze beleving of zo.

anything in return, he has grown up. To have compassion with the other is at the foundation of Groot's worldview, as he tells several times during our conversation, and he illustrates this through the Parsifal story. At first, it seems that things cannot be brighter: we can, so to speak, put the Parsifal opera on Groot's life story. However, the last sentences of the above-mentioned quote show that this is not really the case. Groot is not quite sure how the *Mitleidsfrage* relates exactly to his religious experience. His words "in one way or another" demonstrate this. Groot does not give a further explanation but uses a vague clue "or something like that," and here the story remains stuck. Groot does not succeed in talking about his religious experience on the basis of the Parsifal story, while initially this really seemed to be his intention. He had lost his grip on the narrative he took as his starting point.

This is not unusual for the life story of an artist: it is an idealistic picture of oneself based upon a real or literary character, such as Parsifal, but also Tristan or even Superman. A thorough analysis is needed to prevent the researcher from uncritically engaging in the creation of an idealistic picture or life story. A researcher might come to the conclusion that the religious experience of Groot is indeed based upon the story of Parsifal. A critical analysis, however, yields different information. Groot is more than a Parsifal character and several sub-identities (Mishler 1999: 108–109) resonate as well. We might call this way of interpreting ludistic. One tries to come as close as possible to the respondents and on the other hand one tries to keep distance. Instead of assuming coherence in the life stories, we then see how important sub-identities are for the narrative of several other artists.

COMPETING AND SWITCHING IDENTITIES

It is often assumed that one of the most important goals of telling one's life story is to persuade others and oneself that the life that one leads is a coherent one. In the above-mentioned quote Wuthnow suggests that "these narratives of spiritual journeys remain significant as ways of finding coherence in a tumultuous world" (Wuthnow 2001: 106). By telling a coherent life story informants experience their life as meaningful, which brings about the conclusion that they matter as a human being. They do live, however, in a tumultuous and fragmented world in which they are confronted with a multitude of options from which they have to choose. In this chaotic society they fulfil multiple roles, each with its sub-identity. By telling their life stories they seek coherence, in order to understand the world and their part in it and, retrospectively, give meaning to it.

For their life stories however, being an artist means that they can play with circumstances that matter for others but not for them, precisely because such an attitude emphasizes their originality. For artists and writers play is an important tool to emphasize that they are different from other people. Play enables them to show their creativity in, for example, the way they tell their stories; they use a playful way of constructing them. But, as mentioned above, they also play when they construct their worldview. Furthermore, they play in their studio: they play with materials, and they make up stories. Artists often do not seek wholeness in a fragmented world, but call attention to the incomprehensiveness or disorderliness of their existence and to their double role as a human being and artist. The French writer Albert Camus stated: "If the world would be comprehensible, there would be no art." In particular the older respondents (the younger artists, born in or after 1970, do in fact struggle with this) are able to play with the disorderly circumstances of their lives. Mishler's statement, "If our stories are to represent our lives with any adequacy, then they must leave room for the complex interplay of multiple, and sometimes competing, plot lines" (1999: 80), seems to be the adagium for artists born before 1970. Mishler collected life stories of craft artists and in his analysis it also appears that continuity is the exception rather than the rule. In their life stories artists try to cope with tensions and contradictions in life and to seek solutions for it: "How they define their respective partial or sub-identities and how their ways of accommodating them to each other changed over time" (1999: 108–109). These "partial or sub-identities" produce dilemmas and the way people deal with these dilemmas provides important information. In particular the life stories of writer Peter Verheugd (1969) and artist Marjolijn van den Assem (1947) are worthwhile to analyse in this regard.

Verheugd attended a fashion academy and worked in the fashion industry for years. When his last employer went bankrupt, he lost his job and received unemployment benefit. During that time he wrote some lengthy books on the lives of people in their 30s. Publishers rejected these manuscripts however and deemed them unfit for publication. I talked to him twice and from these conversations it is clear how he struggles with his different sub-identities. Among other things he is a husband, father and writer. As a husband and father he finds himself to be deficient because due to his unemployment his family struggles to make ends meet. This troubles him even more so because as a writer he does not seem to be able to fulfil his role as a husband and father. When he opts for his family, the "intense personal expression" that he regards essential for himself as a writer disappears.

More than 30 years ago artist Van den Assem lived in similar circumstances. From her life story we learn that age matters for the construction of the story and in dealing with "partial or sub-identities" such as being an artist and motherhood. One identity does not necessarily rule out the others (Mishler 1999: 109). In retrospect the older respondents such as Van den Assem, have learned that contradictory interests and fragmentations can be of value and can make life and work more intense and interesting.

Van den Assem had two children by the end of the 1960s. Her oldest was born when she was still studying at the art academy and although she did not finish her education she remained active as an artist. She tells us that at the time it was unusual for female artists to become mothers.

That was almost a taboo: your work had to be zero then. Really. You can hardly imagine that now anymore, but it was really the case and it was quite a struggle, but I always believed in such intensity. And being something, what is that for god's sake, who constructs these standards? I still know that my gallery owner once said to me: having children makes your work immensely profound. Because you have children, you work has the layers it has. Damn, yes, she is right. So yes, I do not have a "burning" ambition to become world famous in that job, that is sincerely true, although it is doubted sometimes. I think I find being a good mother and a good grandma more important than being world famous, I really feel so, but I would die without that work and as I already told you, I think one is born as an artist.[4]

In her life story Van den Assem emphasizes how the different roles taken up by her in her career have influenced, strengthened and complemented each other. Nevertheless, a paradox arises because it has never been Van den Assem's ambition to become a "world famous artist" – she always deemed it to be more important to be a good mother (and grandmother), yet at the same time she cannot live without being an artist because that would amount to death for her.

Verheugd, by comparison, tries to bring just one role to the fore of his life story, although he experiences that several identities compete for the first place. He seems to think that he must pass over one identity to light up the other. Van den Assem, on the other hand, has experienced that this is not necessary. She easily alternates her identities as mother and grandmother with her identity as artist, and vice versa. Obviously, this yields a form of continuity, because she varies, apparently effortlessly, the many roles she fulfils in her life.

Whereas anthropologists have thought about the ways people shape their identities, literary scientists help us to discover how artists display these identities in their life stories. When combining these perspectives, we realize that we should reckon with the fact that artists try to meet the image that others, but they themselves as well, have created when telling their life stories. This image is an idealized image that never corresponds to actual reality. The first discrepancies between their idealized and real life stories soon turn up. They remain, however, invisible for the researcher, in case he or she lacks the appropriate research instruments to analyse texts. Among fiction analysts it is thus very common to look for sudden changes of style or changes

---

4. Dat was bijna een taboe, dan kon je werk niks zijn. Echt waar hoor. Dat kun je je nu niet meer voorstellen, maar dat was echt zo en dat was ook een hele worsteling, maar ik heb altijd geloofd in die intensiteit. En wat is iets zijn, wat is dat nou in godsnaam, wie legt die maatstaven aan? Ik weet nog dat mijn galeriehoudster een keertje zei: het hebben van kinderen is voor jou een enorme verdieping voor dat werk. Doordat je kinderen hebt, heeft dat werk die lagen die het heeft. Ja verdomd, daar heeft ze gelijk in. Dus ja, ik heb niet zo'n brandende ambitie om wereldberoemd te zijn in dat werk, dat is oprecht waar, ook al wordt het wel eens anders gezegd. Ik denk dat ik goede moeder zijn en goede oma zijn belangrijker vind dan wereldberoemd zijn, dat vind ik echt, maar dat ik dood zou gaan zonder dat werk en ik je al zei: volgens mij word je als kunstenaar geboren.

in time (see, among others, Van Boven and Dorleijn 1999). The appearance of such changes is often significant, for they may, for instance, indicate that the author wants to emphasize a particular aspect of his or her story. This is not different for life story narrators, although they might be less conscious about it. Besides, we should be aware of our influence as interviewers on the narration of this story, as well as on the story itself. To illustrate this:

During my conversation with visual artist Jan Murk (1919), something occurred that I could not immediately understand. When I rang his doorbell, his partner – Jan Murk lives with a man – opened the door. From out of the long hall that divides the house, the artist, completely dressed in black, strode to me while extending his hand. It seemed a scene from a film house movie. Jan Murk gave me a solemn welcome, yet at the same time his reception was so warm that I immediately felt at home.

This welcome foreshadowed something that would frequently occur in our conversation, something that I could not grasp until I analysed it more profoundly. During our meeting, Jan Murk presented himself as the type of artist we know from books, films and television series. Striding to me out of that impressive hall in his monumental house did not keep him from greeting me as an old friend.[5] During our conversation, Jan Murk kept switching between these two roles. This is in particular illustrated by his alternating formal and informal forms of addressing me during our conversation, which I found really unpleasant and difficult to grasp at the same time. Different from English language, there is a polite and an intimate form of addressing other persons in Dutch language. Older, highly placed and unknown persons are, according to linguistic etiquettes, addressed by the word "u," while intimates and acquaintances are addressed by "jij"; English speakers use in both cases "you." Jan Murk used both "u" and "jij" during our conversation. Was it to create distance, and if so, why did he do that? When I transcribed the interview recording, I initially thought that the artist changed from the informal "jij" to the formal "u" when he floundered. Yet later on I realized that he used the formal "u" when he answered questions that were patently obviously related to my research. Foregoing our conversation, I had informed Jan Murk about my research and I had told him that I as a researcher would like to discuss his work, life and worldview. At moments that we were discussing these topics, he addressed me with the formal "u." These were apparently the moments that I was perceived as the researcher. At these moments, he seemed to show an idealized image of himself and to present himself as an artist. He used the informal "jij" when we were not talking as interviewer and interviewee, but as two persons with a shared past, involved in a pleasant conversation that could have happened by accident.

5. Jan Murk and I know each other from the time that his ex-fiancée was my neighbour. Jan Murk was then a well-known figure in our street, because he visited her very often.

"SEARCH-AND-REPLACE" WORLDVIEWS

A life history contains a lot of information about the work, life and the world-view of its narrator. Wuthnow argues that we can find patterns in different worldviews. These can best be explained "in terms of artists' religious upbringing, the crises they have faced, and the spiritual practices in which they engage" (Wuthnow 2001: 8).). As mentioned before one could consider this construction a form of play.

My fieldwork data show indeed that the background of the respondent time and again is the basis on which the current worldview is built. Yet, the worldview evolves. The artists develop their very own way of dealing with these givens. For the artists authenticity and originality remain the core characteristics of their narratives. This influences their worldview. I found that artists do not reproduce existing worldview repertoires, but pick and choose parts of different worldviews which they then replace with and transform into their own interpretations. I saw this happen on three levels: in the use of sources, in worldview practices and in language.

SOURCES

An artist, like every other person, may of course have what is called a reading autobiography. A reading autobiography is a type of autobiography in which people tell about reading experiences that are important to them. They connect these experiences to memories they have of a certain period (see, among others, Andringa 2004; Charlton et al. 2004; Graf 1997; Pette 2001). My analysis of reading autobiographies of artists shows that they construe their world-view by going sideways. Straightforward and obvious paths are avoided as much as possible. This can be seen in their use of sources. While in bookshops the "spirituality," "new age" and "esotery" sections grow larger and at least in floor space dominate the formerly much more popular sections "religion" and "theology" (Heelas and Woodhead 2005: 69), artists ignore this trend. On their shelves I did not find large quantities of spiritual books, although there were exceptions to the rule. More often artists sought substitutes for the popular spiritual literature that others bought. For example, ego documents and poetry provided the artists with spiritual insights. Also fiction, essays, as well as books on philosophy and psychology provided them with insights, whereas others consulted spiritual and esoteric works.

Books are especially valuable because artists not only identify with their content, but equally with the life of their authors. Graphical artist Christina de Vos (1965) suffered a great loss when her partner died. Her artistic work came to a halt. This period came to an end when the Dutch poet and writer Anna Enquist published a collection of poems about what she had experienced when her daughter died. Enquist's poems and Enquist's case offered De Vos consolation.

THE PRACTICE OF WORLDVIEW

Many artists start each day in the same manner. Every morning respondent Boudewijn Payens (1951) sits down at his turntable and makes a pot. Wuthnow connects this regularity in artistic practice with worldview. "The essence of spiritual practice is engaging in a regular pattern of activities to deepen one's understanding and experience of the sacred, to strengthen one's relationship to God, or to establish a closer connection with the ultimate ground of being" (Wuthnow 2001: 127). In my research however, it became clear that those who had turned away from traditional religion replaced such practices with less explicitly religious practices. This is aptly illustrated by the "search-and-replace" worldview of Toine Horvers (1947). The artist says to seek the quiet in churches, although he only visits them for funerals or on a cultural excursion.

> I notice that every time I sit there, I find something beautiful, a service like that, yes, yes, the whole ritual and then you think god yes, he does it in this way, and he does it in that way, but everybody in his way has his ritual, so I think it is nice too, and I like churches when I am travelling somewhere or something, I always go and take a look in churches, there is something that in some way fascinates me in that, that gives me a sort of spiritual, spiritual peace. I would not be able to explain what it is, but, well I don't know, I don't go there myself or anything, church services.

Horvers does not necessarily need to go to church for this peaceful experience. As soon as he is taken out of his daily activities, he feels in a similar contemplative mood. "Well, that doesn't have anything to do with the church or religion" he suggests, but in the same breath he adds: "but well, I do have the same feeling in church sometimes, that I, during a service, during a funeral or whatever, that I, that I feel a kind of peace that, that I actually miss." This peace Horvers used to find also in his sports activities. "There has been a time that I went swimming twice a week in the morning and that I found also very beautiful, also because just swimming laps is a kind of, has something meditative, a sort of inner peace." Being an artist also gives him this. "So when I'm working on those drawings, that also gives a kind of peace," he thinks.

WORLDVIEW LANGUAGE

Worldview touches on experience and feeling. Usually it is difficult, also for artists, to find the fitting words for this. They are often drawn to spiritual expression because they, as artists, experience life in a way that cannot easily be reduced to words (Wuthnow 2001: 59). In the interviews he held, Wuthnow distinguished four worldview narratives: "recovery," "journey home," "spiritual conversion" and "reinventing oneself." Worldview language, in his view, is connected to these different narratives. Thus "The language of recovery," for example, indicates the struggle of humans to achieve continuity and wholeness in a tumultuous and chaotic world. The language is characterized by recovery. Wuthnow's division in four narratives means that one can speak of a certain systematization in the worldview of artists. I used his division for a first, orientating analysis of the life stories that I collected. But what emerges out of my research is that artists are not able to stick to one narrative.

For example, if one asks double talent John Huxley a question – he makes plastic arts and writes – one runs the chance that he answers with: "Do you know, Voltaire he said..." and what follows is Huxley's answer in the words of Voltaire. Huxley easily quotes from a repertoire of narratives, all of great artists, scientists or thinkers, and used freely. Huxley positions himself as an outsider, but paradoxically, his language is nevertheless shaped by others. The distance that he creates by not using his own words, is partially negated because he views the words of others as those of so-called partners or friends.

TYPES OF WORLDVIEW

With the background of the artists, the sources they use, their worldview practice and their worldview language are the elements that point the way towards charting their worldview. Taking these elements as leading criteria, I was able to group my informants in four types. The first type I labelled "Worldview à la carte," the second one I called "*On the high one*"; the third type is indicated by "And yet I am not alone" and the fourth type I named "Because all this is my religion." This division of types of worldview should be seen as ideal types. The interesting thing about these four types of worldview is that gender and age play a significant role. Type 1 is represented by the youngest respondents, from 2 to 4 the average age increases. Moreover it is interesting to note that type 2 is only represented by women, and type 3 only by men.

"WORLDVIEW À LA CARTE"

This type of worldview is represented by artists that are born in or after 1970. For the most part they grew up in church-going families. They do not cherish this religious background. Religion, for them, is associated with dogmas, rules, narrow-mindedness and superficiality.

The representatives of "worldview à la carte" use different sources for the construction of their worldview and they mix high and low literature. Insights from Herman Hesse are combined with quotes from new age books by former actress Shirley MacLaine. These artists not only draw on these books but sometimes literally use the terms of these books in their interview statements.

The worldview practice of the representatives of this type of worldview is especially connected to their way of working. Irene X (1971), for example, thinks that the way her sculptures are created is similar to meditation.

The worldview language of artists that I group around this type can be typified by opposites such as "positive" against "negative." "Good" and "evil" (replaced by "trust" and "mistrust" respectively) from the church language they grew up with seem to be the starting point for this dualist thinking.

"ON THE HIGH ONE"

The representatives of "*On the high one*" are all female. They feel the urge "to come home." In other words: they want to return to the religion they grew up with. Their way home is not a literal way home. Instead it is a place where they "value a space that combines something of their personal history with tangible symbols of religious meaning" (Wuthnow 2001: 85). This can be their studio but also a painting or a statue they have made.

Poetry especially is important for the respondents of this type. The artists that belong to "*On the high one*" use poetry to construct their current worldview. Caren van Herwaarden (1961) identified her worldview by explaining and analysing the poem "*On the high one*" to me.[6] The representatives also identify themselves with certain aspects from the lives of the writers they quote. They do not model their lives after these lives but they look for certain aspects that could help them in difficult circumstances. As Christina de Vos, already mentioned, is one of the respondents of this type. For these representatives the Bible is also a source.

Their way home also influences their worldview practice. Religious elements are thus also found in their work. Van Herwaarden spent half a year as an artist in residence in a monastery. Furthermore, she uses religious images in her work – a former taboo. The title of one of Jacolien de Jong's (1961) expositions is: "En God dacht dat het goed was" ("And God thought it was good").

The use that the representatives of "*On the high one*" make of language is personal. They frequently employ words such as "vulnerable," "openness," and "trust." They also use the words of poets to express their most existential feelings. They use poetical metaphors to speak about their insights on worldview.

"AND YET I AM NOT ALONE"

Most of the especially male representatives of this type come from non-religious, intellectual backgrounds. The relationship with their parents was often difficult. The artists I group around this type quote from mostly literary and philosophical works. The representatives of this type do not combine high and low literature. They quote important writers and thinkers and in this way show their erudition. Furthermore, they are interested in the lives of others. They love to read autobiographies and biographies. These books are

---

6. "*On the high one*" is written by the Dutch poet and writer Willem Jan Otten.

used to direct their own lives, because they offer the artists answers to important questions.

The representatives of this type are strongly opposed against religion. They were not raised with a religious practice and therefore are not looking for substitutes.

Painter and writer John Huxley (1951) emphasizes that he does not believe in life after death. He is constantly aware of the final character of life. Painting and writing are his ways to cope with it: "a daily way." Reading and thinking about life is the worldview practice of these respondents.

The representatives of this type often speak in a critical way about the other and the society she is part of. These artists detest society although they also speak in an ironic way about it. Their language is influenced by the above-mentioned writers and thinkers, whom they quote frequently.

"BECAUSE ALL THIS IS MY RELIGION"

Not all respondents of this type grew up in religious families. In some cases the church was visited incidentally and in other cases (grand)parents were also interested in other forms of worldview and religion. None of the artists I group around this type are negative about their religious roots. Yet this does not mean that they still visit the church. Rather it implies that religion in the most general sense is acknowledged and cherished by the representatives of this type. They find religion everywhere around them.

Poetry, literature and philosophy are important sources for the construction of their worldview and work. Reading is also an important part of the way they spend their day. Reading gives them rest and it offers the opportunity to think about their work and life. The artists see a similarity between the construction of their work and religion. Van den Assem thinks her being an artist is her "signification," "comfort" and "religion."

The other plays an important role in the way representatives of this type use language, yet in another way than is the case for "And yet I am not alone." The representatives of "Because all this is my religion" tell about valuable encounters with others. They consider the others as God sent.

CONCLUSION

The longing of artists towards authenticity and originality is mirrored in the way they have constructed their worldview. They do not copy already existing repertoires, but look for replacements. In this process their religious background plays an important role, because it turns out to be the fundament on which their "search-and-replace" worldview is built. They have found substitutes for sources, worldview practice and worldview language. In this way they have been able to create their own unique and exclusive pattern, thereby fitting into their individualized and secularized society.

These findings are mirrored by their life stories. Because of the interdisciplinary methodology of my research – a combination of methodological insights from literary studies and the cultural anthropology of religion – I was able to point out similarities between the individual life stories, which at first all seemed to be very authentic and personal. Based on these similarities I was able to distinguish four types of worldview. I discussed the difficulty of extracting a typology of worldviews from narratives that are meant to be unique and exceptional. Despite their authenticity, the narratives can be shown to have roots in existing worldview repertoires and to copy available life story models. Yet, elements from these repertoires are substituted and story models are used in an inconsistent manner.

At first sight the artist's life stories seem to present us with new and unique worldviews. However, a more thorough research, not misled by their way of storytelling, shows that they obey the regularities of four types. Besides, although many are very critical of the worldview of their youth and parents, some continuity can be observed as well in the dynamic way in which they construct their current views.

Chapter 8

Fieldwork on Morality: Gossip and Secrets[1]

KIM KNIBBE*

Please don't tell anyone what I just told you.
I never talk to anybody about this.
I don't know what happened, why I told you this.

(Various interviews, 2001/2002)

That priest has some characteristics of a psychopath. He always wants to be right.
He twists everything in such a way until people fall for it. The former bishop was
really a psychopath. They showed Dr Terruwe (a psychiatrist) one of his letters,
without telling her who wrote it, and she said immediately: this was written by a
psychopath.

(Interview 24 September 2002)

The young priests, they are the worst.

(Conclusion of a group discussion)

INTRODUCTION

Doing research on the role of religion in moral orientation through fieldwork
and later in analysing it and writing about it felt to me like a long series of
small betrayals. Trained as an anthropologist, I was very much aware of the
criticism on "grab and run" data collection, of objectifying my "informants,"

* Kim Knibbe is a University Lecturer at the Department of the Comparative Study of Religion, Groningen University. She has recently published a monograph entitled *Faith in the Familiar: Religion, Spirituality and Place in the South of the Netherlands* (Brill 2013), based on her research
into Catholicism and contemporary spirituality in the Netherlands. Furthermore, she has co-
edited with Anna Fedele the volume *Gender and Power in Contemporary Spirituality* (Routledge
2013). Alone and with Peter Versteeg and with Andre Droogers she has written reflective articles on the practice of doing ethnographic research on religion. In addition, she has carried out
research on Nigerian Pentecostalism in Europe and published widely on this topic.

1. This article is a reflection on the research I did for my PhD thesis, defended in 2007. Some of
these reflections were part of the text of the thesis. I thank André Droogers and Els Jacobs for their
supervision during this process, and André Droogers and Marten van der Meulen for their comments
on much earlier versions of this article. The fieldwork on which I draw here took place over a period
of one and a half years, in 2001 and 2002. I participated in several religious contexts during this
period, all centred in one area of rural Limburg around a village I will call Welden (not its real name).

of writing about them in a way that was alienating, of the need to be reflexive (Jackson 1989; Knibbe and Versteeg 2008; Stoller 1997). However, being aware of these pitfalls did not change the fact that doing fieldwork and then writing about it always involves an instrumentalization of human relationships: for a while, I participated in the social processes of a place (without actually doing anything very useful), and then I went away to write about it, which is an act of objectification. This predicament of how to deal with this instrumentaliza-tion was further complicated by the important role of "suppressed" genres of speech in the context of my fieldwork.

Within the research project "Between Secularization and Sacralization" it was my task to focus on changes in moral orientation in relation to religious change. In the classical research on religious change, certain changes in moral orientation have been statistically chronicled. To a large extent through its own doing, the Catholic Church had lost its grip on the moral life of Catholics in the Netherlands (Coleman 1978: 85; Kennedy 1995; Knibbe 2013; Simons and Winkeler 1987).

I found that one of the challenges of doing anthropological research on religious change in the Netherlands was to find a way of doing qualitative research on this subject, going beyond the methodological individualism of quantitative research on secularization (e.g. Halman and Riis 2003; Houtman and Mascini 2002; Schepens and Spruit 2001) without limiting oneself to a case study approach. By basing itself on the data provided by individuals through questionnaires, this type of research makes it appear as if social and cultural developments are the sum of many individual decisions, caused by individ-ual characteristics such as educational level. But it obscures the context in which these decisions are made. On the other hand, qualitative research on religion to a large extent focuses on case studies, limiting the scope of quali-tative research on religion. Navigating between these two extremes, I chose to start from a geographical location rather than a religious group, to develop a perspective on the ways in which various religious contexts related to each other, and to gain new insights into the nature and place of religion. I chose a region that had always intrigued me, since I grew up there: the South of Lim-burg, the Netherlands.

The province of Limburg is the most Catholic province of the Netherlands, being 99% Catholic until recently (Knippenberg 1992: 174). During the height of pillarization this meant that to people living in Limburg the Catholic pillar practically encompassed the whole of society. The presence of socialists in some mining towns and a tiny protestant minority only intensified the efforts of the Catholic Church to ensure that the Limburg people remained "Catholic in everything." Since the 1960s however, the power of the church has declined markedly. According to the studies available then, Catholics in the whole of the Netherlands (of which a very large part live in Limburg) are more liberal in their moral orientation than (former) Protestants (Dekker et al. 1997: 57–76).

As shown by the research mentioned above, and according to most people I spoke to in Limburg, the Catholic Church was of no importance anymore to people's moral orientation. That fact alone seemed to me so puzzling, that I wanted to go beyond these bland observations and dig a little deeper. Common sense dictates that this rather sudden irrelevance is impossible: only 50 years ago, the church had seemed all powerful in Limburg, and Catholics were confident that they would soon become the majority in the Netherlands. The clergy dictated what was taught in schools, professional education, medicine, and had created an efficient network of organizations to cover all areas of life. This formative power of the church cannot simply vanish overnight.

To prove the persistence of religion I could point to the many processions, yearly celebrations and life cycle rituals that are quite clearly part of life in Limburg, and to the roadside chapels and crosses everywhere (e.g. Nissen 1996, 2000; Wijers 2000). They have become bound with the identity of being a Limburger, but they also neatly distinguish insiders from outsiders, participants from spectators. Culturally, Catholicism is very much alive. But in terms of moral orientation, it seemed to be gasping its last breath. Everybody I spoke to quite clearly said that they had no wish to "turn back the clock" as they put it, and let the priest, in conjunction with the mayor, decide how life should be lived by everybody. Although older people, especially women, were a bit worried about the ways relations between the sexes nowadays seemed to be completely unregulated, they generally said that their children and grandchildren had "their own morals" and that that was fine. In terms of moral orientation, they felt no need for the church or the priest.

During my fieldwork I discovered that this irrelevance might be true on an overt level, but that there were genres of speech in which the church and the priest had a significant role in defining what is good and what is to be rejected. However, these were typically "repressed" genres of speech: secrets, gossip, rumour. It took me a long time to recognize the importance of these genres of speech to my research, yet they eventually provided the key to understanding the continuing role of "the church" and "the priest" in moral orientation. During my fieldwork, but especially in writing, I mostly worried about what to do with these forms of speech, how to take them seriously in a way that would not harm people, betray their confidence, or repeat slander.

Anthropological and sociological studies have paid attention to these genres, although not as much as might be expected, as giving important insights into "what really matters" to people, but also into how groups function, and how moral orientations are reinforced (e.g. Stewart and Strathern 2004; Straating 1998). Interestingly, the subject of gossip is often linked to witchcraft, a subject explored very thoroughly in the anthropological literature (e.g. Evans-Pritchard 1937; Geschiere and Roitman 1997; Gluckman 1963, 1968; Merry 1997; Stewart and Strathern 2004). Equally, the subject of secrets is often linked to initiation into secret societies, cults, witchcraft and magic. In this literature, the treatment of the subject of gossip and witchcraft is quite established and a respectable scholarly topic. In the way that this is discussed, the notion of witchcraft is so exotic to the academic world that there seems to be no danger that it will seem dangerous and painful to discuss in an anthropological work (although there is a notable exception in the work of Jeanne Favret-Saada 1980). The chance that anyone from "the field" in "faraway Africa" will actually read the work of the anthropologist writing about them is remote, so that the issue of repeating slander does not seem very important. The issue of betraying confidence comes up in the sense that the anthropologist may be initiated into a cult or secret society and sworn to secrecy.

My position as a researcher was very different: I was doing research in my own society, there was every chance that the people I spoke to would read my work later on, especially those priests who were the subject of the most vicious gossip such as that quoted in the first part of the article. Furthermore, the "secrets" that seemed so crucial to understand what was going underneath the bland statements that religion was not important any more were very private, painful and personal, not recognized secrets that were the prize to be had after a process of initiation.

The many small acts of betrayal that come with doing fieldwork and writing about it, are not often a subject for discussion in the handbooks for qualitative research. Yet for me, they were very real. Moreover, in discussing my experiences with students it is this exactly that they find difficult as well, especially if they are very close to their subjects. One could dismiss this as "over-identification," but if we conceive of fieldwork as a relational exercise in establishing intersubjectivity, or in terms of "serious play," moving between different worldviews, then it is important to look more closely at the complex relational dynamics at work in doing fieldwork, in analysis and in writing up. What are the ethical implications of moving between different worlds?

In the following I will unpack these issues in more detail as I encountered them during fieldwork. Section 2 will deal with the question of how I came to know these personal, painful secrets and how I dealt with them. Section 3 will deal with the question of whether and how we should take gossip seriously, whereas section 4 will deal with the difficulties I had in dealing with the guilt that accompanied analysing the role of gossip in a context to which I felt very close, among people that I felt were doing really wonderful work.

HOW TO DEAL WITH OTHER PEOPLE'S SECRETS?

My original plan was to confine my research to participant observation and in-depth interviews within the boundaries of this village. Soon, it became clear that this was an unrealistic plan, since many people participated in religious contexts outside the boundaries of their village and parish, although close by. By following the leads from Welden,[2] to other religious contexts, my research turned out to include two religious contexts located within the same municipality: a "spiritual society" and a (Catholic) pastoral centre. Further-

2. This is a pseudonym.

more, I conducted about 25 life-history interviews with people of different generations: men and women who were coming of age during the war, and people of later generations. I was always the youngest person around: there were not many adults under 30 living in that area.

Initially, I had planned to find people of roughly three generations to have life-history interviews with. Ideally, they would be grandparents, parents and children. I found that this was quite difficult to realize. All my key informants had warned me about this: according to them Limburg people are quite closed, especially to someone from "above the rivers"[3] (i.e. someone who did not speak the local dialect, was not a Catholic). Although individuals consented to be interviewed, snowballing meant that I ended up with extremes: either very pious people, or people who hated the church for a particular reason. While this was very informative, I was not satisfied with this. Through the local school I found some people of the post-war generation, but their family members refused to be interviewed. However, through a very helpful contact with the secretary of the society of seniors, a substantial number of people of the older generation consented to be interviewed. It helped that, while not speaking the local dialect I was not actually from "above the rivers," I had grown up in the area and could at least understand the local dialect.

While interviewing people of the older generation, I became the receptacle of secrets. Initially, I was very confused by these interviews. On the one hand, the uniformity of what people said about the role of the church in their lives was astonishing. On the other hand, there were some very personal, painful and private stories. My respondents felt that these painful stories happened only to *them*, that nobody else had had these experiences, and they were anxious that these stories should not become public. But then, why did they tell them? And why did they sound so familiar to me, why did it seem I had heard them so many times already? Why did I immediately recognize the pain that they felt?

Robert Kahn and Charles Cannell compare the dynamics of an open-ended interview to the therapeutic interview, since in both situations it is especially the *non-judgmental context* created by the interviewer that encourages the respondent to open up, by eliminating the need to defend oneself (Kahn and Cannell 1967: 70–75). This non-judgmental context is unusual in daily social life, and in my experience it does indeed lead people to open up and start to enjoy telling their stories. Besides, dwelling on memories and personal opinions builds up its own momentum, and creates an atmosphere of familiarity and intimacy between the interviewer and the interviewee.

---

3. By the expression "above the rivers" the Netherlands is divided into two: the Catholic South below the Rhine, and the Protestant North above it. Although this is strictly speaking not correct (there is a Bible belt of strict Protestantism that reaches far below "the rivers") it is used to indicate people who are not "familiar," have different ways and will never really understand the ways of the people below the rivers.

Although I reassured people that I would protect their anonymity (hence the pseudonym for the location), I did not quite know how to handle the responsibility that came with being entrusted with these stories. Somehow, the very private nature of the grief expressed in these stories asked for a response, a connection that extended beyond the interview situation. I recognized their stories because my family from my mother's side comes from Limburg (although not from the same region). But to redress the balance was impossible: ultimately, the intimacy created in the interview situation is a false one, whatever the common ground between interviewer and interviewee may be. There is a definite power-relationship present in the interview, since it is the interviewer who defines the context and the purpose (Kvale 1996: 126). Besides, I did not plan on sticking around to help them, as a friend, to come to terms with these painful secrets. Even if I could have been in a position to do so, I was much too young to take on that role for them anyway.

So I felt guilty for being entrusted with these secrets without being in the position to reciprocate this trust. Although one might argue that open interviews grant more space to the respondents to set the pace, context and topic (as opposed to structured or closed interviews) the sense of empowerment that comes from "telling one's own story" can quickly turn into a sense of deflation when attention turns once more to the day-to-day life. I tried to end each interview with more reciprocal talk, letting them question me about my life and background, but it was hard to shake off this feeling that somehow, by using my own knowledge and background, I had tricked them into telling me details of their life they had not wanted to reveal.

While writing my thesis I had to decide whether or not to use the stories that contained what people thought were only their own private shameful secrets. On the one hand, my respondents had asked me to keep them secret. On the other hand, I felt that they revealed something very crucial about the power of the Catholic Church, its practices and its doctrines: many years after the actual social power of the church had dwindled to a shadow of its former power, people still felt ashamed, emotional, and anxious. I felt I had the responsibility, not to "unmask" how horrible the church was, but to analyse the ways the former power of the church is embedded within the experience and memories of people, and how it affects the ways they relate to the Catholic Church and other forms of organized religion. It seemed I had the choice between violating their trust by being truthful, or being untruthful but keeping their secrets.

I decided to leave out those stories that were obviously still painful to tell for my respondents. Instead, I paid more attention to some stories that were very similar, but were less painful for the respondent to tell. In fact, they were part of the repertoire of stories they *wanted* to tell and it was noticeable that they were already polished and smooth, since they had been told more often. Whether they were still painful or not, they have in common that they show another, individualized, side of the coin of the shared narratives about the past: they concerned events that people had tried to forget because they were too shameful, or too painful or both, related to the mechanisms of control by the church. These stories were similar to those in the collection of letters edited by Marga Kerklaan (Kerklaan 1987). These letters were written by Catholic women from all over the Netherlands in response to a television programme discussing the question of whether the church's rules on sexuality could be seen as the cause of the massive emptying of the churches starting in the 1960s.

Although people thought their secrets to be private, shameful and extremely individual, they show an important side of the moral dominance of the church in their life: its power to keep the suffering that this dominance caused out of the public domain, its power to summon mechanisms of social control to its cause. They contrasted sharply with the general efforts of the narratives of the past that people tried to impress on me: that although the past might seem "bad" by present day moral reasoning, "it was just the way things were," a state of affairs nobody had an opinion about. The past and the present seemed to be separate moral universes. The painful stories show how this past moral universe was created and maintained, and tell of the casualties that fell by the wayside.

Instrumental to enforcing this state of affairs was not only the cooperation between the church and the "notables" of a community, such as the mayor, landlords and the doctor, but also the threat of being excluded from the sacraments. The causal chain of events implied by this exclusion was instilled in people from elementary school onwards. The mechanism of the sacraments often affected women disproportionately because of the strict Catholic doctrine on birth control: if a woman indicated during confession that she wanted to practice birth control (whether actively or through abstention) she risked "getting the shutter": the priest would close the shutter between himself and the confessant without giving absolution. Without absolution, one could not participate in the sacraments such as communion.

Exclusion from the sacraments meant that one was living in a state of sin. Living in a state of sin meant that if one should die suddenly, heaven (and the church graveyard) would be closed to you. In the same vein, children who had not had the stain of original sin removed by baptism were barred from heaven and had to be buried outside hallowed grounds. People who told me this emphasized that this should remain a secret. After more than 60 years they still did not want anybody to know about this. Some people remember being taught to do emergency baptisms to prevent this tragedy, especially during the Second World War. After "getting the shutter," a woman would often not dare to go into church during mass again.

Although it was ethically complicated to use these stories, I felt that I should analyse them and represent them even if only in very "generic" ways, to gain a deeper understanding of the ways in which the moral power of the church lives on, long after the actual worldly power of the church has decreased. Individual secrets too, are usually the products of social processes and cultural ideas.

HOW TO TAKE GOSSIP SERIOUSLY

Geographically, the parish, the pastoral centre and the spiritual society were located close to each other, although not in the same village. The people frequenting the pastoral centre and the spiritual society were mostly local, and the few "imported" people participating in these contexts had been living in the area for a long time or were committed to becoming part of their local community. The difference between "locals" and "import" is usually keenly felt, but of course this difference fades over time as people get used to each other. Other differences were just as important in the two contexts: the difference between lay people and priests, between lay pastors and priests, between professionals and priests, between those with a higher education and those without, between city people and rural people, between neoconservatives and progressives.

Doing participant observation in the parish life of Welden was complicated because of the history of polarization between a "neoconservative" priest and "progressive" Catholics in that parish. This polarization had affected the whole community: most people felt that after the polarization, "it was never the same again" and the parish church was not "their" church anymore. They referred me to the pastoral centre two kilometres away from Welden instead. They felt I would be better off with the people of the pastoral centre, because in contrast to the parish priest, the pastoral centre had "kept up with the times." Even the parish priest (who had, supposedly, not "kept up with the times," and had a problematic relationship with this centre) referred me to them. His argument was that "his" (neoconservative) brand of Catholicism did not make for a very lively parish life, so there would not be many interesting things for me to observe. It was also clear that my presence was not comfortable to him, since I was not a Catholic and he assumed (correctly) I did not share his neoconservative views on morality.

Asking people directly about the role of the church in their own life and in social life in general usually produced quite bland answers. People found it important to have a local church, as a centre for the ritual life of the local community. However, they did not really take the doctrines of the church very seriously, except in a very general way: religion stands for decency, a reminder that there is good and evil, something they want to pass on to their children but not in the particulars of Catholic doctrine. Indirectly, however, people had quite a lot more to say about the church and its priests. It was through gossip that it became clear how the different contexts related to each other and how people themselves navigated these contexts. Since my subject was moral orientation, I grew very interested in a particular type of gossip: "bad priest stories."

Through these stories a strong stereotype of usually "young"[4] neoconservative priests was created. The persons telling these stories were usu-

4. They were called "young" relative to the middle-aged mostly liberal priests and the very old priests educated in pre-Vatican II times. However, some of the priests figuring in these stories

8. Fieldwork on Morality   135

ally women and quite often their narratives had to do with funerals. They described their experiences with the arrangement of the funeral of a loved one as a process in which they had to "haggle" with the priest about the extent to which their own input was allowed, and there was a constant fear that the priest would upset the ideal of a good Catholic death, including the last sacraments.

Following up on these "bad priest" stories was a distinct decision on my part, that was not taken lightly. There were in fact some quite good arguments against it. I did not want to get caught up in a mud-slinging competition between progressive and conservative Catholics by repeating stories that put priests in a bad light. Furthermore, these stories are not quite representative of how things normally go. After all, the great majority of funerals seem to go by without making headlines in the papers. There were, however, also reasons for paying more attention to these stories. One of them was the moral outrage they embodied. Since the focus of my research was on the role of the church in moral orientation, it seemed that here was an example of a case where the church, or at least some of its representatives, played the role of the classical "bad guy" in moral tales. By analysing these stories, the moral values against which these bad guys sinned could be deduced. Moral values reveal themselves most strongly around a crisis, and death is such a crisis (Zigon 2008: 17). Another reason was that I encountered these kinds of stories (sometimes the same ones!) in many different contexts: during life-history interviews, during interviews with key informants, but also during participant observation in the courses and reading groups of the pastoral centre and the informal conversations before and after these sessions.

Just before defending my PhD thesis I gave two interviews, one to a national paper, and one to the regional paper of Limburg. Ironically, the attention I gave to "bad priest" stories led to a small media hype: people recognized them and came out with more "bad priest" stories. The bishop felt that he had to protect "his priests" and said he did not agree with my research, while admitting that he had not read it. Some people expected that I would do more research, "unmasking" bad priests in the church. Although I had expected some publicity, the huge public interest in Limburg took me by surprise. However, it was very difficult to bring across the difference between an academic interest in "bad priest stories," the question why many priests were the subject of intense moral disapproval, and the popular impression that I had *confirmed* people's opinion of these priests. I had merely given them voice.

The local newspapers on Limburg bundled the letters from the general public with a few commissioned articles by experts, and reactions by priests and the bishop in a special supplement to one of the weekend editions. There

were in fact not so young at all, but their career had only taken off after Bishop Gijsen came to power in 1973, an extremely conservative bishop who, according to his critics, tried to "turn back the clock" and himself was the subject of extremely vicious "bad priest" stories. See also Knibbe (2013) on the polarization caused by his appointment.

was also a public debate to which I and other "experts" were invited, televised by the local media. During this debate, many people came forward with their own stories about how they had been hurt by the church through its hard line of refusing the sacraments to anyone not living in accordance with the guidelines of the church, especially concerning burial.

The bishop declined the invitation to this debate, and accused the newspaper of being biased against the church. In the past, the bishop had a considerable influence with this newspaper, and there was a gentlemen's agreement that the newspaper would not publish articles that were detrimental to the reputation of the church, and report positively on celebrations and processions. This had led to the state of affairs that important news concerning the Catholic Church (such as the reassignment of a priest with a history of paedophilia to a new parish) was usually published by a national highbrow newspaper. In recent years however, scandals had broken out in some local parishes located in my research area and the newspaper had become more determined to follow up on this news and report on it seriously. The special edition, with reactions to my PhD thesis, gave rise to a website maintained by the newspaper that was in the air for a few years.

Via the post and e-mail, I received many requests for my thesis and had some discussions with priests, who generally did recognize that my analysis was more complex than the popular reaction that it had generated. Personally, I did not want to feed the media interest in this topic, nor contribute to polarization, so I refused further interviews. Aside from my own inclination to mistrust the media, especially television, I was afraid that they would exploit the opposition between a Catholic bishop and a young female researcher. In my view, the public debate did not go beyond a repetition of grievances between adversaries that had reached a stalemate a very long time ago.

GOOD PEOPLE GOSSIP TOO, AND BAD GUYS ARE HUMAN

In analysing the role of gossip, one of the most difficult things was to recognize my own complicity in gossip and then to "break" the trust generated through this complicity. Gossip, after all, is a way to create trust between people, a shared moral universe in which you both agree that what this person said or did is bad, creating a warm glow. There were many small ways in which I broke out of this atmosphere of complicity. For example, I detached myself from the temporary moral universe created by being taken into confidence and told that "that this priest is a psychopath" by scheduling an interview with him and other priests that were the subject of gossip. Another "betrayal" took place during the analysis: to show that gossip, something that goes against the "doctrines" of the pastoral centre, was in fact crucial in the boundary-making processes that took place there and in deciding "what version of Catholicism is right": the liberal version that was taught in the pastoral centre, or the neoconservative version enforced by the "bad young priests."

On the level of doctrine, the emphasis on uncertainty crucial to the discourse of the pastoral centre meant that there could be no definite answer to this question (see Knibbe 2013). The tension created by the enormous discrepancy between the liberal Catholicism of the centre and the neoconservative policy of the diocese and its priests could only be resolved through stereotyping the priests who carried out this policy too strictly as inhuman, devoid of feeling.

I felt this betrayal of complicity quite keenly because I was mostly sympathetic to what the group leaders at the pastoral centre were doing and how they were doing it. However, as with the question of whether or not to "betray secrets," I felt that I had a responsibility to something that I hesitatingly call the "truth" that I had been looking for. In my view, it is not objectivity that is the goal in the practice of fieldwork, but to gain insight into the production of social and cultural reality, preferably from as many different positions as possible. Gossip, in this case, was crucial to see how this context was linked to other contexts around Welden.

As in most fieldwork, the requirement to gain insight from different positions was difficult because there were issues of trust: all those actors knew I was in touch with the other ones. Although I had the impression that I could have established a working relationship with one of the "bad priests," the rift his style of behaviour and his views had caused in the local community was a significant obstacle to getting cooperation from other people: people were afraid that my research, because it focused on religious life, would open old wounds and rivalries. So I had to tread carefully: clearly local parish and community life did not amount to an environment that I could hope to navigate safely with just one year of participant observation if I was doing research on religion. The different factions that had emerged through the process of polarization after the appointment of the current priest had each cut their losses, and settled down into a status quo that minimized contact and conflict between them. To gain an impression of parish life therefore, I stuck to doing interviews with individuals.

In contrast, the people of the pastoral centre welcomed my research and were very interested. Although this was very nice, it also made things difficult for me. There was a tension between difference and familiarity on various levels that was usually not explicitly recognized. First of all, there were issues of confidentiality: they had to trust me not to tell anything damaging to "religious rivals" (neoconservative clergy), and I had to be careful not to tell them too much about their "religious rivals" as well (neoconservative clergy and the spiritual society). Second, although on the face of it, the people of the pastoral centre and the background I come from are similar in values and general outlook on life, and the professional staff shared a strong sociological interest with me, this sometimes made me even more aware of the differences between them and myself: I was not a Catholic, not even baptized, and I did not want to become a Catholic either.

As part of my fieldwork, I participated in several courses and discussion groups, and interviewed the pastors. The courses I participated in involved training lay persons from the surrounding parishes to put together family services, wake services for the bereaved held the night before burial, and to help in the pastorate for elderly people. The courses were either commissioned by the diocese or by a cluster of parishes cooperating in order to pool resources.

Although I had access to all these courses and discussion groups for observation, it was hard to really do "participant" observation. In most cases, my role was confined to taking notes during the discussion. In rare cases, I joined in the discussion. Participation was made more difficult because of the formalized character of the meetings and the fact that everything centred on talking (which meant, of course, that I wanted to write it all down). Everybody knew I was a researcher and why I was taking notes. They did not really expect me to join their discussion, because my motivation to be there was considered to be completely different from theirs. In the context of the courses and discussion groups the fact that I was young, not involved in parish life, and had a different background and an "urban smell" automatically put me outside the group at the informal level.

In the informal interactions with volunteers and supporting staff, I also remained an outsider. Although everybody was friendly, they had known each other for a long time and spoke in dialect among themselves, which only included me as a listener. Speaking "proper" Dutch is a "front stage" activity, which automatically breaks the complicity created through gossip. Here also, a difference in background and experience, and of course age, played a role. Nevertheless, through hearing the stories about "bad priests," through listening to other types of gossip, I became complicit, I shared in the moral universe created by this gossip, although temporarily.

The tension between mutual recognition and familiarity and the underlying differences was reinforced by the very inclusive ideology of the pastoral centre. This ideology made me feel that I would spoil the atmosphere if I insisted on signalling that I was not the same, I did not belong to them, was not a Catholic. Besides, this inclusiveness was to the advantage of my research because it facilitated access to the courses and discussion groups.

CONCLUSIONS

During my research, gossip and secrets turned out to be important genres of speech to analyse the place of religion in moral orientation. Furthermore, these genres of speech showed how the various contexts of my research were connected, enabling me to go beyond the "case study" approach to see how locality is produced through the circulation of gossip, but also through the painful secrets that are not shared, but sensed among each other. This created two dilemmas. The first is the dilemma of how to bring these genres of speech out of the shadows and give them the proper place in analysis. The second is the ethical implications of this process, the sense of betrayal that accompanies this process. As already outlined in another publication, moving between worlds "playfully" involves many ethical isues (Knibbe and Droogers 2011).

At first sight, the question of how to deal with secrets seems simple: don't betray them. The same goes for gossip: don't repeat it. However, as researchers we do have a responsibility to give insight into the life worlds and contexts in which we do research, in the most complete possible way. In order to do this, I found that looking at the productions of secrets and the role of gossip was very important. The stated aim of fieldwork is often to go beyond the "front stage," to gain insight into the "unofficial" everyday practice of social life. In view of the recent publicity on the topic of sexual scandals in the church, including in the Netherlands,[5] it is perhaps time to turn to the question of how these "secrets" were produced and kept secret so long. Methodologically, it begs the question why researchers did not pick up on the systematic nature of the sexual and psychological abuse that went on in Catholic institutions. These stories have been around for a long time, it is a public secret that homosexuality and sexual abuse took place and takes place. Of course, the Catholic hierarchy has played a role in covering up these issues. But there is also a methodological "block" for researchers of Catholicism who are, in the Netherlands at least, from a Catholic background themselves and are read by other Catholics. If I, a relative outsider, felt the research process to be a series of small betrayals, this must be doubly so for researchers who are to a much larger extent part of the world they study. The question is, why did the process of research feel like a series of small betrayals?

Both secrets and gossip create in-groups and out-groups, they create an atmosphere of complicity and reciprocity. Sharing secrets and gossip with a researcher means that the researcher is drawn into this atmosphere of complicity. Suppressed genres of speech such as gossip are by their nature "hard to prove," highly subjective accounts that are constructed in such a way that one may agree with it privately, but not in the "official" representation to the outside world. In taking seriously the role of gossip and secrets, the researcher is doomed to betray this complicity. With hindsight, it seems that the trust and complicity established during interviews and informal talks was merely instrumental, the fieldwork a classic example of the "grab and run" method of data gathering. On the other hand, as I argued above, I felt that by ignoring the role of secrets and gossip I would omit something that was quite crucial to the understanding of the role and place of religion in moral orientation.

Through a hundred small decisions during fieldwork, during the analysis and during the writing, I decided to step outside this sphere of complicity and take up my own position. I was prepared for the eventuality that people would get angry with me. As it happened, the bishop did get angry (although he did not read my thesis) but I have not heard any negative reactions from other parties. Doing fieldwork on religion involves a complex process of becom-

---

5. http://www.onderzoekrk.nl/english-summery.html

ing involved, disengaging oneself, creating a position from where one can move around most freely. As I have argued elsewhere, with Peter Versteeg, the ethnographic imperative to stay close to people's life world, when taken to extremes, can obscure the fact that researchers in fact move between life worlds, and thereby create a unique vantage point from which to write and create insight (Knibbe and Versteeg 2008).

In this article, I have attempted to show in detail what this means in practice. Throughout the fieldwork, intersubjectivity is created, maintained, but also betrayed. During the process of writing, other encounters become relevant: those with colleagues, and with certain bodies of literature. Here, other mechanisms come into play again: what ideas are fashionable, what theoretical approaches are popular. In this article, the focus was on the relationship between the researcher and researched, regarding the ways in which the researcher becomes part of the moral universes he or she researches. With hindsight, my considerations during the whole process of doing research, analysis, writing and making public my research can be summarized as follows: (1) how will it affect the people involved, (2) how will it affect my relationship with them, and (3) how will it affect the representation of the reality "out there" if I leave out the "highly individual" and the "highly subjective" embodied by suppressed genres of speech such as secrets and gossip (in this case: are they as individual as they seem, and what is the role of these very subjective judgments?).

Chapter 9

Fieldwork on Identity: Contested and Politicized Research

MARTIJN DE KONING,* EDIEN BARTELS,** DANIËLLE KONING***

INTRODUCTION

One of the most interesting and challenging aspects of doing fieldwork is that the field site is a space of encounter. Moreover, doing fieldwork actually derives its strength and weaknesses from the fact that the researcher is part of the encounter. It is in this encounter that the researcher and his/her personality interact with his/her interlocutors' personalities and worldviews. Contrary to quantitative research the anthropologist is not anonymous. In the field an anthropologist carefully tries to construct his/her identity, seeking to come close to his/her interlocutors while at the same time maintaining a certain degree of distance. In turn the interlocutors play their part categorizing the researcher as an outsider, but also allowing him/her to come closer. In this encounter the symbolic order of each other's worldviews can be rearranged. It comes with challenges for every researcher.

* Martijn de Koning studied anthropology at VU University and defended his PhD thesis there on religious identities among young Moroccan-Dutch youth. He is a participant in the Radboud University research project "Salafism as a Transnational Movement." In his project he looks at how young Muslims actively engage with the writings of major Salafi religious leaders in the Middle East and their representatives in the Netherlands. He maintains his own weblog: http://religionresearch.org/martijn.

** Edien Bartels received her PhD in 1993 (on the topic of Arabic women, symbols and power relations between men and women) and is a senior research fellow at VU University, Department of Social and Cultural Anthropology. Together with Martijn de Koning she conducted research on Moroccan and Islamic youth, and on partner choice. She also did research on Islam, female circumcision, Islamic law, and Dutch Moroccan women and children who have been left behind in Morocco. Recently she started a research project on Islam, consanguineous marriages and preconceptual testing.

*** Daniëlle Koning studied cultural anthropology at VU University and graduated with an MA thesis on Muslim students in Amsterdam and their engagement with the religion versus science question. She recently completed her PhD at the same university, discussing Christian immigrant churches in the Netherlands and their involvement with evangelism. She is currently a career missionary with Adventist Frontier Missions (project Central Thai of Thailand).

In this article, research on religious identity and accompanying methodological problems will be illustrated by three cases of researching Muslims in the Netherlands. After having settled in the Netherlands, the first generation of Moroccan migrants started to redefine their religious identity and to institutionalize Islam. For the second generation of Moroccan-Dutch youth, Islam proved to be an important identity marker as well, but in a different way. This generation wondered about the meaning of their religion in Western society, and did not identify with the Islam of their parents. After 9/11, the 2002 election campaign that ended with the assassination of the populist anti-multiculturalism politician Fortuyn, and the murder of the film director Theo van Gogh in 2004 by a young Moroccan Muslim, Islam became one of the most important topics in public debate. Accordingly, problems in researching Islam and Muslims increased. We will introduce three cases here: research among Islamic scholars participating in an Islamic organization by Edien Bartels, research among Muslim students at VU University by Daniëlle Koning, and research among Moroccan-Dutch youth in a mosque by Martijn de Koning. First of all we will briefly elaborate on the political and societal context of these research projects. In the next section we discuss questions pertaining to intersubjectivity such as the relation between the identity of the researcher and the identity of the researched, and the different ethnographic roles researchers can take up in order to relate to the respondents and avoid controversies. In the following sections we show how the consequences of the politicization of Islam directly influence the insider/outsider positioning of the researcher. Within this framework, we will concentrate on (a) the necessity and predicaments of going public and dealing with public issues, (b) the relation between the worldviews of informants and those of the researcher and (c) processes of inclusion and exclusion during fieldwork. These three cases, all concerned with research on Muslim identity and religiosity, reveal the difficulties of fieldwork, the problems of establishing rapport, and the illusion of neutrality in a politicized research field. At the same time they point to the usefulness of an ethnographic approach in a contested field, because it may enable the very access to this field and, by playing with insider/outsider boundaries, yield additional information. This chapter tries to contribute to the debates about the methodological challenges and opportunities that come about in worldview studies. More in particular the three different cases deal with issues of power that both limit and enable the possibilities of researchers for "playful" meaning-making.

THE POLITICIZATION OF ISLAM, MIGRANTS AND CULTURE

During the 1990s, the topics of migration and integration became increasingly politicized in the Netherlands. This resulted in a gradual awakening of the public that had hitherto been rather silent or felt unable to speak out on migration and integration (Sniderman and Hagendoorn 2007; Scholten and Holzhacker 2009). Though this politicization already started in the 1990s (Mepschen, Duyvendak and Tonkens 2010; Stolcke 1995), it took a new turn with the above mentioned populist leader Fortuyn in 2001. Fortuyn effectively used already existing frustrations of native citizens on issues concerning migration and integration in a confrontational debating style. Fortuyn was followed by Hirsi Ali (a Somalian refugee woman and member of parliament for the conservative-liberal party VVD) and Wilders (leader of the right-wing Freedom Party – PVV), which led to an even stronger confrontational style in public debates on Islam. Several opinion leaders argued in favour of this style, for example, by claiming that it is a matter of freedom of expression to criticize or even insult Muslims' religious convictions and feelings. Vliegenthart (2007) shows how after 9/11 the focus in media and politics, shifted almost entirely from integration in general to Islam and Muslims and their alleged threat to Dutch society. These discussions and debates led to a growing "Islamization" of the public debate about migrants. This "Islamization" is a process in which people from Moroccan and Turkish origin (i.e. those ethnic groups in the Netherlands in which Muslims are most strongly represented), are increasingly categorized as primarily Muslims and in which the abandoning of Islamic beliefs and practices has become the standard to measure integration.

Along with the Islamization of migrants, according to Moroccan-Dutch youth, native Dutch usually categorize them negatively. They note that Islam is portrayed as backward, suspicious, related to terrorism, intolerance, and oppression of women. This leads to a confusing situation for these youths, since their search for a Muslim identity initially meant an attempt to transcend the perceived dichotomy between "Moroccan" and "Dutch" (Bartels 2000). The debate about Islam however rendered such a strategy futile because a new dichotomy arose: Muslim versus Dutch. The result was not only that being Muslim became an identity imposed upon these youths by outsiders, but also that the former tried to find another identity that would create distance both between them and Dutch society and between them and their parents. This process resulted in a search for a "true" Islam, an Islam they perceived as undiluted by cultural adaptations or traditions such as, in their view, the Islam from their parents. The aim of this searching for a "true" Islam was to create coherence between identities and loyalties that others (and sometimes they themselves) perceived as conflicting. Yet, paradoxically, this strategy only resulted in a reproduction of the dichotomy between "Muslim" and "Dutch" (De Koning 2008; Ketner, Buitelaar and Bosma 2004; De Koning and Bartels 2006).

INTERSUBJECTIVITY AND INSIDER-OUTSIDER ROLES IN A POLITICIZED FIELD

To a certain extent every field is political, since for both the researcher and the researched, ethnographical fieldwork means building alliances and affiliations and a constant shifting between being inside and outside of the field (Gupta and Ferguson 1997; Clifford 1997). This makes issues of neutrality, social roles, and the identity of the researcher pertinent. In a positivist approach, the researcher's identity is that of the scientist using "objective" approaches. According to Ghorashi the desire to be objective and neutral led researchers to claim that they represented "truth" (2001: 3). In this approach, the researcher intends to be invisible during the research. However, Ghorashi states that this professed invisibility has not been a means to diminish the importance of the role of the researcher, but a "trick" to maintain power – mostly used by white Western male researchers (2001: 32–33). The emphasis on objectivity and claiming the truth gradually shifted to giving more attention to the subjectivity of the researcher. The anthropologist was no longer the only voice of the *Other*, the *Other talked back* and thereby had the power to categorize the anthropologist as insider or outsider. From the single voice of the researcher, the focus shifted to interaction between the researcher and the researched, notions of power, the context of the research site and the various voices of the researched. Reflexivity about the researchers' identity and its influence on the information gathered therefore became necessary (cf. Arendell 1997; McCorkel and Myers 2003).

Reflections on the relationship between researcher and researched should take into account that research concepts (such as religion, culture and identity) play a role in public debates too. For example, the term culture in popular discourse is clearly connected with migration, the increase in travel, new communication techniques, and cultural globalization. The same can be said for identity. Both concepts, culture and identity, have become politicized with time: they have been used by scholars and politicians alike to legitimize or question marginalization or hegemonization (Wright 1998). Especially in cases of strong ideological connotations, it is necessary to analyse not only the meaning of these concepts for the researched but for the researcher as well. Moreover, doing research is not working in a vacuum: macro-events influence the research, sometimes directly. The politicization of concepts such as culture and identity therefore has ramifications both on the macro-level as well as on the micro-level. The macro-level pertains to the actual debate: how can anthropologists engage with issues relevant to public debates without taking for granted the political agendas behind these debates? In this article we will however concentrate our reflections on this subject as far as it is relevant to the micro-level.

As anthropologists we try to make the lives of the researched comprehensible to ourselves by translating them into categories such as identity and culture. Since not only our informants' understandings of the world are influenced by politicized concepts of identity and culture, but inevitably our own worldviews as well, how do we come to assume to understand the researched? The politicization of identity and culture creates a particular ambiguity that makes reflection on the interaction between the researcher and the researched (between the researcher as a subject and the researched as subjects), that is, the issue of intersubjectivity, pertinent. Jackson (1998), in analysing the dialectic between the universal and the particular between him as a researcher and his informants, sets out to explain these ambiguities. He sees intersubjectivity as a field of "constructive, destructive and reconstructive interaction" (1998: 8). Within the interaction between researcher and informants, "idiosyncratic, ideational, and impersonal elements commingle and coalesce" (1998: 8). Furthermore, independent from modalities and degrees of social inequality, the self and the other are "existentially dependent on and beholden to the other" (1998: 9). While the interaction between the self and the other is the basic structure of the interaction between researchers and informants, this dyad is always "mediated by...a third party, a shared idea, a common goal" (1998: 9). Not everything within the dialectic interaction between self and other being is conscious and Jackson emphasizes the role of the "taken-for-granted dispositions" (1998: 9). Ambiguity is caused furthermore by the "instability of human consciousness" (1998: 9–10). These ambiguities create and are also produced by the aforementioned problem of knowing the other. According to Jackson (1998: 7), a focus on intersubjectivity makes it possible for the researcher to come closer to the details of the everyday lives of informants. First, it helps to see identities as "mutually arising" rather than as particularities that are taken for granted. Second, it helps to shed light on how we as subjects construe extra-psychic processes as intra-psychic. Third, it enables us to reveal and analyse the relationship between the individual subject and abstract categories that are part of our anthropological toolkit, such as society, class, identity, culture, nation and so on.

As intersubjectivity concentrates on relations and interactions, reflection should not only focus on the researcher as subject but also, and perhaps even more, on the interaction between the researcher and the researched. Questions then arise, like what is the effect if one of the interacting persons is a member of a majority group in society, while the other is a member of a minority group in that same society? Or, more focused on the cases here, what consequences does it have that the researchers are part of the religious and ethnic majority (secular/Christian and white Dutch), while the infor mants belong to religious and ethnic minorities (Muslim and of Moroccan/ Turkish origin)? An interesting example is Reis (1998), who did research in Swaziland and the Netherlands on perceptions of epilepsy. Reis noted that in Swaziland she had to overcome being an outsider, while in the Netherlands she was "too much" of an insider. In Swaziland it was necessary to create an intersubjective emotional space in order to interact, while in the Netherlands she needed to restrict the emotional space in order not to be engulfed by it (Reis 1998).

Reis' work on Swaziland and the Netherlands makes clear that the categorization by informants has ramifications for the ethnographic roles researchers play in the field as insiders or outsiders. In a special issue of *Fieldwork in Religion*, Adogame and Chitando (2005) discuss the methodologi-

cal challenges they faced in their research on the African religious diaspora in Europe and the USA. Since they are both Africans and Christians,
their attempt to establish themselves as outsiders was questioned by participants who saw them as (partial) insiders and asked them for advice and
support. In the same special issue, Yip (2005) reflects on his research on British Lesbian, Gay and Bisexual (LGB) Christians and Muslims. Like Adogame
and Chitano, he shows how the expectations of the research group often
served a political end and how the research group expected his research
to be a form of advocacy on their behalf. In both cases the issue of accurate and careful representation of the research group became an important
issue. No matter what kind of social role a researcher chooses, it will affect
data collection, the functioning in the field, and the possibilities of getting
access to respondents (cf. Hayden 2009). Researchers usually try to take up
and develop a social role which is recognizable by the researched and is not
too controversial (Johnson, Avenarius and Weatherford 2006). As Knibbe,
Van der Meulen and Versteeg show in Chapter Five, the participation of a
researcher may cause participants to reflect and (re-)interpret their own
practices. In our research those interpretations are strongly influenced by
the politicization (and its accompanying polarization) in Dutch society. In
a politicized context, however, controversy seems to be almost a matter of
fact and in some cases, as we will show below, focusing on and becoming
involved in moments of interaction among informants can become valuable
research input, because it directs our attention to how ordinary and taken
for granted routines, social order, and hierarchy can become contested and
challenged, sometimes resulting in changing the social order (Emerson
2009: 538, see also Knibbe, Van der Meulen, and Versteeg in this volume).
In fact as we propose, together with the other authors in this volume (see,
for example, the chapters by Versteeg and Roeland, and by Knibbe), the
qualitative approach is, given the researcher's capacity to "play," very well
suited to map and analyse internal disagreements and contestations. It
also addresses political sanctions and taboos, which limit and enable people's opportunities. These insights only come during a long stay in the field
(without disregarding the often proclaimed openness, inclusiveness and
tolerance, yet commonly serving as mere window-dressing). The roles we
take up as researchers will therefore be influenced by internal and external disputes. In this article, we concentrate on efforts to manipulate the
boundaries between insider and outsider in the ongoing interactions with
informants and the purposeful selection of particular roles.

THE RESEARCHER AS PARTNER

With the influx of Muslim immigrants, several relatively new practices have
entered Dutch society, such as female circumcision and particular marriage
arrangements (Bartels 2003; Storms and Bartels 2008). These practices change

through the migration process but have not disappeared. They receive new meanings and can become partly institutionalized in a new environment, which occurred for example with the establishment of mosques, burial arrangements, and ritual slaughtering. Practices considered more problematic by the Dutch public range from women wearing a *niqab* (the face veil), forced marriages, and consanguineous couples. One of the consequences of the politicization of migration, integration, and culture, is benchmarking integration by these practices. Cultural integration then means the abandonment of those practices that are considered to be at odds with Dutch identity and culture. One could argue that in times of the culturalization of citizenship (Mepschen, Duyvendak and Tonkens 2010) and the politicization of culture, religion, and identity, there is a need for anthropological knowledge that can shed light on exactly those issues related to cultural practices of migrants and natives.

As Versteeg and Roeland have already made clear in this volume, analysing disputes and contestations is a more outspoken role for the researcher. One avenue of pursuing such an approach is what Calhoun has dubbed "Real time social science" (Calhoun 2009), or engaging with issues that are part of the public debate at that particular moment and using an idiom that is contested in that same debate. This is also very demanding for researchers, however. Participating in research activities determined by the public debate and policy concerns, implies the risk of politicizing the research agenda and thereby compromising the "neutral" position of researchers. This, of course, is far from new. Already in the eighteenth and nineteenth centuries, anthropologists – sometimes in ethnographic roles as missionaries or civil servants – played a huge role in colonial projects. Sometimes their involvement was complicit, other times it was an unintended consequence. The current debates about Islam and integration in which culture is used by some political entrepreneurs to exclude people on the basis of perceived incompatible cultural differences with the Dutch, bring this issue back to the fore. At the same time, research that aligns itself with matters of interest in the public debate can play a role in deconstructing prevailing prejudices and distorted notions among both non-Muslims and Muslims. Given the confrontational style of the public debates, which has led to a strong "us versus them" division between Muslims and (non-Muslim) native Dutch, religion scholars are frequently asked to position themselves as "with us or against us" by Muslims and non-Muslims alike. Researchers should be careful not to reproduce this "us versus them" opposition, but this does not mean we cannot take up an engaged mode of anthropology.

As an anthropologist, Edien Bartels was asked by researchers from the genetics department of the medical faculty of her university to participate in a research project about consanguinity. Moroccan-Dutch and Turkish-Dutch migrants show a high number of consanguineous marriages, mostly cousin marriages. The risk for disabled children to be born from these marriages is on average two to three per cent higher than in non-consanguineous marriages (Bennett et al. 2002; Stoltenberg et al. 1997).[1] The medical faculty is developing tests to differentiate between high-risk and low-risk consanguineous couples. One of the relevant issues here is that the view of Turkish-Dutch and Moroccan-Dutch people on pre-conception testing is unknown. Prenatal testing has already been introduced but, for various reasons, is not yet fully accepted by most Moroccan-Dutch and Turkish-Dutch pregnant women.

During the start of the research on consanguinity among Moroccan-Dutch and Turkish-Dutch migrants in the Netherlands, an Amsterdam alderman started the discussion in a daily newspaper on the prohibition of consanguineous marriages. From that moment on, consanguinity was a political issue. Half a year later, the minister of integration announced his proposal to restrict migration in the case of consanguineous marriages, in order to prevent the birth of handicapped children. At that time, Edien Bartels wanted to start fieldwork among Muslim religious scholars and leaders to discuss the ethical aspects of pre-conception testing from an Islamic perspective. The problem was how she could approach these religious leaders with the request to interview them. How could she be accepted as a researcher on a religious ethical question in a sensitive, politicized field, and at the same time maintain an independent role as researcher?

The solution was found in a partnership with a Muslim organization working on integration from a Muslim perspective and specialized in discussing public questions in a Muslim context in the Netherlands. A partnership was set up to lead a discussion on consanguinity, without repeating the political arguments from the public debates, but starting from an ethical, medical and social perspective. This entailed working as a researcher affiliated with and on behalf of that Muslim organization, on the one side. On the other side, it meant providing the organization with research results necessary to start discussions on consanguinity and Islamic ethics of pre-conception testing.[2] The only condition of the organization was to receive a report written in a scientific rather than confrontational, political style. Though this was self-evident for the researcher, it showed the fear of the Muslim organization to be criticized even by researchers from the university. Because of her earlier scientific work, the executive committee of the organization trusted Edien Bartels as a "neutral" researcher. In the partnership, she could go beyond political questions and interests and attempt to de-politicize the subject of the research theme. The partnership became a way of crossing insider-outsider boundaries. The report was offered to the executive committee of the Muslim organization and the researchers of the genetic department of the medical faculty.

---

1. This is an average percentage; most consanguineous couples have a risk comparable to non-consanguineous couples, while few have an increased risk of 25% or more (Bennett et al. 2002; Stoltenberg et al. 1997).

2. There is of course more to the topic of pre-natal testing than only the issue of Islamic ethics. Whereas the concerns about handicapped children are understandable, they also raise questions about how people value human life, more in particular the life of handicapped people. This is however beyond the scope of our article.

The report included elaborate discussions with Muslim scholars (who had stayed aloof from the political debate) about medical possibilities and testing.

Drury and Stott (2001) discuss several examples of researchers trying to show sympathy and establish close alliances with particular factions in order to get the research started and to gather information that otherwise would not be accessible. In this project, Edien Bartels sided with a Muslim organization while at the same time trying to engage with a topic deemed important by politicians and opinion leaders. This worked well and all activities needed for the research were accepted and carried out without any objection. All Muslim leaders, imams and scholars who were approached gave the opportunity to discuss the subject. Interviewees felt free to discuss and express their doubts. Access to the research group and yielding of detailed and sensitive information could not have been realized without Edien Bartels taking up an active role as researcher-in-partnership. At the same time she maintained her position as an independent researcher, which guaranteed she had a wider range of resources for gathering reliable information than she would have had if the research were controlled by the Muslim organization. She did not so much remove the boundaries between her as a female, white, non-Muslim researcher and her two Dutch student assistants (one of them from Moroccan-Dutch origin), on the one hand, and the mostly male, Muslim-Dutch informants on the other hand, but tried to make the boundaries permeable by re-defining them in dialogue with the Islamic organization. Edien Bartels was very careful not to reproduce the opposition between Muslim and Dutch society, but instead engaged in a dialogical re-definition that came about by downplaying differences between groups, focusing on the joint cause of the welfare of children, and establishing an atmosphere of dialogue and cooperation.

THE RESEARCHER AS BELIEVER

As Edien Bartels' case shows, researchers have to balance between the need to take up socially relevant issues and the sensitivities that exist among informants. As explained earlier, some groups may try to use a researcher and the research for advocacy purposes, but in a politicized field one may encounter potential informants who are afraid of a negative image and harmful representation. Another way of taking up a role as a researcher is to emphasize the similarities in life-worlds, personal trajectories, and beliefs. Like all other social sciences, anthropology and sociology operate within a secular premise pertaining to empiricism, logic and rationality (Stewart 2001). Researchers can of course choose to hide their (lack of) religious ideas from their informants. But is this really necessary or truly helping the research? Very often the people we study are well aware of the secular or religious worldviews of the researcher, or at least they think they are. Using one's religious identity then can be a means to relate to the people we are studying and as such constitutes an attempt to shift insider-outsider boundaries. This brings up the issue of the role of the secular or religious identity of the researcher when trying to study people.

As a student, Daniëlle Koning did research among Moroccan-Dutch and Turkish-Dutch students in the Fall and Winter of 2004–2005, focusing on their religious beliefs and the impact of academic education thereon. She interviewed students of VU University in Amsterdam where she studied herself, discussing their views on the relation between religion and science, ontological issues (e.g. what is true: creation or evolution? do miracles and spirits exist?), epistemology (e.g. can we access absolute truth and an absolute understanding of Islam?), and methodology (e.g. is religion based on evidence and critical thought, or on faith and feeling?). She also did participant observation in Moroccan-Dutch and Turkish-Dutch student organizations, classroom discussions, and the female student mosque, and studied student essays and student society emails, flyers, online discussions, and reports (Koning 2005).

The context of this research was highly delicate. Daniëlle Koning's research was carried out at the height of the anti-Islam debate in the Netherlands after the murder of film director Theo van Gogh in November 2004. Furthermore, an incident at VU University made tensions rise. In December 2004, local and national media in the Netherlands were stirred by a group of Muslim students in the bio-medical sciences of VU University. They were said to have written their essay assignment for the course "Man and Evolution" by uncritically copying anti-evolutionist scripts from supposedly anti-Western Muslim authorities such as Harun Yahya. More generally, lecturers complained that Muslim students refused to even consider evolution theory. The debate that followed cannot be understood by solely looking at the national Islam debate. It was also related to the rapid secularization of Dutch society in the last 20 years, characterized by loosening the ties between religious institutions, other groups within civil society, and the state. Religiosity has not disappeared but it changed and adapted to the secular framework of society. As Asad (2003: 25) argues, the secular and the religious are not fixed categories. In secular societies, particular modes of reasoning and argumentation, behaviour, knowledge and sensibilities are seen as the embodiment of a universal reason with which religious people have to comply, while only modestly expressing their religiosity (cf. Asad 2006: 515). The discussion about the anti-evolutionist essays spiralled from a local concern about the scientific attitude (or lack thereof) of Muslim students to various national debates on Islam and integration, on evolution versus creationism and intelligent design, and the permissibility of mixing religion and science in a public academic institution (Koning 2006).

Though Daniëlle Koning studied at the same university, the move to conversations with Moroccan-Dutch and Turkish-Dutch fellow students was far from easy and even psychologically stressful. These students formed ethnic enclaves in the university and were hardly ever seen to be mingling with

Dutch students. Some told her later that the negative political climate had reinforced their retreat within these ethnic groups. In consequence, in many attempts to make contact, Daniëlle Koning was looked upon with suspicion and sometimes literally ignored. What is more, her outsider status made it difficult for her respondents to understand her position vis à vis the Islam debates. Her unexpected presence in these closed groups demanded an explication of her role, which quickly led her to explaining her research project by referring to Islam and Muslim identity. This Islamic element in her study even heightened the difficulty of accessing the field. Another researcher who did research among Turkish-Dutch students around the same time had significantly easier access, most likely because her study was not on Islam but on the students' views on academic careers.

In order to break down the fences brought up by her very presence and specific interest in Islam, Daniëlle Koning intuited that she could divert the political connotations of her research theme by linking the topic to her personal story. This diversion became a way of trying to negotiate insider-outsider boundaries. Since she was interested in the way in which these students viewed the relation between Islam and science, she brought up her own history with the topic. Raised as a Christian, she lost her trust in faith when she absorbed theories of religion in anthropology courses at VU University. She explained how she herself had known the dilemma between faith and science, and that now she wanted to understand how adherents of a religion other than Christianity viewed this same topic, in order to complement a Christian bias in the religion-science debate. She thereby introduced her research interests as personally and academically rather than politically motivated. Moreover, she in fact engaged in a shared discourse of "finding your own way" and "following your own personal path," well known to both her and her informants (see also the chapters in this volume by Versteeg and Roeland, and Van Harskamp). Instead of focusing on the often politicized perception of antagonistic differences between her Muslim informants and the researchers, she focused on the ethos of authenticity, personality and individuality. Daniëlle Koning experienced this diversion of the political connotations of her research topic as helpful in winning a certain level of trust and being able to conduct interviews that probed rather deeply into students' religious convictions. She noted, for example, that students' body language became more open and that they became more willing to express their views.

The rather defensive introductory talk that was necessary revealed how much effort Daniëlle Koning needed to invest to receive sufficient "insiderness" in order to have access to the field. Both a strong ethnic and a strong religious boundary had to be overcome by creating shared identities in different realms: that of being a religious student wrestling with academic theories, and that of being a well-trained student who recognizes that biases in any study are undesirable. In one case, a male Turkish-Dutch student who responded cynically to the presentation of her research theme and completely ignored her afterwards, became more open to converse with Daniëlle Koning after he burst out in laughter in response to a joke he overheard her make to another person. This joke evoked another shared identity that had been hidden until then: that of persons with humour. Rather than being another Islam critic, Daniëlle Koning was neutralized by the discovery of this common human trait. In addition, the specific act of sharing her faith journey did not just help by creating new forms of identification. Her adoption of a vulnerable, self-disclosing position was in itself a strong negation of the possibility that she was one of those many "Islam bashers" and produced trust among her respondents that her research results would be sensitive and honest. In the tense climate of the day, self-disclosure helped temporarily break through a spiral of mutually emergent offensives. Thus, in a politicized environment, students came to view Koning as somebody who was trustable, through alternative forms of identification and the reseacher's vulnerability, which led to a greater openness in the interaction between the researcher and researched.

THE RESEARCHER AS YOUTH WORKER

The third research project started in 1999, before the politicization of Islam, and ended half a year (July 2005) after the murder of Theo van Gogh by a Moroccan-Dutch Muslim extremist. In this project, Martijn de Koning explored and analysed the religious beliefs and identity of Moroccan-Dutch Muslim youth (De Koning 2008). He started working at a mosque in the small Dutch town of Gouda (near Rotterdam) as a researcher and simultaneously as a coordinator of youth work activities. These activities meant that he worked in the mosque and received young boys and girls (teenagers) who came there for homework support and for support with socio-emotional problems. All of them knew Martijn de Koning was "writing a book about them" but often the roles of researcher and youth worker mixed. The youth activities were carried out in the mosque by Moroccan-Dutch and native Dutch volunteers. De Koning's double role as researcher/youth worker provided the basis for establishing a relationship of trust between him and his research group. It provided him with access not only to the mosque but also in schools and at the youngsters' homes. It also means that as researchers we are not just witnesses of internal disputes and differing interpretations, as other contributors to this volume have already shown, but that we can become part of those disputes as well. Moreover, in a politicized environment, it is almost by definition that the researcher is perceived by his/her interlocutors as part of the ongoing debates and contestations.

It is important to bear in mind that the presence of non-Muslims in the mosque has always been a bone of contention and that it can be considered a symbolic issue of "struggle" (Gerritsen and De Vries 1994: 13). In a symbolic way, the presence of Martijn de Koning and a few native volunteers involved with the youth work project in the mosque, violated several norms and values that are considered to be important in the mosque in Gouda. For some critics it meant the presence of the negative approach many Moroccan-Dutch experienced in the broader society. For others (especially those working with the Moroccan-Dutch girls) it signalled an agreement with Dutch standards of freedom, which in the eyes of parents and children went too far. And again for others it meant that Dutch are *kafirs* (infidels) breaking the rules of ritual purity. Finally, since Islam had become a political issue, the presence of native Dutch brought politics into the mosque: something most Moroccan-Dutch did not want. Notwithstanding these objections, the youth work programme's principle, to work on the problems of children by including the parents, was appreciated by the majority of the visitors of the mosque. As a result, Martijn de Koning was able to maintain his position and was recognized as a partial insider. During his research he was, for example, nicknamed "Dutch Berber," which meant he was to a certain extent included on an ethnic level (but still excluded on a religious level).[3]

This way of inclusion by joking contrasted sharply with moments of exclusion during the fieldwork. The first of these moments was in December 2000 when there was a conflict between several frequent visitors and the board of the mosque. A meeting organized by Muslim youth and the board of the mosque disrupted the normal procedures in the mosque on Sundays and it was in particular the researcher (who was there with the permission of the board and at the request of the Muslim youth) who stood out. Instead of directly engaging with the board of the mosque, the visitors took offence because of his presence as an "infidel" among believers. During other previous meetings Martijn de Koning always stayed after the end to chat with the visitors of the mosque. After this particular meeting however, he was requested to leave immediately after the meeting's end, and so he did. Remarkably, there was no problem in returning to the mosque the next day. Most people agreed he was welcome and the complete board of the mosque supported him and apologized for the conflict and the sending away. The whole event was linked with internal affairs between regular visitors and the board of the mosque. The direct consequence of this event was that Martijn de Koning tried to establish stronger relations with other factions within the mosque community, including those who opposed the board of the mosque.

In 2002 an internal mosque conflict once again triggered the categorization of the researcher as an infidel. A new imam, Abdallah, was very popular among the Moroccan-Dutch youth in the mosque but was fiercely denounced by first generation visitors and the board of the mosque. The latter judged the imam as too strict and moreover ignorant of Dutch society. The case of imam Abdallah is exemplary for Moroccan-Dutch Muslims in several respects. First of all, the case shows the high level of involvement of Moroccan-Dutch youth with Islam. Although, like all other people, Moroccan-Dutch youth can identify themselves on the basis of numerous categories such as ethnicity, gender,

---

3. Most of the Moroccan migrants in the Netherlands ascribe themselves not as Arabs but as Amazigh or Berber.

age, lifestyle, and so on, since the second half of the 1990s they have increasingly identified themselves as Muslim, and are categorized as such by outsiders, despite the enormous variety among them in the way they practise their faith. Second, Moroccan-Dutch youth have since the end of the 1990s become more vocal about their quest to purify Islam of what they see as its "contamination." Notwithstanding the differences among Moroccan-Dutch youth, most of the young people in De Koning's research expressed the necessity to purify Islam from both Dutch and Moroccan culture. They attribute this "contamination" to Moroccan traditions and "bad integration" in the Netherlands, the latter especially pertaining to the failure in upholding Islamic rules in regard to gender relations. This purification trend does not only appear among Muslim youth but also among Evangelical and New Age youth (Roeland 2009) and is one of the examples of changing religiosity in a secular, individualized environment. Third, imam Abdallah, as part of one of the Salafi groups in the Netherlands, was trying to revitalize Islam in this mosque by propagating a return to the example of the Prophet Muhammad and the first generations of Muslims.[4]

The imam did not like Martijn de Koning's presence at his Qur'an lessons for children. At first he mentioned this to one of De Koning's Moroccan-Dutch colleagues. This colleague stated in response that it was not too late for Martijn de Koning to become Muslim. The imam did not agree because after several years of presence in the mosque Martijn de Koning "still did not realize what a wonderful religion Islam was." For the imam this implied that Martijn de Koning would probably never come to full understanding. After this consultation the imam went to Martijn de Koning himself and stated the same in more polite words. This led to anger among the board members of the mosque. As there was already a huge conflict between the imam and the board at that moment, Martijn de Koning decided to keep a low profile and not to interfere. The board accused the imam of telling things that were "not Islamic" and "not fitting for Muslims living in the Netherlands."[5] The conflict with the imam escalated in June 2002. Factions within particular groups are not stable and can shift during the research, making their positions difficult to anticipate and predict. These shifts take place in particular during moments of social change within the community and society at large (Cohen 2000: 320). Developments in the public debate about Dutch Islam (then heavily influenced by 9/11 and the election campaign with Fortuyn) played a prominent role in this. In June 2002 a television programme aired a short story about

4. The Salafi movement in the Netherlands (but also in the rest of Europe and the Middle East) became controversial after several violent events such as 9/11, the Casablanca bombings and the murder of Theo van Gogh, although certainly not all Salafi networks (including the one in Gouda) engage in violence (De Koning 2009).

5. Interestingly Martijn de Koning was able to publish about these internal conflicts without any interference of the board of the mosque. The board was very concerned about the publication of his PhD, given the strong reactions during the imam controversy, but it refrained from any attempt to censor it.

Salafi imams from other cities whose sermons were secretly taped. In these tapes they threatened the "enemies of Islam" and stated that the beating of women was allowed. The public controversy about these tapes was an important trigger for the board of the mosque in Gouda, since they were afraid of negative publicity, which already surrounded Salafi imams elsewhere. When the board openly declared to fire the imam, the conflict rose to huge proportions with death threats and people being (temporarily) expelled from the mosque. De Koning's response to this situation was to emphasize his presence as an objective, neutral outsider engaged with the societal position and future of the children. It was, however, exactly this self-identification that triggered the question: "Whose side are you on? The board's or the imam's?" His attempt to disengage was not accepted right away because his social role and identity became unclear. This only changed after he made sure he was seen in public with representatives of all factions within the mosque community, including the imam. Although this could have led to even more suspicion, the long-standing presence of Martijn de Koning and his prior reputation as an unbiased figure, meant that he could maintain his position in the field. He was then recognized as an outsider but without the derogatory connotations attached to labels such as "infidel."

DISCUSSION AND CONCLUSION

What makes these three research projects notable is the fact that during the projects, the public debates about Islam in the Netherlands flared up and Islam became a politicized issue. The field of interaction between researcher and researched is influenced by politicization, which means that the researcher has to reflect even more than usual on how to construct and perform one's role in the field. As we have shown in this chapter, the politicized environment yields paradoxical results in terms of the relation between the researcher and his/her interlocutors. In Knibbe's research (this volume), it is the issue of using gossip in research, breaking the trust that results from (and is expressed by) participating in gossip, that produces the paradoxical result of betraying trust whereas the fieldworker's intention is to do fieldwork that is as neutral as possible. In our three cases the tension between distance and proximity yields similar paradoxical results. The researchers' loyalty became important and the expression of it was asked, sometimes even forced, both by Muslims and non-Muslims. Notions such as identity, religion and culture are not only used by social scientists but also by the researched, the people who are the subject of social-scientific research. Moreover, these notions are central in the political debate. They are therefore by definition politicized, rendering a neutral position impossible. In fact, in all three cases it appeared that neutrality itself was subject to interpretation.

Our analysis here is the result of trial and error during the fieldwork, as there are no clear-cut solutions to the questions and challenges that come up during the research. We went from engagement to distance and from proximity to being categorized as the representation of a hostile outsider. Similarly the research sites changed in unexpected ways. Our focus here on intersubjectivity makes it clear that both the researchers' and the informants' identities are not static and given, but mutually emerging and developing, for example by downplaying differences between identities or by establishing a clear identity. Our ethnographic approach is particularly suitable for analysing such dynamics and to discover the meanings informants attach to labels such as Muslim identity and Islamic religiosity in a secular environment that is negative or even downright hostile towards Muslims and migrants.

In a politicized environment the researcher's capacity for play is tested, because it is not just two different worldviews coming together in the encounter but several – sometimes antagonistic – worldviews meet and/or are imposed upon the researcher. The perceived differences between the worldviews involved gain extra weight, because people often experience that their individual lifestyles and the integrity and safety of their own group are at stake. Different factions within one community use different categorizations for the researcher in order to include or exclude him/her from their factions which has important consequences for intersubjectivity. Daniëlle Koning in her research among Muslim students had to emphasize her "sameness" with regard to her respondents and Edien Bartels had to take up a partnership with a Muslim organization, both in order to make clear that they were not "islambashers" but open and honest in their approach. Martijn de Koning was categorized both as outsider and insider during his research, but the meaning of these labels varied with changes in the local community and society at large. Furthermore, the cases make clear that it is not sufficient to reflect upon the researcher as subject. A focus on the interaction between researcher and informants is necessary because the informants have the capacity to exercise power and exclude or include the researcher.

Reflection on the interaction between researcher and informants can serve as an extra means of validating research material and establishing its reliability (Davies 1999: 85–92). It seems to be quite normal for "native" (read non-Western) researchers to account for their "nativeness" in doing research among their "own" group, but not for non-native researchers to account for their "non-nativeness." The whole idea of "native" researchers is actually quite strange, because all anthropologists and all informants live out multiple identities (cf. Narayan 1993). Our emphasis on intersubjectivity reveals how changes in religiosity, identity, the religious and the secular are experienced and interpreted at both on an individual and on a group level. Sudden changes, for example after 9/11 and the murder of Theo van Gogh, influence local identifications and allegiances. In our case these changes produced a politicization of the field which in turn led to the construction of the researchers as "natives" by the informants. Reflection on the construction of nativeness in the interaction with informants is a means to adequately represent the researched and to analyse their role. As we have tried to show here, the politicization of the research field does complicate the way a researcher can engage in a particular type of play. To a certain extent it certainly limits the researcher's capacity to construct his/her own identity, and it frustrates attempts to reconcile what may be conflicting worldviews. Yet, reflecting about the relationship between researcher and research group can also serve as an additional means of gathering material. Therefore, the way people for example give meaning to concepts such as "*kafir*" in relation to the researcher gives us more insight in processes of signification among Muslims. This reflection also helps furthering the field of anthropology, since our methodological assumptions with regard to the relation between the researcher and the researched need to be adjusted to new and ever changing circumstances.

Part III

Moving Parameters

Introduction to Part III

ANDRÉ DROOGERS*

If scholars face the task to make sense of people making sense of their lives, then researcher and researched meet on common ground. Two worldviews encounter. Once the two sides are identified as worldviews, our perception of the methodological dynamics of the meeting between researcher and researched takes a new dimension. The usual contrast between science and religion becomes less important. Scholars and their subjects, who for a long time were considered to belong to mutually exclusive categories, can now come closer to each other. Common characteristics and interests can be uncovered from the deeper layers in which they were hidden. The implications of this new perspective can begin to be considered. The parameters start moving.

In the case of secular worldviews, inspired by scientific insights, for example regarding empirically obtained knowledge or the creation and evolution paradigms, the difference between science and worldview was always negligible, although, in a more subtle way, the relationship is not in principle one of identical views. In both science and secular worldviews presuppositions may play a role, and not always the same. Yet, secular worldviews obviously owe their current existence to the role of science in the modernization process of the last two centuries.

In any case, the distance between the scholar and her or his interviewees has been reduced. This means that intersubjectivity becomes important as a methodological attitude. Especially when qualitative methods are reappraised, the nature of the relationship between researcher and researched needs attention. Even when quantitative methods are preferred, it can be an issue.

In Chapter 10 André Droogers shows that when the study of religion is transformed into worldview studies, new challenges and opportunities present themselves. As soon as the distance we keep with regard to the adherents we study diminishes, and moreover our knowledge is found to emerge in our encounter with them, we will inevitably also take part in their worries, since

*   André Droogers is Emeritus Professor of Cultural Anthropology, especially the Anthropology of Religion and Symbolic Anthropology, at VU University, Amsterdam. He is co-editor of *"Studying Global Pentecostalism: Theories and Methods"* (University of California Press, 2010). A selection from the articles that he has written over the last 30 years was reprinted, together with an autobiographical Introduction, in *"Play and Power in Religion: Collected Essays"* (De Gruyter, 2012).

these are part and parcel of their worldview, whether religious or secular. This means that we will become more aware of the role that power mechanisms play in their worldviews. Besides, the negative effects of the modernization process will show. Again the playful approach may be helpful, not only in understanding the adherent's intimate motivation, but also because play can be understood as inherent in any worldview, since leaders and followers play with interpretations and possibilities. However, they do so within a setting in which power is a crucial factor, usually limiting the possibilities of playful meaning-making. Since power often is an element in the worldview, the example of religious and profane powers has become an organic part of the worldview's symbolic expression, preferentially containing power metaphors.

If worldviews are studied from this perspective, the researcher, identified as homo ludens, must weigh anchor off the safe academic harbour and dare to embark on an adventurous voyage. New coasts and landscapes can be discovered. The adventure is not without risk if the researcher, taking power and play as diagnostic instruments, decides to seek engagement, instead of keeping the usual distance. The role religions play in solving but also causing humanity's current problems regarding poverty, violence, pollution and conflicts, can no longer escape notice. The existential questions that lead to the creation of worldviews – what is beautiful, good, significant, true and authentic? – are closely connected to these problems. In taking the format of a research project in the study of worldviews, the consequences of a different methodological perspective can be made visible.

The phenomena we study have changed more rapidly than the discipline. We must catch up and overtake the arrears. With a new methodology for a newly defined field our profession must adopt a more engaged mission. The discipline needs to be reinvented.

In Chapter 11, the Epilogue of this volume, Anton van Harskamp points to this need for continuous reinvention of the discipline by reflecting on the idea that doing religion research is an activity in which the very own (social scientific) worldview is at stake. He first makes an inventory of the aspects that demand our attention when we start considering intersubjectivity. What does it mean that in our era secularization and sacralization are both present, in a paradoxical way? Can autonomy and heteronomy be combined successfully, without frustrating the late modern call for authenticity? Or is this the typical virtue of present worldviews?

Subsequently the question must be raised of how the researcher, with his or her academic worldview, can work effectively in such a paradoxical setting. If the sacred and the secular co-occur, the task to understand worldviews becomes even more challenging – and exciting. The simultaneous working of the secular and the sacred must have methodological consequences. We must bid farewell to the contrast between science and religion, between the secular and the sacred, by which we have been conditioned for as long as our trade exists. If people, through their worldview, seek to bring order to their reality, how shall the researcher understand that order correctly, while imposing his or her own view of order, using the scholarly methods of one's own academic worldview? Intersubjectivity, including an ample use of qualitative methods, will from now on be needed. Intimacy with religion is no longer a methodological sin, but detachment of religion can also be needed. As Droogers has made clear in this volume: in the study of worldviews religion has to be learned and...unlearned. The same is applicable, in a different way, to secular worldviews.

There may even be an ideological side to this, with Western secular culture tending to look at religious worldviews as backward. Especially when religions seem to oppose modernization, as happens in fundamentalist forms, the student of religion runs a real risk of contamination with this superior attitude. The hegemony of the modern worldview and ideology easily enters the worldview of our discipline. The celebration of the contrast between science and religion has contributed to this tendency.

Still, wanting to make up for this habitus of decades, it is not easy to find an effective alternative methodology. This is not a matter of either or, but much more of determining a position on a spectrum of possibilities, especially since in concrete situations the secular and the sacred are mixed up. The complementary side of contrasts must be explored. When the researcher's self and that of the worldview adherent meet, a complex set of dynamics takes over, in the end a dynamics in which both researchers and religious believers go beyond their very own worldview.

One possible new attitude in moving our parameters that Van Harskamp recommends is that of methodological ludism, as presented by Droogers in Chapter 4. In combining two perspectives, secular and sacred, scientific and religious, but also academic and ideological, to mention but a few of the binary oppositions at stake, the playful attitude may open possibilities that have remained hidden for as long as the contrast between perspectives have been emphasized.

Chapter 10

The Future of New Worldview Studies

ANDRÉ DROOGERS*

MAKING A START

Let us return briefly to the start of our book so as to be able to look to the future. In the first chapter of Part I, the terms and concepts highlighted throughout our discussion were introduced, including worldviews, religions, secular worldviews, ideologies and spiritualities. In defining these concepts, a particular way of looking at worldviews and their manifestations emerged. In fact, if we were to alter this perspective, the concepts and their definitions would also have to be adapted. I proposed that we should take the term "culture," by which I mean the human capacity for meaning-making, as the general framework for our analysis and worldview as a sub-category of it. Together with a constructivist perspective, this allowed us to see the dynamics at work in worldviews. As a consequence, we were able to give the notion of meaning-making a good deal of attention, not only in relation to the adherents of worldviews, but also in relation to those who study them. In studying worldviews we make sense of people making sense of their world and their lives.

We have also seen that over the course of the last two centuries the state of worldviews has undergone a sea change. A transforming world, with always new worldviews, demands new worldview studies. Our trade must adapt itself accordingly (Davie 2007, Droogers 2010). Modernization, by which we mean the application of science and technology in society, has generated a series of processes, both general and more specifically religious, each exerting a massive impact on the worldview situation, as evidenced by processes of colonialism, globalization, migration, individualization, de-institutionalization, secularization and syncretism. Scholarly interest in the study of religion emerged as one consequence of these processes, colonialism

* André Droogers is Emeritus Professor of Cultural Anthropology, especially the Anthropology of Religion and Symbolic Anthropology, at VU University, Amsterdam. He is co-editor of *"Studying Global Pentecostalism: Theories and Methods"* (University of California Press, 2010). A selection from the articles that he has written over the last 30 years was reprinted, together with an autobiographical Introduction, in *"Play and Power in Religion: Collected Essays"* (De Gruyter, 2012).

having provided an important impetus. In reaction to these processes, brand new worldview identities have emerged and old identities had to be adapted to new circumstances. The range and variety of worldviews has increased significantly.

In several regions of the world, power has taken a different form with migration and de-institutionalization, allowing more scope for individual meaning-making, including the formation of secular views. We suggested that in order to make room for secular worldviews, the concept of worldview should substitute religion as the main category in our field of study. Under the new circumstances the usual cultural dynamics of externalization, objectivation and internalization received extra impetus and went into overdrive. As Robert Bellah has argued, "We are now adapting so fast that we can hardly adapt to our own adaptations" (Bellah 2011: xxiii). Several once neat boundaries and categories are being perforated and eroded. In a rapidly and profoundly changing world, people are struggling to make sense of relentlessly altered meanings. For many people, modernization has been experienced as a hardship, not as progress. Rather than putting an end to the practice of religion as some scholars predicted it would, modernization has acted as a stimulus to religion, particularly in affliction-ridden contexts, but not only there.

To many people, the answers to the five existential questions mentioned in Chapter 2, about what is beautiful, good, significant, true and authentic respectively, have changed under the impact of modernization. This in turn led to a different construction of the seven dimensions discussed, including ritual, experiential, mythical, philosophical, moral, social, and material dimensions. In the instances where people refused to change, they may have attached much weight to a tradition that is dear to them. They may view modernization and its effects as a real threat to their worldview. Orthodox or fundamentalist beliefs were sometimes the result, beliefs that are at once seemingly traditional and very modern.

In Chapter 3, we learned that in view of this new situation, the family of qualitative methods needs urgently to be rehabilitated, while also recognizing the value of quantitative methods. Individualization does not put an end to the social dimension, even though it is less visible and takes new forms. The complementarity of the quantitative and qualitative approaches was investigated. Thus the role that qualitative methods may play in the empirical cycle was discussed. Moreover, qualitative methods were shown to serve a purpose beyond this particular role, simply because now, more than ever, important personal aspects of varied and fragmented worldviews cannot be expressed in numbers. Nuanced worldviews are expressed via language and narrative. We also saw that the appreciation of the two families of methods depends on what mission one attributes to science, and which philosophy of science one prefers, typically either neo-positivist or constructivist. These positions have cultural roots, and meaning-making among scholars takes different forms. Changing times with changed cultural constellations and new forms of behaviour make new demands. Though a (neo-)positivist tradition has been dominant for a long time and remains so, the advantages of a constructivist approach were emphasized, especially in studying new, less rule-driven worldview behaviours.

Chapter 4 highlighted the need, especially in the context of our time, to find a considered way of dealing with all the dualisms, contrasts and conflicts that dominate both the field we study and our trade. Qualitative and quantitative methods express these dichotomies differently. Each approach positions itself near one of the poles of a spectrum. In the constructivist mode, in qualitative work, acquired knowledge is the result of the interaction between researcher and researched, an interaction that the neo-positivist recipe prescribes. The role of the researcher is key and inter-subjectivity is viewed as a benefit. However, in quantitative methods, where objectivity prevails as a neo-positivist norm, any form of subjectivity is considered to be an undesirable variable and a risk to the production of reliable knowledge.

I proposed the use of methodological ludism as a way of dealing with these and other dichotomies. The playful attitude acknowledges the value of any position, since play demands seriousness, yet at the same time is aware of the relative, constructed nature of any position, thus creating a win-win situation. In this way the importance of dualist thinking is recognized, while at the same time rigid positions are avoided. Both polarity and similitude are appreciated.

The truth claims cherished by religious followers and scholars, were taken as a springboard from which my approach could be tested. Knibbe's experiences, in studying the healing sessions of medium Jomanda, highlight some methodological benefits and hazards, as described in Chapter 4. The capacity to deal simultaneously with two – or more – perspectives can be activated by worldview adherents as well as worldview scholars. Thus the merits of seemingly contrasting positions can be acknowledged and burning problems, whether of the discipline or the field, can be addressed. Homo ludens is rehabilitated.

In Part II, the reader was introduced to everyday research practice, illustrated via a number of case-studies on key themes: ritual, experience, language, morals and identity. Qualitative methods and the researchers' intersubjectivities proved to be indispensable. The authors showed how they dealt with dichotomies including the individual and the social, authenticity and conformity, distance and participation (all chapters), mind and body (Chapter 5) and social power and spiritual experience (Chapter 6). They also addressed religious and secular views, different disciplinary perspectives (Chapter 7), public and suppressed genres of speech, loyalty and betrayal (Chapter 8), researcher's identity and researched identity as well as inclusion and exclusion (Chapter 9). In each case the double perspective that honours both poles was sought. The pitfalls of unilateral choices were shown. The authors experienced and sought to deal with the new methodological challenges that the current worldview situation presents. Moreover, the reader was given the opportunity to become acquainted with the concrete forms that modern worldviews take in a range of contexts.

In the next chapter, Anton van Harskamp elaborates on the role of inter-subjectivity in qualitative research on religious and secular worldviews, a recurring theme in this volume. He explores what happens between meaning-makers in the space opened by fieldwork in the constructivist mode, and especially what happens when the impossibility of expressing the experience with the sacred is acknowledged. In his approach, the religious and the secular are not depicted as contrasting positions, but as being deeply connected.

What then, in light of this overview, is our methodological harvest? What are the consequences of our book for the study of contemporary religious and secular worldviews? If we live within a context of worldviews that needs qualitative methods and where problematic dichotomies need playful atten-tion, what type of methodology should we choose? How should the face of our trade be reshaped? How do we remake the tools of our discipline?

It seems to me that for too long we were obsessed with contrasts of various kinds, and especially the divide between science and religion. As scholars, we were taken hostage by a view of modernization that put the scientific world-view at the forefront of knowledge and which led us to accept science as "the most prestigious institution of the modern world" (Taylor 2007: 28). Concep-tual representation gained higher status than narrative or symbolic representa-tion, at the expense of insight. Since Descartes, "the vestiges of pre-conceptual thought" have been removed (Bellah 2011: 39). This is why the use of qualitative methods needs always to be justified, in contrast to quantitative methods, which do not. As academics, scholars of religion were tempted to accept, consciously or implicitly, this hierarchical science versus religion framework. This dichot-omy and others have certainly helped us to map our field, but they have also kept us from seeing resemblance and connectivity. To compensate for this long-term blinkered way of thinking, the similarities between approaches should be granted our full creative attention from now on. By helping to break down the dichotomous bias in the worldviews we study, this commitment should form the basis for the contribution our discipline could make towards solving some global world problems. In doing this, we may seek new answers to the questions of what is beautiful, good, significant, true and authentic. These new answers will reform the ritual, experiential, mythical, philosophical, moral, social, and material dimensions of our discipline.

Moreover, in reformulating our trade, we might well ask ourselves whether the acquisition of "pure" knowledge is really our main goal. This question, however, might remain secondary to the more urgent need to out-line and devise the fundamentals for engaged studies. The pure science of religion is not an area in which most graduates will find employment. The applied side of the discipline offers far greater opportunity and could market itself as such.

If we make the "cultural turn," adopting a constructivist perspective, we come closer to the people we study as our fellow meaning-makers, and to their concerns. Global issues touch them in their day-to-day life. Precisely because some problems have become global, they are also our problems. The applied side of our discipline could be given new impetus. The fact that religions play a double role in the current world situation, by both causing and solving problems, may serve as a reason to focus on applied studies.

Consequently, in view of the changes in the current global context, it seems to me that we should be ambitious, not just in selecting more appropriate and effective methods for the study of religious change, but by being more programmatic. We should do more than simply translate the instructions from the most recent textbooks on general methodology into our particular discipline. I suggest that we play with the challenges and potentials provided by our current situation.

Working from this perspective, I will try to explore some passable paths. First of all, I make an inventory of the themes that the late modern era puts on the agenda. Second, I discuss the ethics of our profession. I consider not just the question of how we behave towards the people we seek to understand, but ask more broadly what the mission of our discipline ought to be if we want to contribute to the solution of the problems of contemporary global society. Third, I argue that we should give careful attention to finding the best fit between approaches, theories and conceptual frameworks, since these direct our attention in specific ways. These general recommendations will then be fleshed out by walking through the stages of a research project. I will summarize the methodology needed and point to some likely consequences of this approach.

CURRENT THEMES

As described in Chapter 2, the last two centuries have brought an unprecedented transformation of worldview contexts. Subsequently, scholars of religion may experience difficulty deciding what to study first. There are too many ways to enter the field. Let us create an inventory of the possibilities.

Modernization has not caused religion to disappear, but it has certainly changed its manifestations. Non-secular worldviews have made it into the public sphere and have gained institutionalized status in some contexts. Different continents, regions and countries reacted differently to the impact of the various processes that came with modernization, thereby contributing to an increased variety of religious forms. In fact there are multiple modernities at work, each having a different impact. Accordingly, we should dispense with the dominant North Atlantic perspective of modernity, along with the assumption that what happens there is relevant elsewhere (Eisenstadt 2000, cf. Davie 2007: 106–109). Secularization in Europe differs from secularization in the USA or in Latin America, and so does sacralization. The re-emergence of religion in some countries and regions is a new topic of interest. World religions have changed, sometimes drastically, as in the case of Christianity, with its centre of gravity shifted to the Southern Hemisphere (Jenkins 2002). Christian missionaries from the global south now operate in the north. With increasing migration, and better access to transport and communications, including satellite TV, transnational networks have come to be added to traditional religious frameworks, uniting adherents across national borders.

Choices in worldviews are more diverse today than ever before. Individuals, to varying extents, are now "entrepreneurs of their own lives" (Elliott and Lemert 2006: 3). De-institutionalization, migration and the new media have contributed to this increased freedom for meaning-making. New religions have emerged, in a variety of contents and contexts, some remaining local, such as cargo cults or prophetic movements, others rising to global status, such as Pentecostalism. Syncretistic views, though often already part and parcel of world religions, are gaining momentum.

To a greater extent than in the past, religions and their adherents play a role in conflicts, sometimes obfuscating the political, economic or ethnic dimensions of a clash. Even during the colonial era, religion served as a vehicle for rekindling indigenous initiative, just as it became a means to enable grass roots participation in the expanding world. Religion continues to play a political role. Despite being too essentialist in his analysis, Samuel P. Huntington (1997) is right in suggesting that world religions will play a major role in conflicts of the twenty-first century, replacing the Cold War tensions of the second half of the twentieth century. Religion and terrorist violence have become relevant, especially in the wake of 9/11. The relationship between religion and evil is receiving attention. Fundamentalism as a concept was coined within the US Christian context and was later employed in the study of other world religions as well. Religion has recently also been studied as a source of inspiration for ecological action.

In summary, this book has shown that the worldviews that existed two centuries ago have been deeply changed by the dynamic processes unleashed by modernization. Currently there is a great need for new worldview research and innovative practices. On a large scale, worldviews have become significant in the life of nations and global society. Focused attention is urgently needed if the study of worldviews is to catch up with the metamorphosis that has taken place in the field.

THE ETHICS OF THE TRADE

The first association that one makes when thinking about "the ethics of the trade" may be in relation to the researcher's behaviour in dealing with respondents, data and reports. There is a growing awareness in the humanities regarding the demands that need to be made of the researcher. Rights and duties are narrowly prescribed. However, what I am demanding extends much further than this. As Bellah (2011: 42) has argued, "ethical reflection...unites conceptual thinking with forms more deeply embedded in human experience." My demand for increased engagement is inspired by a few key presuppositions stemming from the constructivist approach.

The characteristics of the constructivist approach were outlined in Chapter 2. One basic element of this approach is that knowledge is the result of the interaction between the researcher and the researched (Guba 1990: 24–27). As a consequence, the researcher, to a varying extent, is personally involved with respondents and their lives. Research may be undertaken in a distant and more or less objective manner, or in a more subjective and personally involved manner. Depending on the particular issue being studied, the fieldworker will, as a matter of course, touch on problems that the people being researched experience in their daily lives. It is possible that the fieldworker's religious, secular or ideological views play a role and form the basis of differences or similarities with the respondents. When fieldworkers are told about experiences of affliction and calamity, their response may either be matter-of-fact or more empathetic. The researchers will describe their own role in relating to their subject to the extent that it is relevant to their research.

I do not suggest that a constructivist attitude inevitably leads to more engaged interaction, or that a neo-positivist perspective would hinder the display of compassion. The question is much more about the degree to which researchers, of any conviction, may feel limited in their capacity to identify with the people being researched. What do perceptions of distance or proximity do to a researcher? It may even be that a fieldworker with constructivist leanings, in the interests of sheer self-preservation, must maintain a professional distance from the people he or she is studying. Of course historians of religions, for lack of living witnesses, would not readily concern themselves with such a problem, but may nevertheless find a way to manage distance and proximity.

Being aware of the subtleties of the distance-proximity spectrum, one may nevertheless wish to look beyond the specific setting of one's own research project, simply because the researchers' adventure may bring them into confrontation with the misadventures of the people they research. The practical implications must then be allowed a place within the scientific setting. It might even be that a fieldworker, by adopting an objective, independent stance and abstaining from opinion or action, might be interpreted by respondents as having taken sides against them within a complex field of power positions. A constructivist approach would consider the researcher's attitude to be a form of meaning-making, thereby making explicit what may remain implicit when objectivity is routinely presupposed.

Power relations provide an excellent theme when one wishes to uncover what is at stake in a specific context. If the exercise of power is able to redirect people's behaviour, or even make them act against their will, this is of great significance in worldview contexts, whether religious, secular or ideological. This exercise of power may result in respondents acting in solidarity, but it could also lead them to resort to violence, or the repression or exploitation of others. Adherents may be ready to sacrifice themselves for a good cause, but they may also resist the demands of the leadership and dream of a better solution. The whole process of meaning-making may be disciplined and controlled to a limitless extent. Yet, adherents often maintain their own discourses and practices, in secret if need be. The difference between official and popular religion is a symptom of the power constellation in religious worldviews. The production of religious meaning may result from a clergy's monopoly on power and yet their followers inevitably develop their own versions and experiences. In combating popular religion, the clergy may use the need for stability and order to justify the repression of free signification. This may happen in the context of secular worldviews and ideologies as well. Control and discipline could be limited to the internal conditions of a worldview, but they might also have repercussions for society as a whole, especially if a worldview serves as a blueprint for the organization of a society. Secular and worldview leaderships may coalesce or coincide.

In taking stock of power mechanisms, we must return to the notion of play. In considering alternatives to the existing order, followers play with possibilities. They look for forms of meaning-making that those in power experience as a threat to their position. Human beings show a paradoxical combination of capacities and needs, requiring a degree of order, but also having the means to consider alternatives and reflect on the need for change. It may be in the interests of an established leadership to ignore or forbid such exercises in alternative meaning-making. The desire to do so may even be used to justify the killing of people for a "good cause." Human history abounds with examples of murders and even genocides that were orchestrated by the proponents of particular worldviews. Since power retains power through controlling meaning-making, meaning-making can be used to legitimize the powers that be. Playful meaning-making in this context is literally marginalized, that is, it can only be enacted at the margins of society.

To this dim picture we must add that modernization has been instrumental in creating a number of seemingly unmanageable problems in the global world of the present. I see that there are four types of such problems in existence. The first is the problem of the inequitable distribution of wealth and the battle against poverty. The second relates to the control of violence, modern arms being unlike those of previous eras. Third, there is the ecological crisis. And finally there is the problem of how people of different origins and orientations can live together, having been thrown together without choice through colonial and global processes. These problems could be left to the specialists of the disciplines that already seek solutions to them. But students of worldviews occupy a special place within research contexts because worldviews are frequently implicated in causes or solutions. Moreover, worldviews contain a paradoxical combination of exclusive, non-negotiable strongly held convictions mixed with universal humane values and compassion. For these reasons, the researcher stands a good chance of being confronted with the problem of trying to unpack the role of worldviews in relation to one of the four problem areas just mentioned.

In the instance that a scholar wishes to address these issues, an appeal to any of the humane values that worldviews share may provide some scope (cf. Droogers 2010). Tentatively, and in line with the emphasis on meaning-making, a first criterion would be that the freedom of meaning-making should be guaranteed. A second criterion is that (the quality of) human life should not ever be sacrificed to ideals of a "higher," sometimes supernatural, sometimes secular, order. Again the power-play set may serve as a moral barometer, using these two criteria to check the room for safe meaning-making. Recently, efforts have been made to initiate a considered approach to the contemporary study of worldview changes (e.g. Borofsky 2011, Davie 2007, Rappaport 1999: 451–61, Stausberg 2009: 276, see also http://charter-forcompassion.org). However, a more systematic approach that would reconsider established views on the mission of the discipline is still required. Our toolkit should be adapted to new tasks. A considered methodology will help to overcome the objection that utopia will always drift away with the horizon. It may also draw into question the views of those scholars who argue that scholarly objectivity should exclude engagement. The urgency of finding solutions to the problems just mentioned demands a revised perspective on objectivity. It also necessitates taking steps in the direction of concerned action.

THE NEW STUDY OF WORLDVIEWS

If indeed scholars of religion are to mirror the current themes in their theoretical and conceptual frameworks, then what should that framework look like? Moreover, if they wish to take up the challenge of giving their work a more applied and engaged profile, what is needed to contribute to a solution to the problems listed above?

Scholars of worldviews, who so far have focused mainly on religions, have either shown an interest in a particular (world) religion, sometimes with an emphasis on its history, or have adopted a comparative perspective. In all cases, existing religions, especially world religions, were the starting point for this division of labour. Across the different disciplines, such as religious studies and the phenomenology, history, sociology, psychology and anthropology of religion, different choices have been made, but usually within an early modern framework.

To understand the present state of late modern worldviews, a meaning-making perspective is needed. It will allow room for syncretism, new religions and secular worldviews, and addresses issues related to the four current problem areas. Admittedly, and fortunately, these phenomena receive attention already, but this has not altered the general early modern perspective from which we look at worldviews. Just as cultural anthropology has moved from the study of more or less autonomous cultures to culture as the human capacity for meaning-making, the study of worldviews will make headway via an emphasis on meaning-making processes. This will also liberate the trade from its current North Atlantic perspective and will end the explicit or implicit dominance of the Christian religion as a general model for comparative and monographic work. Essentialist pitfalls can be avoided. Accordingly, the phenomenology of worldviews can rethink the categories employed so far in the phenomenology of religion, doing away with the current Christian bias. Work that is done on specific religions need not be abandoned, but can gain depth by locating that particular religion within the global worldview context of which it has become an integral part.

The addition of secular worldviews to our field will legitimize a move to the meaning-making perspective. The similarities between religious and secular worldviews may be explored, instead of focusing exclusively on contrasts, as inspired by the disenchanted scientific worldview. This will have consequences for the significance given to the religion-science dichotomy, and may reveal some unexpected similarities.

The central question is how both worldview adherents and scholars will use their meaning-making competence to find their way through this continuously changing world, answering the five questions mentioned in Chapter 2. As suggested previously, dualisms and dichotomies tend to structure the worldviews and the disciplines that study them. Some of these play a role in both the field and in academia. This happens not only because scholars of worldviews, for reasons based on descriptive simplicity, adopt categories that are basic to the field, but also because scholars tend to think in terms of binary opposites. Moreover, scholars are prone to focusing unilaterally on official views, thereby reiterating the perspective of the day. As I suggested previously, when Christian theologians were first converted to the study of religion, official Christianity served implicitly as a model for exploring other world religions and writing theological treatises and textbooks, and in creating copies of theological sub-disciplines.

Among both adherents and scholars, the following dual sets play a role: subject and object, individual and social, doctrine and behaviour, belief and ritual, and knowledge and experience. Their list of binary oppositions might also include oral tradition and holy scriptures, institution and movement, institutional control and freedom of reflection, orthodoxy and heterodoxy, and truth and heresy. It may be further extended to include pro and contra, religion and magic, centre and margin, official and popular, participation and distance, and religious and secular. So far in both the worldviews themselves and in the discipline that studies them, these options may lead to a balanced view on the relevance of both extremes or on synthesis, but more often a choice is made that privileges one side of a binary pair. Adherents as well as scholars will differ in their way of using these sets and in how they give meaning to them.

Alongside the sets that occur in both, there are specific pairs. The scholarly sets of the neo-positivist and constructivist positions, of quantitative and qualitative methods, of participation and observation are examples of this, although even here the worldview sets of orthodoxy and heterodoxy, true and false, pro and contra, may serve at least as a metaphor and sometimes as something more. On the other hand, among the followers of a religion, the dual sets often represent existential bodily experiences, such as being lost or saved. Scholars are more cerebral in dealing with their dichotomies.

If dichotomies are abundantly present, a protocol for their responsible management must be devised. Worldview scholars can act as advisors to worldview leaderships and in dialogue conferences between worldview representatives. Incidentally, if our task were to focus on policy matters, we could more easily fund what we do by reappraising of the mission of our discipline. If Huntington's prediction on the clash of civilizations (Huntington 1997) is even partly correct, worldview students could very well assert themselves as experts in the matter.

The two criteria proposed in the previous section, those guaranteeing the inalienable freedom of meaning-making and safeguarding the quality of human life, can be of help. The dichotomies that form the basis of a worldview's role in causing any of the four global problems mentioned earlier must be studied in order to devise better policy. An appeal to the humane core values of a worldview, especially when related to the two criteria just mentioned, can bring about a breakthrough. This is not an easy task. There is a diabolical dilemma contained within the human condition, between the need for a workable social order and for freedom of meaning-making. This is a double-bind. Like all animals we are part of the herd, and yet we cannot help but behave as individual self-reflective animals, acting both with and against each other, and even ourselves. We have difficulty in managing the disparity between our social and cultural outfits. Modernization and all its consequences have hammered this message home on an unprecedented scale. This has repercussions for the object-subject dichotomy. Both the adherents and the scholars of worldviews interpret the modern human condition and seek to make sense of it. The two criteria should form part of this interpretation.

The power-play barometer may serve to explain when and where, as a consequence of a unilateral emphasis on one pole in a dichotomy, the two criteria are not being respected. To understand these occurrences, theoretical paradigms that accommodate conflict must complement the frequently used functionalist harmony models. There is a surprising similarity of interests between functionalist thinking on the one hand, taking equilibrium as the normal human condition, and the leadership's need to maintain order and control on the other. A particular emphasis on order in society has taken precedence. The dynamics of aberration and strife could however also be taken as a starting point, in which case order would be more the exception than the rule.

This perspective may, for example, stimulate interest in the friction that emerges between official and popular versions of worldviews. Inter-worldview strife can also be studied from such a perspective, with inter-worldview dialogue serving as a counterpoint. Marginal worldview situations represent promising fields of study, since it is in this context that change happens, outside the power centre, with innovations that at least at the outset obey the two criteria just mentioned. These reform movements often seek to restore what their supporters view as the original order. Once they wish to return to that stage, the power centre will seek to repress their efforts, since the reform movement is viewed as a threat to the institutional framework that has been erected in the meantime. Subsequently it is important to study what institutionalization and routinization do to such worldview reform movements, since their success often brings them to the very place that was severely criticized when they began, until the cycle makes a fresh start.

In managing the dichotomies that divide the discipline as well as its object, the field of worldviews is understood as not only including worldview adherents, but also those who study them. In fact the latter are often the inventors of the field. Adherents typically stick to their preferred worldview and contrast it with other worldviews. Once aware of the role of dichotomies, all stakeholders can develop a position that may better serve both researchers and the researched, as fellow-meaning-makers. In Chapter 4, a strategy was proposed, starting from the gift for play that all human beings, whether adherents or scholars, share. Very often, depending on the two criteria, it will become clear that a preference for one of the poles need not rule out an appreciation of the other end of a spectrum. In this manner paradoxes can be rehabilitated and put to good use. The ludist perspective lends itself to an applied design in the study of worldviews (Droogers 2010).

WORLDVIEW METHODOLOGY

And then how do I move from the general and abstract recommendations contained within this chapter to a more concrete methodology? Taking the chronology of a project as a framework, what should the research process be?

A theme is chosen, preferably as part of a larger programme, with many researchers and supervisors involved. Cooperation between different departments and universities from several countries is advisable, for the purposes of both mutual inspiration and comparison. The theme that is selected will reflect one of the four global problem areas with which religions are involved. A research proposal is then developed, to be used to obtain academic approval and funding. Funding sources must be explored, including Non-Government Organizations (NGOs) and government agencies, as well as supra-national bodies such as the European Union. Funding agencies could take the lead by preferring to fund applied applications. A theoretical and conceptual framework must be chosen that corresponds with the topic, while simultaneously remaining open to allowing for alteration in light of new findings as they arise, thereby combining deduction and induction. In meeting consistently rigorous standards, a theoretical framework for applied studies will evolve (cf. Trotter and Schensul 1998: 697–700).

The approaches as well as the research teams selected for the applied and engaged study of worldviews must be multidisciplinary and preferably interdisciplinary. The complexity of the phenomena to be studied as well as the urgency of the problems that worldviews are involved with, are more than a single discipline can manage. The whole range of themes, theories, concepts, methods and practices must then be mobilized. Ergo the worldview methodology must be eclectic and hybrid, using the full potential of and honouring, within the parameters of the two criteria, both poles in the many dichotomies that play a role in worldviews and disciplines. The playful ludist attitude is almost by definition eclectic and hybrid. Policymakers from the government agencies or NGO's that subsidize the project must be involved. In addition, the people studied must be included in some way in the design and process of the research, depending on the topic and the circumstances.

This new study of worldviews has consequences for the way future studies of worldviews are set up, influencing the courses that are on offer in universities, the ways scholars interact in journals, associations and conferences, and the ways they fund their work. More interdisciplinary initiatives must be taken. Although vested interests may seek to slow the rapid pace of change, in the long run we will all have to adapt to the brisk changes taking place in the worldview field. To do otherwise would mean to estrange scholars from their object and limit them to conducting historical analysis. All this must in the end influence the training of future researchers.

To prepare for the actual fieldwork, and before finishing the text of the research proposal, a short period for exploration is needed. A preliminary knowledge of the theme and the available literature is required before a proposal can be written. It may be necessary to raise a small sum of money to make the pilot period possible. Funding agencies could take initiatives in this regard, and some are already doing so, thereby steering research policies.

In preparing for the fieldwork, team meetings can be held, for example on a weekly basis. Working in teams, peer learning is as important as supervision by seniors. It is important to formulate an appropriate research question, as this will lead to choices with regard to location and methods. That question must reflect the available knowledge and theories, but also highlight the missing data.

It is also important to make a good choice in relation to the methods that will be used. In the research proposal these decisions must be adequately justified. The research team will have to decide whether to use a combination of qualitative and quantitative methods or just one of the two families. Projects can complement each other. Policymakers, if involved, may insist on using surveys and quantification in order to legitimate the translation of the research into policy and law. As far as this choice is concerned, the different aspects mentioned in Chapter 3 may serve as a checklist. The emerging methodology, drawing from a wealth of possibilities, has the benefit of being tailormade, demanding creativity in its application. The focus on meaning-making and its dynamics will demand a different research design. Comparative studies that focus on the comparison of processes of meaning-making more than on that of particular worldviews or specific categories, will challenge scholars to reform the phenomenological methodology. Depending on the theme to be studied and the questions raised, choices can be made that go beyond the old disciplinary exclusivity. The engaged applied scope will inspire a creative search for new methods. A normative approach will find ways to implement the two criteria which seek to ensure freedom of meaning-making and of the quality of human life. Accordingly, methods can be chosen or developed to play a unique role in studying a particular theme, just as they can be combined in ever new ways.

This approach will result in more direct contact between the researcher and the people that are being studied. Since knowledge is the result of the meeting between the researcher and the researched, the role of worldview adherents in research must be explored and exploited. This may lead to new methods. New forms of participation, as Knibbe tested in her research on the healer Jomanda, can also be explored. This may include action research (Huizer and Mannheim 1979, Trotter and Schensul 1998), in which the research serves to improve the position of the people being studied. Lay experts may take part in the actual fieldwork and, if possible, in the research design. The closer participation of fieldworkers will also bring new problems. Efforts may be made to convert the researcher to the religion studied. Personal involvement may also go beyond the interests of the research project, influencing the researcher's private life. Careful training of fieldworkers must prepare them for these eventualities.

Once the fieldwork has been completed, typically at the point when no new information seems to emerge, the research report can be written, as an article, memorandum, book or thesis. The application of the research will lead to a different type of reporting. While obeying academic conventions, the respondents must be served as well as the academic audience. Dissemination of research outcomes could be via popular reports, documentaries or theatre presentations. Provisional outcomes could be discussed with respondents, especially those already collaborating with the project. The public presentation of results may form part of this type of research. Compassion can be included among the researcher's virtues. Subjectivities can be made explicit and valued for their role in contributing to the understanding of what motivates the adherents of worldviews.

Though tentative, this overview outlines a blueprint for an applied and engaged research project that characterizes the study of worldviews in a new way. Besides going beyond the "pure" research that is typical of much work in the study of religion, new research that in itself seeks out socially useful results may prove to bring much more satisfaction to the individual researcher and his or her team, as well as greater empowerment to respondents.

CONCLUSION

There is a lag between current methodology in the study of religion and the changing worldview situation. Changes in wordviews have outpaced the organization of our discipline. The field must be expanded to include secular worldviews and ideologies, and also the global context with its four fundamental problems. Rethinking our discipline is a challenge that should be undertaken on a much wider scale than has been possible here. Just as worldviews are being constantly reinvigorated, the disciplines that are used to study them need to be rethought and retooled from time to time. Catching up with the changes of the last two centuries will keep the members of our trade busy for a good part of the twenty-first century. Extrapolating from recent developments, one gets the impression that the already urgent need to make the trade more applied in nature will only become more compelling over time. Joint forces will be needed. Courage and creativity will be required to reinvent our discipline from the various branches that now exist. The result will make us better scholars and the global world will become more habitable as a direct result of our efforts.

Chapter 11

Epilogue: Studying Religion as our Intimate Stranger

ANTON VAN HARSKAMP*

THE INSIGHTS

Three foundational insights are highlighted in this volume.

In the first place there is the insight that human beings are essentially meaning-makers. We are beings who by acting, thinking, feeling, experiencing, in short by "living," try at any time and in any place to give meaning, that is order, to the world. We give meaning by worldviews. Worldviews are culturally produced and individually internalized networks of culturally constructed significations of the world, out of which, or better, *in which* we live our lives. These worldviews are basically descriptive and normative symbolic representative significations of our world. Worldviews may be considered to be images *of* and ideals and norms *for* the world, while these images, ideals and norms are simultaneously the culturally shaped, mental apparatuses for our being *in* the world.

In the second place there is the insight that there are many distinct cultural systems in which we may live, and in which we can try to give meaning to the world: ideologies, politics, works of art, technologies, economic activities, science, and so on...and, not to forget: religion! Religion/s is/are one specific form of worldview construction. It is a form of worldview construction in which an ultimate Gestalt of reality, the real Reality, that is the Sacred, is imagined to play a decisive role.

In the third place there is the insight, that when we study religion with qualitative methods, and when we try to think and even feel ourselves into the inner life of religion, into the signifying, worldview making capacity of the religious "other" (cf. in this volume the contributions of Knibbe; Knibbe,

* Anton van Harskamp is a philosopher of religion, and Emeritus Professor of "Religion, Identity and Civil Society" at VU University, Amsterdam. He is co-editor of *"Playful Religion: Challenges for the Study of Religion"* (Oberon, 2006) and author of books on new religions and civil society. He is the co-editor of volumes on conflicts in social science, on individualism and on moral philosophy. His main research interest is the social theory of the impact of new religions on civil society.

Van der Meulen and Versteeg) – so when we position ourselves on the continuum between distance/detachment and closeness/participation closer
to Geertz's famous "village preacher" than to his "village atheist" (Geertz
1973: 123) – then we enter a "space of encounter" with religion (Keane 2003).
It is a space in which an encounter takes place between the worldview(s)
of the researchers and the worldview(s) of the researched believers. It is a
space which renders researching religion an intersubjective enterprise. It is
an enterprise in which not only the researcher will be interdependent with
the researched believer – Droogers in this volume even suggests that the
researcher can be a temporary "stakeholder" in the researched religion –
but in which the researched religious "objects" are also subjects that can be
triggered to deepen or to change their very own religious worldviews (cf. de
Koning, Bartels and Koning in this volume). For real intersubjectivity always
implies reciprocal cognition and recognition of both the researching "self"
and the researched religious "other" (Hayden 2009).

Here we propose to stand still a moment at the methodological consequences of the insight that doing qualitative research in the field of religion is
to enter a space in which two distinct worldviews not merely encounter each
other, but potentially may influence each other. The question is: what kind of
methodological attitude is required, when we accept that qualitative religion
research is a form of intersubjectivity?

THE FIELD

In order to be able to think further about the researcher's attitude in religion
research, let us first try to give a general impression, an anticipative construction, of the kind of field on which we wish to apply our methods: what kind of
general orientations are present on the field of contemporary religion?

Elsewhere in this volume André Droogers referred to both the processes
of secularization and sacralization. These processes are of crucial importance
for our view on the status of "modern," contemporary religion. One may
think today that "God is Back" and that the secularization thesis is not valid
anymore, the thesis which once "foretold" the social and cultural decline
of religion and the expansion of "the secular" in society (Micklethwait and
Wooldridge 2009). However, while the theoretical secularization thesis may
not be valid, it is nevertheless clear that we live in an age in which some forms
of real *Verweltlichung*, of "the coming of worldly matters" (= secularization),
have had their effects. For we definitely live in what Charles Taylor calls a
Secular Age (Taylor 2007). That is, an age in which our life world is not struc-
turally religious anymore: we live not anymore as a matter of course in a religious universe. The implications of secularization are that religiosity seems to
be primarily an issue of human choice and endeavour and that religion seems
to be a purely "worldly" symbolic practice. So our age is still coloured by secularization, by processes like rationalization, individualization, globalization

and so on, while we also may observe a growing significance of (transformed, secularized) forms of religiosity and modern religion. So there is a paradoxical concurrence of secularization and of sacralization, and of the effects both these processes have: "the secular" and "the sacred" (Willaime 2006, cf. Kearney 2010).

Now anthropologist Talal Asad once observed in his *Formations of the Secular* (Asad 2003) that "the secular" and "the sacred," effects of the cultural movements towards secularization and sacralization, cannot be considered to be completely separated societal and cultural domains of life. The secular and the sacred are "moving things," continuously changing "things" which mutually influence, even penetrate each other. These "moving things," being cultural undercurrents towards "the secular" and towards "the sacred," are also working in what we call religion. So, even that domain of life that we call "religious," is shaped by "secular" forces – and, it goes without saying, by "sacred" forces. This observation of Asad can bring us to the assumption that in many "modern" religions in the West, not only in, for instance, "classical" new religions, such as New-Age spiritualities, but also in renewed and reshaped "old" religions like protestant evangelicalism or western Islam, "secular" as well as "sacred" orientations are at work.

This assumption can be established if we take a bird's eye look at the work of the authors of this volume on "modern" religion. It then becomes possible to assume that in many contemporary religions two broad, distinct, but yet simultaneously acting orientations are actively present: a "secular" orientation towards human autonomy, in so-called new religions a strong accent on the authenticity of the self (Heelas 1996; Houtman and Aupers 2012) on the one hand, and a "classical" religious orientation towards heteronomy on the other. So, we may suppose that on the field of contemporary religion a desire for "worldly" self-determination is active, *as well as* a desire towards bonding, bonding with a determining Other, embodied in a spiritual tradition, a holy book or an (imagined) religious community.

American sociologist of religion Wade Clark Roof once pointed at this inherently paradoxical pattern of a double orientation in "modern" forms of religion. He made use of Robert Jay Lifton's views on the predicaments of the modern, multifaceted and "protean" self (Roof 1999: 9, 132). He argued that the subject in "modern" religion wishes to be fluid, not to be pinned down to one identity, he/she wishes to be free to be his/her own authority, master in his/her own life – modern "subjects" are "entrepreneurs of their own lives" (Elliott and Lemert 2006: 3) – while at the same time the modern subject craves after being grounded in a framework, a tradition, a "Scripture," a community, in something that transcends his/her autonomy. Another American sociologist writes that this double constellation in modern religion, this orientation on being a fluid (secular) "entrepreneur" of his own life and the orientation on being grounded in a religious "something" that transcends the secular master, is very difficult to explain (Hoover 2006: 148). And yet, these two orientations may be observed in distinct expressions of contemporary religion. For neo-evangelicals, Pentecostals, western Muslims, neo-pagans, spiritual artists, liberal Catholics, even orthodox believers and fundamentalist religionists, all seem to be, each in their own way, affected by secularizing and sacralizing cultural forces. For all are using their religion in this "age of authenticity" in order to become an autonomous human being and at the same time a being that is grounded in another reality, a reality that transcends the autonomous individual human being.

STARTING RELIGION RESEARCH

What should happen then, when we, students of religion, enter that field of religion, when we *encounter* religious practitioners, when "events of intersubjectivity" are possibly going to occur? What kind of disposition is required if we really wish to meet religion intersubjectively?

Let us begin by realizing that when we enter that field, we may encounter a religious life-world in which claims are presented that real life, "real Reality," will be actively present. Religious practitioners can claim that fullness, totality, healing, wholeness, in short, all those experiences which form a touchstone for evaluating the quality of our life, are grounded in a "non-worldly," sacred reality. This sacred reality may be for us "another" imagined reality, but is for religious people the "really Real." It is a reality that often is only to be touched upon in a momentary experience, but which nevertheless can be considered to be more "real" than "normal," "worldly" reality. Anthropologist Mattijs van de Port recently dealt with that "really Real," in his study of Bahian Candomblé. He suggests that we, students of religion, can get intuitions of the "really Real" when we meet "religion" (Van de Port 2011). Let us follow his arguments for a while.

We have to realize at first that most students of religion are inevitably entrapped in a constructivist (or constructionist) epistemology. We are after all no epistemological realists anymore. We cannot consider social-cultural reality, say religion, to be a reality which expresses itself directly in our cognitive articulations. And for the constructivists who we are, there can be in the last resort no real "givens," no foundation, no absolute truth (cf. Jensen 2011: 42), simply because we know that the things we know, and the things other people know, are always and ever tainted by the cover of our meanings and our significations which we continuously put upon reality. And we presuppose that not only we, researchers of religion, are continuously covering the world with symbolizations, but we approach even religions and ideologies as being essentially human ways of making symbolized worldviews. So we approach religions as being ways of covering up a supposedly chaotic, in itself nonsensical, reality with human symbolizations. We may, however, also realize, that thinking about the inevitable human ways of meaning-making by worldview constructions, eventually brings us to the question: but do we really know reality, are we really in touch with the "real Reality" by means of our worldviews and cognitive articulations? Are our worldviews after all nothing more than a cover on reality?

Van de Port suggests that specifically in religion, the "real Reality" is sometimes to be met and that in religion the "ordinary" meaning-making processes can be broken. We can sometimes encounter the beyond of all meaning-making symbolization in the excesses of religious experiences, in the always bodily "mediated," mystic or ecstatic or plainly spiritual experiences of being there, that is, of being elsewhere, at "the sacred," which is a beyond, while simultaneously being here in this world, in "real Reality." And in this context Van de Port can write, that when the student of religion meets this, in itself "meaningless" and non-apprehensible centre of religious experience, he/she may meet the reality of the absence of our human truth, the reality of our not-knowing. For the "really Real" is according to Van de Port a dimension of being that is exterior to all symbolization, exterior to our very own social-scientific form of meaning/worldview-making (Van de Port 2011: 19–35). So he can bring forward that

> ...the structures of meaning that allow us to come to terms with the world do violence to the experience of being; that sense-making goes only that far; that "symbolic closure" – the total capture of experience in a structure of meaning – is an impossibility; that the symbolic constructions we have at our disposal are lacking; that at the bottom of all meaning lies a residue of nonsense (Van de Port 2011: 256).

These views have consequences for the way we are going to study religion. Van de Port concludes for the methodologically "qualitative" study of religion, which basically is the study of human meaning-making, that "the study of human sense-making, has much to gain by taking the failure of the symbolic order as a starting point for analysis" (Van de Port 2011: 259). So, when we follow the suggestion of Van de Port, and when we as students of religion enter the religious life-world, we should *start* with realizing, that our view on religion as being a (human) way of constructing a meaningful worldview will not work, because the sacred goes beyond the reality we can apprehend with our covers of symbolizations?

Now, let us look for a somewhat more nuanced advice for religion research, and let us be careful with "starting" by considering the failure of our "symbolizing" approach to religion. We've mentioned that religion is a field on which not only "the sacred" can be met, but also "the secular." Religion actually always is a dynamic mixture of "the secular" and "the sacred." And in religion there is not only sheer experience of the sacred. Actual religions are not only carriers of the sacred, but also "this-worldly" institutions, human practices, ideologies, so "secular" carriers for worldviews. Which means that we could better "start" with considering religion as being a field which asks us to explain it as a "normal," human way of worldview-making, but, however...let us after starting to study religion as a worldview, also infuse our study with the intuition, that when we come close to the believers' embodied experiences of the sacred, it will be very hard to understand "it" in terms of "symbols" (verbalized significations). For our language, our means of understanding, are simply not adequate to grasp the sacred "real Reality." So when we study religion and enter that field, let us, to begin with, assume that religion is in the first place a human way of worldview construction, of "giving" reality a cover of human meanings, but let us also be aware of the inadequacy of our very own intellectual ways of meaning-giving to the experiences of the sacred.

FINDING OUR INTIMATE STRANGER?

And when we, students of religion, are going to participate in religion, when we try to perform an "epistemology of intimacy" (Keane 2003), may we then really meet the mystery of religious experience, the "really Real"?

We think that although we should try to come close to an understanding of the worldview-making capacities of the religious "other," we should not reach for complete identification with experiences with "the sacred." "The sacred" may come close, may be recognized as a "mystery," but has also – also! – to remain strange for the researcher. Let us consider a few more thoughts about the undesirability of seeking for identification with religion.

As we may know, not very long ago, it was a criticism to say that an ethnographer/anthropologist had become intimate with the strange world of religion. Especially "going native" was considered to be "going wrong." In recent years however, in our postmodern era, philosophers and other students of religion, like anthropologists, began to think that researching religion could be considered to be a form of Western hegemonic "scientific" thinking: from a "scientific" distance religion was thought to be objectified and devalued as a "primitive" performance. And an increasing number of students of religion, in particular anthropologists, having taken on board the postmodern critique of naive epistemological "realism," empiricism and objectivity, advocate rather than criticize the breaking down of the traditional barriers that separate the detached, objectifying, observing "self" of the researcher, and the engaged, subjectivist, observed religious "other" (Robben and Sluka 2012: 21). We may think of Katherine Ewing who argued in a "classical" article ("Dreams from a Saint: Anthropological Atheism and the Temptation to Believe," 1994) that the epistemological gulf between the researcher and the subject of study was more or less created by anthropologists themselves, anthropologists who were not able to take the believer's practices seriously (Ewing 1994). And we may think of anthropologist Charles Lindholm, who once pointed out a possibility for bridging the epistemological gulf between the researcher's "self" and the belief-performing "other," by suggesting that anthropologists should remember that the religion researcher is a seeker, who just like religious people, is seeking for groundings. Lindholm actually suggested that we, religion researchers, can create an adequate disposition for our religion research by realizing that we are just like religious people "seekers and purveyors of the relics of lost divinity" (Lindholm 2002: 336–37). Other "postmodern" ethnographers of religious phenomena did report on having religious experiences during their research and about their existential entries into the field of religion – for instance Susan Harding (2000) and Thomas J. Csordas (2012) in their research into fundamentalist and Pentecostal groups. And the aforementioned Dutch anthropologist Van de Port tells us of the seduction he felt, to immerse himself in religious practices, while doing research on Candomblé: a seduction to "go native" all along (Van de Port 2011: 37–67). But although he tried to become close to religion, he actually did not immerse himself completely into the world of Candomblé. While practicing an epistemology of intimacy, he did not "fall" completely in that world! Why didn't he give in to the temptation to reach for complete immersion, that is, for absolute intimacy with Candomblé?

It goes without saying that we cannot get into Van de Port's personal motivations, but we may surmise that if one wishes to remain a religion researcher, it will not be wise to seek for absolute intimacy with religion. There are two major strategies for performing an epistemology of intimacy in religion research (Keane 2003: 235–36). One strategy is to present oneself as a mere reporter of other's stories, the other is to claim some form of identity with the religion represented. Both strategies however will not work satisfactorily. Stories are never transparent, and even the most simple narrative transcription implies theoretical choices, and will "betray" by distance and objectivity the religious experiences of the "really Real." And in what way, on what grounds, and in which dimensions could a researcher claim to have reached identity with religion? The point is that when we accept that qualitative religion research is an encounter, an intersubjective enterprise, this does not lead to an absolute intimacy with religion: intersubjectivity does not imply identification of self and other. Also in everyday life any encountering of subjects implies a dialectic, sometimes even "a drama" of alternate estrangement and intimacy!

This insight into the dialectic of estrangement and intimacy has been stressed a few years ago by the anthropologist Bridget Hayden. She proposed that any encounter on the field of research and religion, is inevitably fraught with perils and dangers (Hayden 2009: 87–89). The life-worlds of religious practitioners which shape the religious "other," are often loaded with contradiction, strife, doubt, conflict – if only because in every contemporary "religion" there will be contradictory movements towards "the secular" and towards "the sacred" (see above) – so how could we fully identify with religion, if religion is a complex mixture? Besides that, in any intersubjective encounter, there can be some hardly removable barriers between the "self" and the religious "other," if only because of the possibility that not only the researcher will "betray" the religious "other" by objectifying research – see in this volume Kim Knibbe's view on research as being "a series of betrayal" of the others – but also because there is the actual possibility of "betraying" (or unknowingly deceiving) the researching "self" by the researched "other"!

Also "the other," who actually is another active "self," will betray the research-er's "self"; for religious "others" may try to "convert" the "self," or the religious other may be "a repugnant other" or a self-contradictory, or unknowing deceiver, and so on.

These insights imply that when we are going to perform religion research with "qualitative" methods, we may hope to come close to the experiences of the sacred, of the "really Real," but we, being in the research process will also perform "an epistemology of estrangement": religion will be for us always *also* a stranger. Let us hope religion will become *an intimate stranger.*

SO LET'S PLAY!

And how may we, students of religion, come as close to, as intimate as we can get, with religion, while not trying to reach for an identity with religion? An answer is: by considering over and over the essentially playful character of religion and by performing "methodological ludism" (Droogers 2008).

Anthropologist André Droogers has given here, and in recent work, clues for thinking about playful worldview construction of religion and science (cf. Harvey 2011: 225–26). We may interpret religion, as well as a social-scientific discipline like cultural anthropology, as being encountering "subjective" domains of life, on which the human capacity for playing, serious playing, is acted out (and which has to be intentionally and consciously acted out in religion research). Droogers builds on some insights of the eminent Dutch ethnographer and anthropologist Jan van Baal (1909–1992). Van Baal once proposed that we may interpret religions and ideologies as well as other species of worldview constructions out of which and in which human beings live, as ways of dealing with two radical different situations, the situation of being here, being a unique individual, an isolated entity, *and* the situation of being there, of being encompassed in some the individual and the world transcending "real Reality." It is precisely the playful character of religion, the acting out of the religious believer to play with at least two realities, the exclusively "worldly" and the exclusively "sacred" reality, which should bring the religion researcher to the conclusion that he/she too should play with at least two realities: with being a detached, objectifying researcher and with seeking for some intimacy with religion. "Methodological ludism" implies not only "playing" with and applying distinct methods, it also implies: playing, that is "interplaying" (!) with intimacy with and estrangement from religion. So, let's play with religion, let's come closer to the mystery of "the sacred," knowing that we are dealing with a stranger to remain.

Acknowledgments

We are grateful to Dr Angela Argent (Chapters 1– 4 and 10), Dominic Cronin (Chapter 11) and Audrey Mann (Chapters 5–9) for editorial advice. We also acknowledge financial assistance by the Department of Social and Cultural Anthropology of VU University, Amsterdam. Chapters 5–9 first appeared in the journal *Fieldwork in Religion*, published by Equinox, and are reproduced in this book in revised form with permission.

References

Adogame, Afe, and Ezra Chitando. 2005. "Moving among Those Moved by the Spirit." *Fieldwork in Religion* 1 (3): 253–70. http://dx.doi.org/10.1558/firn.v1i3.253.

Andringa, Els. 2004. "The Interface between Fiction and Life: Patterns of Identification in Reading Autobiographies." *Poetics Today* 25 (2): 205–40. http://dx.doi.org/10.1215/03335372-25-2-205.

Arendell, Terry. 1997. "Reflections on the Researcher-Researched Relationship: A Woman Interviewing men." *Qualitative Sociology* 20 (3): 341–68. http://dx.doi.org/10.1023/A:1024727316052.

Asad, Talal. 1993. *Genealogies of Religion: Disciplines and Reasons of Power in Christianity and Islam*. Baltimore etc. The Johns Hopkins University Press.

Asad, Talal. 2003. *Formations of the Secular: Christianity, Islam, Modernity (Cultural Memory in the Present)*. New York: Cambridge University Press.

Asad, Talal. 2006. "Trying to Understand French Secularism." In *Political Theologies*, ed. H. De Vries, 494–526. New York: Fordham University Press. http://dx.doi.org/10.5422/fso/9780823226443.003.0026.

Aupers, Stef. 2006. "'Beter dan het echte leven.' De aantrekkingskracht van computerspellen op het internet." *Sociologie* 2 (1): 29–52. http://dx.doi.org/10.1347/sogi.2.1.29.

Aupers, Stef. 2008 [2004]. *In de ban van moderniteit: De sacralisering van het zelf en computertechnologie*. Amsterdam: Aksant/Het Spinhuis/Maklu.

Aupers, Stef. 2012. "Enchantment Inc.: Online Gaming between Spiritual Experience and Commodity Fetishism." In *Things: Religion and the Question of Materiality*, ed. Dick Houtman and Birgit Meyer, 339–55. New York: Fordham University Press.

Aupers, Stef, and Dick Houtman. 2006. "Beyond the Spiritual Supermarket: The Social and Public Significance of New Age Spirituality." *Journal of Contemporary Religion* 21 (2): 201–22. http://dx.doi.org/10.1080/13537900600655894.

van Baal, J. 1971. *Symbols for Communication: An Introduction to the Anthropological Study of Religion*. Assen: Van Gorcum.

van Baal, J. 1972. *De boodschap der drie illusies: Overdenkingen over religie, kunst en spel*. Assen: Van Gorcum.

Bartels, Edien. 2000. "'Dutch Islam': Young People, Learning and Integration." *Current Sociology* 48 (4): 59–73. http://dx.doi.org/10.1177/0011392100048004006.

Bartels, Edien. 2003. "Medical Ethics and Rites Involving Blood." *Anthropology & Medicine* 10 (1): 105–14. http://dx.doi.org/10.1080/13648470301270.

Becker, J.W., and R. Vink. 1994. *Secularisatie in Nederland, 1966–1991*. Den Haag: SCP.

Becker, J.W., J. de Hart, and J. Mens. 1997. *Secularisatie en alternatieve zingeving in Nederland*. Den Haag: SCP.

Bell, Catherine M. 1992. *Ritual Theory, Ritual Practice*. New York: Oxford University Press.

Bellah, Robert N. 2011. *Religion in Human Evolution: From the Paleolithic to the Axial Age*. Cambridge, MA: The Belknap Press of Harvard University Press. http://dx.doi.org/10.4159/harvard.9780674063099.

Bellah, Robert N., Richard Madsen, William M. Sullivan, Ann Swidler, and Steven M. Tipton. 1985. *Habits of the Heart: Individualism and Commitment in American Life*. Berkeley, Los Angeles, London: University of California Press.

Bennett, Robin L., Arno G. Motulsky, Alan Bittles, Louanne Hudgins, Stefanie Uhrich, Debra Doyle, Kerry Silvey, et al. 2002. "Genetic Counseling and Screening of Consanguineous Couples and their Offspring: Recommendations of the National Society of Genetic Counselors." Journal of *Genetic Counseling* 11 (2): 97–119. http://dx.doi.org/10.1023/A:1014593404915.

Berger, Peter. 1967. *The Sacred Canopy: Elements of a Sociological Theory of Religion.* Garden City, NY: Doubleday.

Berger, Peter L. 2002. "Secularization and de-secularization." In *Religions in the Modern World*, ed. Linda Woodhead, Paul Fletcher, Hiroko Kawanami and David Smith, 291–98. London, New York: Routledge.

Berger, Peter L., and Thomas Luckmann. 1972. *The Social Construction of Reality: A Treatise in the Sociology of Knowledge.* Harmondsworth: Penguin.

Berlin, Isiah. 1953. *The Hedgehog and the Fox: An Essay on Tolstoy's View of History.* London: Weidenfeld and Nicolson.

Bernard, H. Russell, ed. 1998. *Handbook of Methods in Cultural Anthropology.* Walnut Creek, CA: AltaMira Press.

Bloch, Maurice. 1991. "Language, Anthropology and Cognitive Science." *Man* 26 (2): 183–98. http://dx.doi.org/10.2307/2803828.

Bocock, Robert, and Kenneth Thompson, eds. 1985. *Religion and Ideology.* Manchester: Manchester University Press.

Borofsky, Rob. 2011. *Why a Public Anthropology?* Hawaii: Hawaii Pacific University, Center for a Public Anthropology.

Boudewijnse, Barbara. 1995. "The Conceptualisation of Ritual: A History of its Problematic Aspects." *Jaarboek voor Liturgieonderzoek* 11:31–53.

Bourdieu, Pierre. 1977. *Outline of a Theory of Practice.* Cambridge: Cambridge University Press. http://dx.doi.org/10.1017/CBO9780511812507.

Boven, Erica van, and Gilles J. Dorleijn. 1999. *Literair mechaniek: Inleiding tot de analyse van verhalen en gedichten.* Bussum: Coutinho.

Brightman, Robert. 1995. "Forget Culture: Replacement, Transcendence, Relexification." *Cultural Anthropology* 10 (4): 509–46. http://dx.doi.org/10.1525/can.1995.10.4.02a00030.

Brink, T.L. 1995. "Quantitative and/or Qualitative methods in the Scientific Study of Religion." *Zygon* 30 (3): 461–75. http://dx.doi.org/10.1111/j.1467-9744.1995.tb00084.x.

Bruce, Steve. 2002. *God is Dead: Secularization in the West.* Oxford etc. Blackwell.

Caillois, René. 1958. *Les jeux et les hommes.* Paris: Gallimard.

Calhoun, Craig. 2009. "Social Science for Public Knowledge," *Transformations of the Public Sphere.* http://publicsphere.ssrc.org/calhoun-social-science-for-public-knowledge/. Accessed 13 January, 2010.

Campbell, Colin. 2007. *The Easternization of the West: A Thematic Account of Cultural Change in the Modern Era.* Boulder, CO: Paradigm.

Casanova, José. 1994. *Public Religions in the Modern World.* Chicago, London: The University of Chicago Press.

Charlton, Michael, Corinna Pette, and Christina Burbaum. 2004. "Reading Strategies in Everyday Life: Different Ways of Reading a Novel which Make a Distinction." *Poetics Today* 25 (2): 241–63. http://dx.doi.org/10.1215/03335372-25-2-241.

Clarke, Peter, and Peter Byrne. 1993. *Religion Defined and Explained.* London: Macmillan. http://dx.doi.org/10.1057/9780230374249.

Clifford, J. 1997. "Spatial Practices: Fieldwork, Travel, and the Disciplining of Anthropology." In *Anthropological Locations: Boundaries and Grounds of a Field Science*, ed. Akhil Gupta and James Ferguson, 185–222. Berkeley, Los Angeles: University of California Press.

Cohen, Jeffrey H. 2000. "Problems in the Field: Participant Observation and the Assumption of Neutrality." *Field Methods* 12 (4): 316–33. http://dx.doi.org/10.1177/1525822X0001200404.

Coleman, John. 1978. *The Evolution of Dutch Catholicism, 1958–1974.* Berkeley, Los Angeles: University of California Press.

Cox, James L. 2010. *An Introduction to the Phenomenology of Religion.* London: Continuum.

Csordas, Thomas J. 1999. "The Body's Career in Anthropology." In *Anthropological Theory Today*, ed. Henrietta L. Moore, 172–205. Cambridge: Polity Press.

Csordas, Thomas J. 2012. "Transmutation of Sensibilities: Empathy, Intuition, Revelation." In *Etnographic Fieldwork: An Anthropological Reader*, ed. Antonius Robben and Jeffrey A. Sluka, 540–46. Malden, MA and Oxford, UK: Wiley-Blackwell.

D'Andrade, Roy G. 1992. "Schemas and Motivation." In Human Motives and Cultural Models, ed. Roy G. D'Andrade and Claudia Strauss, 23–44. Cambridge: Cambridge University Press. http://dx.doi.org/10.1017/CBO9781139166515.003.

Davie, Grace. 1994. *Religion in Britain since 1945: Believing without Belonging.* Oxford: Blackwell.

Davie, Grace. 2002. *Europe: The Exceptional Case; Parameters of Faith in the Modern World.* London: Darton, Longman and Todd.

Davie, Grace. 2007. *The Sociology of Religion.* Los Angeles, Atlanta, GA: Sage.

Davies, Charlotte A. 1999. *Reflexive Ethnography: A Guide to Researching Selves and Others.* New York: Routledge.

Dekker, Gerard, Joep de Hart, and Jan Peters. 1997. *God in Nederland, 1966–1996.* Amsterdam: Anthos.

Denzin, Norman K., and Yvonna S. Lincoln, eds. 1998a. *The Landscape of Qualitative Research: Theories and Issues.* Thousand Oaks: SAGE.

Denzin, Norman K., and Yvonna S. Lincoln, eds. 1998b. *Strategies of Qualitative Inquiry.* Thousand Oaks: SAGE.

Denzin, Norman K., and Yvonna S. Lincoln, eds. 2005. *The SAGE Handbook of Qualitative Research.* Thousand Oaks: SAGE.

Desjarlais, Robert. 1992. *Body and Emotion: The Aesthetics of Illness and Healing in the Nepal Himalayas.* Philadelphia, PA: University of Pennsylvania Press.

Dobbelaere, Karel. 2009. "The Meaning and Scope of Secularization." In *The Oxford Handbook of the Sociology of Religion*, ed. Peter B. Clarke, 599–615. Oxford: Oxford University Press.

Droogers, André. 1980. *The Dangerous Journey: Symbolic Aspects of Boys' Initiation among the Wagenia of Kisangani, Zaire.* The Hague: Mouton.

Droogers, André. 1981. "Erosion and Sedimentation: The Changing Religion of the Wagenia of Kisangani, Zaire." In *Secularization in Global Perspective*, ed. D.C. Mulder, 113–62. Amsterdam: VU Boekhandel/Uitgeverij.

Droogers, André. 1996. "Methodological Ludism: Beyond Religionism and Reductionism." In *Conflicts in Social Science*, ed. A. van Harskamp, 44–67. London: Routledge.

Droogers, André. 1999. "The Third Bank of the River: Play, Methodological Ludism and the Definition of Religion." In *The Pragmatics of Defining Religion: Contexts, Concepts and Contents*, ed. Jan G. Platvoet and Arie L. Molendijk, 285–313. Leiden: Brill.

Droogers, André. 2007. "Beyond Secularisation versus Sacralisation: Lessons from a Study of the Dutch Case." In *A Sociology of Spirituality*, ed. Kieran Flanagan and Peter C. Jupp, 81–99. Aldershot: Ashgate.

Droogers, André. 2008. "As Close as a Scholar Can Get: Exploring a One-Field Approach to the Study of Religion." In *Religion: Beyond a Concept*, ed. Hent de Vries, 448–63. New York: Fordham University Press.

Droogers, André. 2009. "Defining Religion: A Social Science Approach." In *The Oxford Handbook of the Sociology of Religion*, ed. Peter Clarke, 263–79. Oxford: Oxford University Press.

Droogers, André. 2010. "Towards the Concerned Study of Religion: Exploring the Double Power-Play Disparity." *Religion, a Journal of Religion and Religions* 40(4): 227–38.

Droogers, André. 2012. *Play and Power in Religion: Collected Essays.* Berlin: De Gruyter.

Drury, John, and Clifford Stott. 2001. "Bias as a Research Strategy in Participant Observation: The Case of Intergroup Conflict." *Field Methods* 13 (1): 47–67. http://dx.doi.org/10.1177/1525822X0101300103.

Dufour, Dany-Robert. 2007. *Le divin marché: La révolution culturelle libérale.* Paris: Denoël.

Durkheim, Emile. 2001 [1912]. *The Elementary Forms of Religious Life.* Oxford, New York: Oxford University Press.

Eisenstadt, S.N. 2000. "Multiple Modernities." *Daedalus* 129 (1): 1–30.

Eliade, Mircea. 1969. *The Quest: History and Meaning in Religion.* Chicago: University of Chicago Press.

Elliott, Anthony, and Charles Lemert. 2006. *The New Individualism: The Emotion Costs of Globalization.* London, New York: Routledge.

Emerson, Robert M. 2009. "Ethnography, Interaction and Ordinary Trouble." *Ethnography* 10 (4): 535–48. http://dx.doi.org/10.1177/1466138109346996.

Eriksen, Thomas Hylland. 2004. *What is Anthropology?* London: Pluto.

Evans-Pritchard, E.E. 1937. *Witchcraft, Oracles and Magic among the Azande.* Oxford: The Clarendon Press.

Everson, Michael. 1991. "The Study of Ritual as an Aspect of Human Religiosity." *Mankind Quarterly* 32(1–2): 57–75.

Ewing, Katherine P. 1994. "Dreams from a Saint: Anthropological Atheism and the Temptation to Believe." *American Anthropologist* 96 (3): 571–83. http://dx.doi.org/10.1525/aa.1994.96.3.02a00080.

Favret-Saada, Jeanne. 1980. *Deadly Words: Witchcraft in the Bocage.* Cambridge, UK and New York: Cambridge University Press. Paris: Éditions de la Maison des Sciences de l'Homme.

Fernandez, James W. 1986. *Persuasions and Performances: The Play of Tropes in Culture.* Bloomington: Indiana University Press.

Flick, Uwe. 2009. *Qualitative Research.* Atlanta, GA: Sage.

Fromm, Erich. 1950. *Psychoanalysis and Religion.* New Haven, CT: Yale University Press.

Fry, Peter, and Gary Howe. 1975. "Duas respostas à aflição: Umbanda e Pentecostalismo." *Debate e Crítica* 6:75–94.

Geertz, Clifford. 1973. *The Interpretation of Cultures.* New York: Basic Books.

Gerritsen, J. W., and G. de Vries. 1994. "Hinderkracht en ondernemerschap. Een historische sociologie van sociale problemen." *Amsterdams Sociologisch Tijdschrift* 21(2): 3–29.

Geschiere, Peter, and Janet Roitman. 1997. *The Modernity of Witchcraft: Politics and the Occult in Postcolonial Africa. Sorcellerie et politique en Afrique—la viande des autres.* Charlottesville: University Press of Virginia.

Ghorashi, Halleh. 2001. *Ways to Survive, Battles to Win Iranian Women Exiles in the Netherlands and the US.* Nijmegen: Katholieke Universiteit Nijmegen.

Giddens, Anthony. 1984. *The Constitution of Society: Outline of the Theory of Structuration.* Cambridge: Polity Press.

Gluckman, Max. 1963. "Gossip and Scandal." *Current Anthropology* 4 (3): 307–16. http://dx.doi.org/10.1086/200378.

Gluckman, Max. 1968. "Psychological, Sociological and Anthropological Explanations of Witchcraft and Gossip – Clarification." *Man* 3 (1): 20–34. http://dx.doi.org/10.2307/2799409.

Goody, Jack. 1977. "Against 'Ritual': Loosely Structured Thoughts on a Loosely Defined Topic." In *Secular Ritual,* ed. Sally F. Moore and Barbara G. Myerhoff, 25–35. Assen: Van Gorcum.

Graf, Werner. 1997. *Lesen und Biographie: Eine empirische Fallstudie zur Lektüre der Hitlerjugendgeneration.* Tübingen, Basel: Francke.

Guba, Egon G., ed. 1990. *The Paradigm Dialog.* London: SAGE.

Gullestad, Marianne. 1996. *Everyday Life Philosophers: Modernity, Morality, and Autobiography in Norway.* Oslo: Scandinavian University Press.

Gupta, Akhil, and James Ferguson. 1997. *Anthropological Locations: Boundaries and Grounds of a Field of Science.* Berkeley, Los Angeles: University of California Press.

Hall, Stuart. 1996. "Introduction: Who Needs Identity?" In *Questions of Cultural Identity,* ed. Stuart Hall and Paul du Gay, 1–17. London: SAGE.

Halman, Loek, and Ole Riis. 2003. *Religion in a Secularising Society: The Europeans' Religion at the End of the 20th Century.* Leiden: Brill.

Hamilton, Malcolm. 2000. "An Analysis of the Festival for Mind-Body-Spirit, London." In *Beyond the New Age: Exploring Alternative Spirituality,* ed. Steven Sutcliffe and Marion Bowman, 188–200. Edinburgh: Edinburgh University Press.

Handelman, Don. 1987. "Play." In *The Encyclopedia of Religion,* ed. Mircea Eliade, vol. 11, 363–67. New York: MacMillan.

Hanegraaff, Wouter J. 1996. *New Age Religion and Western Culture: Esotericism in the Mirror of Secular Thought.* Leiden, New York, Köln: Brill.

Harding, Susan Friend. 2000. *The Book of Jerry Falwell: Fundamentalist Language and Politics.* Princeton, NJ: Princeton University Press.

Harskamp, Anton van. 2000. *Het nieuw-religieuze verlangen.* Kampen: Kok.

de Hart, Joep. 2011. *Zwevende gelovigen. Oude religie en nieuwe spiritualiteit.* Amsterdam: Bert Bakker.

Harvey, Graham. 2011. "Field Research: Participant Observation." In *The Routledge Handbook of Research Methods in the Study of Religion*, ed. Michael Stausberg and Steven Engler, 217–44. London, New York: Routledge.

Hayden, Bridget. 2009. "Displacing the Subject: A Dialogical Understanding of the Researching Self." *Anthropological Theory* 9 (1): 81–101. http://dx.doi.org/10.1177/1463499609103548.

Heelas, Paul. 1996. *The New Age Movement: The Celebration of the Self and the Sacralization of Modernity*. Oxford: Blackwell.

Heelas, Paul. 2007. "The Spiritual Revolution of Northern Europe: Personal Beliefs." *Nordic Journal of Religion and Society* 20 (1): 1–28.

Heelas, Paul. 2008. *Spiritualities of Life: New Age Romanticism and Consumptive Capitalism*. Malden, MA: Blackwell. http://dx.doi.org/10.1002/9781444301106.

Heelas, Paul, and Linda Woodhead. 2005. *The Spiritual Revolution: Why Religion is Giving Way to Spirituality*. Malden, MA: Blackwell.

Hijmans, Ellen, and Adri Smaling. 1997. "Over de relatie tussen kwalitatief onderzoek en levensbeschouwing. een inleiding." In *Kwalitatief onderzoek en levensbeschouwing*, ed. Adri Smaling and Ellen Hijmans, 12–32. Amsterdam: Boom.

Hjelm, Titus, and Phil Zuckerman. 2012. *Studying Religion and Society: Sociological Self-Portraits*. London, New York: Routledge.

Hoover, Stewart M. 2006. *Religion in the Media Age*. London, New York: Routledge.

Horton, Robin. 1993. *Patterns of Thought in Africa and the West: Essays on Magic, Religion and Science*. Cambridge: Cambridge University Press. http://dx.doi.org/10.1017/CBO9781139166232.

Houtman, Dick. 2008. *Op jacht naar de echte werkelijkheid. Dromen over authenticiteit in een wereld zonder fundamenten*. Amsterdam: Pallas/Amsterdam University Press. http://dx.doi.org/10.5117/9789085550037.

Houtman, Dick, and Peter Mascini. 2002. "Why Do Churches Become Empty while New Age Grows? Secularization and Religious Change in the Netherlands." *Journal for the Scientific Study of Religion* 41 (3): 455–73. http://dx.doi.org/10.1111/1468-5906.00130.

Houtman, Dick, and Stef Aupers. 2012. "The Spiritual Turn and the Decline of Tradition: The Spread of Post-Christian Spirituality in 14 Western Countries, 1981–2000." In *Spirituality in the Modern World: Within Religious Tradition and Beyond (Volume One)*, ed. Paul Heelas, 390–412. London: Routledge.

Huberman, A. Michael, and Matthew B. Miles, eds. 2002. *The Qualitative Researcher's Companion*. Thousand Oaks: SAGE.

Huizer, Gerrit. 1979. "Research-through-Action: Some Practical Experiences with Peasant Organisations." In *The Politics of Anthropology: From Colonialism and Sexism toward a View from Below*, ed. Gerrit Huizer and Bruce Mannheim, 395–420. The Hague, Paris: Mouton. http://dx.doi.org/10.1515/9783110806458.395.

Huizer, Gerrit, and Bruce Mannheim, eds. 1979. *The Politics of Anthropology: From Colonialism and Sexism toward a View from Below*. The Hague, Paris: Mouton. http://dx.doi.org/10.1515/9783110806458.

Huizinga, J. 1952. *Homo ludens. Proeve eener bepaling van het spel-element der cultuur*. Haarlem: Tjeenk Willink.

Humphrey, Caroline, and James Laidlaw. 1994. *The Archetypal Actions of Ritual: A Theory of Ritual Illustrated by the Jain Rite of Worship*. Oxford: Clarendon Press.

Huntington, Samuel P. 1997. *The Clash of Civilizations and the Remaking of World Order*. London: Touchstone Books.

Jackson, Michael. 1989. *Paths Toward a Clearing; Radical Empiricism and Ethnographic Inquiry*. Bloomington, IN: Indiana University Press.

Jackson, Michael, ed. 1996. *Things as They Are: New Directions in Phenomenological Anthropology*. Bloomington, IN: Indiana University Press.

Jackson, Michael. 1998. *Minima Ethnographica: Intersubjectivity and the Anthropological Project*. Chicago, IL, and London: University of Chicago Press.

Janssen, Jacques, and Maerten Prins. 2000. "The Abstract Image of God: The Case of the Dutch

Youth." *Archives de Sciences Sociales des Religions* 45 (109): 31–48. http://dx.doi.org/10.4000/assr.20171.

Janssen, Jacques, Maerten Prins, Cor Baerveldt, and Jan Van der Lans. 2000. "The Structure and Variety of Prayer." *Journal of Empirical Theology* 13 (2): 29–54. http://dx.doi.org/10.1163/157092500X00092.

Jenkins, Philip. 2002. *The Next Christendom: The Rise of Global Christianity.* New York: Oxford University Press. http://dx.doi.org/10.1093/0195146166.001.0001.

Jensen, Jeppe Singding. 2011. "Epistemology." In *The Routledge Handbook of Research Methods in the Study of Religion,* ed. Michael Stausberg and Steven Engler, 40–53. London, New York: Routledge.

Johnson, Jeffrey C. 1998. "Research Design and Research Strategies." In *Handbook of Methods in Cultural Anthropology,* ed. H. Russell Bernard, 131–71. Walnut Creek, CA: AltaMira Press.

Johnson, Jeffrey C., Christine Avenarius, and Jack Weatherford. 2006. "The Active Participant-Observer: Applying Social Role Analysis to Participant Observation." *Field Methods* 18 (2): 111–34. http://dx.doi.org/10.1177/1525822X05285928.

Käsler, Dirk. 1988. *Max Weber: An Introduction to his Life and Work.* Cambridge: Polity Press.

Kahn, Robert L., and Charles F. Cannell. 1967. *The Dynamics of Interviewing. Theory, Technique and Cases.* New York: Wiley.

Keane, Webb. 2003. "Self-interpretation, Agency, and the Objects of Anthropology: Reflections on a Genealogy." *Comparative Studies in Society and History* 45 (2): 222–48. http://dx.doi.org/10.1017/S0010417503000124.

Kearney, Richard. 2010. *Anatheism: Returning to God after God.* New York: Columbia University Press.

Kennedy, James Carleton. 1995. *Building New Babylon: Cultural Change in the Netherlands during the 1960s.* Iowa: Iowa City.

Kerklaan, Marga. 1987. *"Zodoende was de vrouw maar een mens om kinderen te krijgen," 300 brieven over het Roomse huwelijksleven.* Baarn: Ambo.

Ketner, Susan L., Marjo Buitelaar, and Harke Bosma. 2004. "Identity Strategies among Adolescent Girls of Moroccan Descent in the Netherlands." *Identity* 4 (2): 145–69. http://dx.doi.org/10.1207/s1532706xid0402_3.

Kloos, Peter, ed. 1990. *True Fiction: Artistic and Scientific Representations of Reality.* Amsteram. VU University Press.

Knibbe, Kim Esther. 2013. *Faith in the Familiar: Religion, Spirituality and Place in the South of the Netherlands.* Leiden and Boston: Brill.

Knibbe, Kim, and André Droogers. 2011. "Methodological Ludism and the Academic Study of Religion." *Method and Theory in the Study of Religion* 23 (3-4): 283–303. http://dx.doi.org/10.1163/157006811X608395.

Knibbe, Kim, and Peter Versteeg. 2008. "Asessing Phenomenology in Anthropology: Lessons from the Study of Religion and Experience." *Critique of Anthropology* 28 (1): 47–62. http://dx.doi.org/10.1177/0308275X07086557.

Knippenberg, Hans. 1992. *De Religieuze Kaart van Nederland, omvang en geografische spreiding van de godsdienstige gezindten vanaf de reformatie tot heden.* Assen, Maastricht: Van Gorcum.

Kolb, Michael. 1989. *Spiel als Phänomen - Das Phänomen Spiel: Studien zu phänomenologischen-anthropologischen Spieltheorien.* Sankt Augustin: Academia Verlag Richartz.

Koning, Daniëlle. 2005. "Encounter of Islam and Science. Religious Beliefs and Academic Education among Muslim Students in Amsterdam." MA thesis, VU University Amsterdam.

Koning, Daniëlle. 2006. "Anti-evolutionism among Muslim Students." *ISIM Review* 18:48–49.

de Koning, Martijn. 2008. *Zoeken naar een 'zuivere' islam. Geloofsbeleving en identiteitsvorming van jonge Marokkaans-Nederlandse moslims.* Amsterdam: Bert Bakker.

de Koning, Martijn. 2009. "Changing Worldviews and Friendship: An Exploration of the Life Stories of Two Female Salafists in the Netherlands." In *Global Salafism: Islam's New Religious Movement,* ed. Roel Meijer, 372–92. London: Hurst.

de Koning, Martijn, and Edien Bartels. 2006. "For Allah and Myself: Religion and Moroccan Youth in The Netherlands." In *Morocco and The Netherlands: Society, Economy, Culture,* ed. P.H.F. Bos and W. Fritschy, 146–56. Amsterdam: VU Publishers.

Kuhn, Thomas S. 1962. *The Structure of Scientific Revolutions.* International Encyclopedia of Unified Science, volume 2, number 2. Chicago: The University of Chicago Press.

Kurth, Stefan, and Karsten Lehmann, eds. 2011. *Religionen erforschen: Kulturwissenschaftliche Methoden in der Religionswissenschaft.* Wiesbaden: VS Verlag für Sozialwissenschaften. http://dx.doi.org/10.1007/978-3-531-93245-3.

Kvale, Steinar. 1996. *Interviews: An Introduction to Qualitative Research Interviewing.* London: SAGE.

Latour, Bruno. 1987. *Science in Action: How to Follow Scientists and Engineers through Society.* Milton Keynes: Open University Press.

van der Leeuw, G. 1956. *Phänomenologie der Religion.* Tübingen: Mohr.

Lindholm, Charles. 2002. "Authenticity, Anthropology, and the Sacred." *Anthropological Quarterly* 75 (2): 331–38. http://dx.doi.org/10.1353/anq.2002.0035.

Lindquist, Galina. 1995. "Traveling by the Other's Cognitive Maps or Going Native and Coming Back." *Ethnos* 60 (1-2): 5–40. http://dx.doi.org/10.1080/00141844.1995.9981506.

Luckmann, Thomas. 1979. "The Structural Conditions of Religious Consciousness in Modern Society." *Japanese Journal of Religious Studies* 6 (1-2): 121–37.

Maffesoli, Michel. 1996. *The Time of the Tribes: The Decline of Individualism in Mass Society.* London, Thousand Oaks, New Delhi: SAGE.

Maxwell, Joseph A. 1996. *Qualitative Research Design.* Applied Social Research Methods Series, vol. 41. Thousand Oaks: SAGE.

McCorkel, Jill A., and Kirsten Myers. 2003. "What Difference Does Difference Make? Position and Privilege in the Field." *Qualitative Sociology* 26 (2): 199–231. http://dx.doi.org/10.1023/A:1022967012774.

McGilchrist, Iain. 2010. *The Master and his Emissary: The Divided Brain and the Making of the Western World.* New Haven, CT: Yale University Press.

McGuire, Meredith B. 1990. "Religion and the Body: Rematerializing the Human Body in the Social Sciences of Religion." *Journal for the Scientific Study of Religion* 29 (3): 283–96. http://dx.doi.org/10.2307/1386459.

Mepschen, Paul, Jan Willem Duyvendak and Evelien H. Tonkens. 2010. "Sexual Politics, Orientalism and Multicultural Citizenship in the Netherlands." *Sociology* 44 (5): 962–79. http://dx.doi.org/10.1177/0038038510375740.

Merry, Sally Engle. 1997. "Rethinking Gossip and Scandal." In *Reputation: Studies in the Voluntary Elicitation of Good Conduct,* ed. Daniel B. Klein, 47–75. Ann Arbor: University of Michigan Press.

van der Meulen, Marten. 2006. "Vroom in de Vinex. Kerk en civil society in Leidsche Rijn." Unpublished PhD dissertation. Amsterdam: VU University.

Meyer, Birgit. 2008. "Religious Sensations: Why Media, Aesthetics and Power Matter in the Study of Contemporary Religion." In Religion: Beyond a Concept, ed. Hent de Vries, 704–23. New York: Fordham University Press.

Micklethwait, John, and Adrian Wooldridge. 2009. *God is Back: How the Global Revival of Faith is Changing the World.* New York: The Penguin Press.

Mishler, Elliot G. 1999. *Storylines: Craftartists' Narratives of Identity.* Cambridge, MA: Harvard University Press.

Momen, Moojan. 1999. *The Phenomenon Religion: A Thematic Approach.* Oxford: Oneworld.

Moore, Sally Falk. 1975. "Epilogue: Uncertainties in Situations, Indeterminacies in Culture." In *Symbol and Politics in Communal Ideology: Cases and Questions,* ed. Sally Falk Moore and Barbara G. Myerhoff, 210–39. Ithaca, NY and London: Cornell University Press.

Murchison, Julian M. 2010. *Ethnography Essentials: Designing, Conducting, and Presenting your Research.* San Francisco: Jossey-Bass.

Naipaul, V.S. 1979. *A Bend in the River.* New York: Knopf.

Narayan, K. 1993. "How Native is a 'Native' Anthropologist?" *American Anthropologist* 95 (3): 671–86. http://dx.doi.org/10.1525/aa.1993.95.3.02a00070.

Newman, Isadore, and Carolyn R. Benz. 1998. *Qualitative-Quantitative Research Methodology: Exploring the Interactive Continuum.* Carbondale, IL: Southern Illinois University Press.

Nissen, Peter. 1996. "Confessionele identiteit en regionale eigenheid." In *Constructie van het eigene.*

196 References

Culturele vormen van regionale identiteit in Nederland, ed. Carlo van der Borgt, Amanda Hermans, and Hugo Jacobs, 155–72. Amsterdam: P. J. Meertens-instituut.

Nissen, Peter. 2000. "Constructie en deconstructie van het katholieke Limburg." *Studies over de sociaal-economische geschiedenis van Limburg* 45: 79–97.

Norbeck, Edward. 1974. "Anthropological Views of Play." *American Zoologist* 14:267–73.

Olson, Carl, ed. 2003. *Theory and Method in the Study of Religion: A Selection of Critical Readings.* Belmont, CA: Thomson/Wadsworth.

O'Reilly, Karen. 2005. *Ethnographic Methods.* Abingdon: Routledge. http://dx.doi.org/10.4324/9780203320068.

Patton, Michael Quinn. 1987. *How to Use Qualitative Methods in Evaluation.* Atlanta, GA: Sage.

Pette, Corinna. 2001. *Psychologie des Romanlesens: Lesestrategien zur subjektiven Aneignung eines literarischen Textes.* München, Weinheim: Juventa.

Platvoet, Jan G., and Arie L. Molendijk, eds. 1999. *The Pragmatics of Defining Religion: Contexts, Concepts and Contents.* Leiden: Brill.

van de Port, Mattijs. 2011. *Ecstatic Encounters: Bahian Candomblé and the Quest for the Really Real.* Amsterdam: Amsterdam University Press. http://dx.doi.org/10.5117/9789089642981.

Possamai, Adam. 2005. *Religion and Popular Culture: A Hyper-real Document.* Bruxelles, Bern, Berlin, Frankfurt am Main, New York, Oxford, Wien: Peter Lang.

Post, Paul. 1998. "Het rituele perspectief." In *De religieuze ruis in Nederland: Thesen over de versterving en de wedergeboorte van de godsdienst*, ed. Anton van Harskamp, 47–55. Zoetermeer: Meinema.

Rappaport, Roy A. 1999. *Ritual and Religion in the Making of Humanity.* Cambridge: Cambridge University Press. http://dx.doi.org/10.1017/CBO9780511814686.

Reis, Ria. 1998. "Resonating to Pain: Introspection as a Tool in Medical Anthropology 'at home'." *Anthropology & Medicine* 5 (3): 295–310. http://dx.doi.org/10.1080/13648470.1998.9964565.

Ricoeur, Paul. 1984. *Time and Narrative.* Chicago: University of Chicago Press. http://dx.doi.org/10.7208/chicago/9780226713519.001.0001.

Robben, Antonius C.G.M., and Jeffrey A. Sluka, eds. 2012. *Ethnographic Fieldwork: An Anthropological Reader.* Malden, MA, and Oxford, UK: Wiley-Blackwell.

Roeland, Johan. 2009. *Selfation: Dutch Evangelical Youth between Subjectivization and Subjection.* Amsterdam: Amsterdam University Press. http://dx.doi.org/10.5117/9789085550198.

Roeland, Johan, Stef Aupers, Dick Houtman, Martijn De Koning, and Ineke Noomen. 2010. "The Quest for Religious Purity in New Age, Evangelicalism and Islam: Religious Renditions of Dutch Youth and the Luckmann Legacy." *Annual Review of the Sociology of Religion* 1 (1): 289–306. http://dx.doi.org/10.1163/ej.9789004187900.i-488.82.

Roof, Wade Clark. 1999. *Spiritual Marketplace: Baby Boomers and the Remaking of American Religion.* Princeton, NJ: Princeton University Press.

Saler, Benson. 1993. *Conceptualizing Religion: Immanent Anthropologists, Transcendent Natives, and Unbounded Categories.* Leiden: Brill.

Schepens, Theo, and Leo Spruit. 2001. *De Rooms-Katholieke kerk in Nederland, 1960–1998 een statistisch trendrapport.* Nijmegen en Tikburg: KASKI and KUB.

Schram, D.H., and G.J. Steen, eds. 2001. *The Psychology and Sociology of Literature.* Amsterdam: John Benjamins.

Scholten, Peter, and Ronald Holzhacker. 2009. "Bonding, Bridging and Ethnic Minorities in the Netherlands: Changing Discourses in a Changing Nation." *Nations and Nationalism* 15 (1): 81–100. http://dx.doi.org/10.1111/j.1469-8129.2009.00350.x.

Seale, Clive. 1999. The Quality of Qualitative Research. London: Sage.

Sharpe, Eric J. 1975. *Comparative Religion: A History.* London: Duckworth.

Silverman, David. 1999. *Interpreting Qualitative Data: Methods for Analysing Talk, Text and Interaction.* London and Atlanta, GA: Sage.

Silverman, David. 2000. *Doing Qualitative Research: A Practical Handbook.* London and Atlanta, GA: Sage.

Simons, Ed, and Lodewijk Winkeler. 1987. *Het verraad der clercken: intellectuelen en hun rol in de ontwikkelingen van het Nederlandse katholicisme na 1945.* Baarn: Arbor.

Simpson, John H. 1993. "Religion and the Body: Sociological Themes and Prospects." In *A Future for Religion? New Paradigms for Social Analysis*, ed. William H. Swatos, Jr, 149–64. Newbury Park, CA: SAGE.

Smart, Ninian. 1992. *The World's Religions: Old Traditions and Modern Transformations*. Cambridge: Cambridge University Press.

Smith, John K. 1993. *After the Demise of Empiricism: The Problem of Judging Social and Educational Inquiry*. Norwood, NJ: Ablex.

Sniderman, Paul M., and Louk Hagendoorn. 2007. *When Ways of Life Collide: Multiculturalism and its Discontents in the Netherlands*. Princeton: Princeton University Press.

Spickard, James V., J. Shawn Landres, and Meredith B. McGuire, eds. 2002. *Personal Knowledge and Beyond: Reshaping the Ethnography of Religion*. New York: New York University Press.

Stausberg, Michael. 2009. "The Study of Religion(s) in Western Europe III: Further Developments after World War II." *Religion, a Journal of Religion and Religions* 39 (3): 261–82.

Stausberg, Michael, and Steven Engler, eds. 2011. *The Routledge Handbook of Research Methods in the Study of Religion*. Abingdon: Routledge.

Stewart, Charles. 2001. "Secularism as an Impediment to Anthropological Research." *Social Anthropology* 9 (3): 325–28. http://dx.doi.org/10.1111/j.1469-8676.2001.tb00157.x.

Stewart, Pamela J., and Andrew Strathern. 2004. *Witchcraft, Sorcery: Rumors and Gossip*. Cambridge: Cambridge University Press.

St John, Graham, ed. 2003. *Rave Culture and Religion*. London, New York: Routledge.

Stolcke, Verena. 1995. "Talking Culture: New Boundaries, New Rhetorics of Exclusion in Europe." *Current Anthropology* 36 (1): 1–24. http://dx.doi.org/10.1086/204339.

Stoller, Paul. 1997. *Fusion of the Worlds: An Ethnography of Possession among the Songhay of Niger*. Chicago: The University of Chicago Press.

Stoltenberg, Camilla, Per Magnus, Rolv Terje Lie, Anne Kjersti Daltveit, and Lorentz M. Irgens. 1 Mar, 1997. "Birth defects and parental consanguinity in Norway." *American Journal of Epidemiology* 145 (5): 439–48. http://dx.doi.org/10.1093/oxfordjournals.aje.a009126. Medline:9048518

Storms, Oka, and Edien Bartels. 2008. *De keuze van een huwelijkspartner. Een studie naar partnerkeuze onder groepen Amsterdammers*. Onderzoeksrapport. Vrije Universiteit, Faculteit Sociale Wetenschappen, Afdeling Sociale en Culturele Antropologie. (The choice of a marriage partner. Research to partner choice under groups of Amsterdam people). (VU University, Department of Cultural and Social Anthropology). Amsterdam. http://www.fsw.vu.nl/nl/Images/huwelijkenamsterdam%20Spdf_tcm30-60514.pdf Accessed 13 October, 2010.

Straating, Alex. 1998. "Roddelen en de verbale constructie van de gemeenschap." *Etnofoor* 11 (2): 25–41.

Stringer, Martin D. 1999. *On the Perception of Worship: The Ethnography of Worship in Four Christian Congregations in Manchester*. Birmingham: Birmingham University Press.

Tashakkori, Abbas, and Charles Teddlie. 1998. *Mixed Methodology: Combining Qualitative and Quantitative Approaches*. Thousand Oaks: Sage.

Taylor, Charles. 2007. *A Secular Age*. Cambridge, MA: The Belknap Press of Harvard University Press.

Trotter, Robert T. II, and Jean J. Schensul. 1998. "Methods in Applied Anthropology." In *Handbook of Methods in Cultural Anthropology*, ed. Bernard H. Russell, 691–35. Walnut Creek, CA: AltaMira Press.

Turner, Victor. 1967. *The Forest of Symbols: Aspects of Ndembu Ritual*. Ithaka. Cornell University Press.

Turner, Victor W. 1982. *From Ritual to Theatre: The Human Seriousness of Play*. New York: PAJ Publications.

Turner, Victor W. 1988. *The Anthropology of Performance*. New York: PAJ Publications.

Versteeg, Peter. 2006. "Marginal Christian Spirituality: An Example from a Dutch Meditation Group." *Journal of Contemporary Religion* 21 (1): 83–97. http://dx.doi.org/10.1080/13537900500382235.

Versteeg, Peter. 2007. "Spirituality on the Margins of the Church: Christian Spiritual Centers in the Netherlands." In *A Sociology of Spirituality*, ed. Kieran Flanagan and Peter C. Jupp, 101–14. Aldershot: Ashgate.

Vliegenthart, Rens. 2007. *Framing Immigration and Integration: Facts, Parliament, Media and Anti-Immigrant Party Support in the Netherlands*. Amsterdam: Vrije Universiteit Amsterdam.

Widengren, Geo. 1969. *Religionsphänomenologie*. Berlin: Walter de Gruyter.

Winnicott, Donald W. 1971. *Playing and Reality*. London: Tavistock.

Wijers, Carla. 2000. "'In een hand de rozenkrans, in de andere hand een glas bier' – de Limburgse identiteit onder de loep." *Studies over de Sociaal-economische Geschiedenis van Limburg* 45: 111–34.

Wijsen, Frans. 2002. *Missie en Multiculturaliteit: Communicatie tussen Europeanen en Afrikanen in Afrika en Europa. Inaugural Lecture*. Nijmegen: Katholieke Universiteit.

Willaime, Jean-Paul. 2006. "Religion in Ultramodernity." In *Theorising Religion: Classical and Contemporary Debates*, ed. James A. Beckford and John Walliss, 77–89. Farnham, UK, and Burlington, VT: Ashgate.

Woodhead, Linda, ed. 2012. *Innovative Methods in the Study of Religion*. Oxford: Oxford University Press.

Wright, Susan. 1998. "The Politicization of 'Culture'." *Anthropology Today* 14 (1): 7–15. http://dx.doi.org/10.2307/2783092.

Wuthnow, Robert. 2001. *Creative Spirituality: The Way of the Artist*. Berkeley, Los Angeles: University of California Press.

Yip, Andrew K. T. 2005. "Religion and the Politics of Spirituality/Sexuality." *Fieldwork in Religion* 1 (3): 271–89.

Zigon, Jarret. 2008. *Morality: An Athropological Perspective*. Oxford, New York: Berg.

Zijderveld, Anton C. 2000. *The Institutional Imperative: The Interface of Institutions and Networks*. Amsterdam: Amsterdam University Press.

Index

CPSIA information can be obtained at www.ICGtesting.com
Printed in the USA
BVOW08s1854190814

363132BV00002BA/8/P

9 781781 790434